Even Pellerud

on

Coaching & Leadership in Women's Soccer

with Sam Kucey

REEDSWAIN PUBLISHING

Even Pellerud

Library of Congress
Cataloging - in - Publication Data

by Sam Kucey
Even Pellerud
on Coaching & Leadership in
Women's Soccer

ISBN No. 1-59164-096-2
Lib. of Congress Catalog No. 2005900334

Art Direction, Layout and Proofing
Bryan R. Beaver

Cover Design
Bryan R. Beaver

Printed by
DATA REPRODUCTIONS
Auburn, Michigan

Reedswain Publishing
562 Ridge Road
Spring City, PA 19475
800.331.5191
www.reedswain.com
info@reedswain.com

CONTENTS

Foreword

by Egil Olsen

There is a long history of the roots and development of the Norwegian style of soccer play, beginning when British sailors came to Norway over 100 years ago. There have always existed different views, schools of how football should be played in Norway. The school that we, Even and myself, belong to now as we did when we were National Team Coaches, never represented the majority of Norwegian coaches. We occupied, for many years, the most important position as National Coaches for women and men and also the U-21 National Team and, therefore, had an opportunity for influence on the game. This was possible due to many accidental circumstances that two of us with similar philosophies would arrive at these important positions at the same time.

In the period Even and I were colleagues in the Norwegian Football Association (NFA), we often discussed football, but we never disagreed on the fundamental questions: the zone orientation defense and the penetrativeness in attack. At the same time it is necessary to challenge positions all the time. The truths of today aren't necessarily the truths of tomorrow. You need to be ahead of your opponents.

This is a large explanation of Even's success and to my success with the Norwegian men's team. Neither the National Women's Team of Canada nor the Norwegian team of the 90s had the best players in the world, but were among the best in the world as teams. That ability to build the team out of the correct players will go a long way to making any coach successful.

Foreword

by Anson Dorrance

My introduction to Even Pellerud was right after a U.S. Women's National Team match with his Norwegian squad back in 1990 in Winnipeg Canada. It was while we were trying to create an American identity at an international level. This was before Hamm, Lilly and Foudy were on the field regularly. We were definitely a work in progress. Honestly, we were not a real threat yet at this level but on this particular day we had played well and had captured a result. There were all kinds of mitigating factors for Norway's loss: they had no real preparation coming in (we had been training and playing for two weeks beforehand), some of their best players had not made the trip; Even had little time to get to know, let alone to work with this new team. What had impressed me about Even right after this match is his lack of excuses and his accurate insights to what had impacted on our success. He could have moaned about lack of preparation or the absence of some of his stars but he did not. He proceeded to congratulate us on our preparation and cited every positive quality we exhibited and complimented the play of several of our players. I remember being struck by his graciousness but also his extraordinary confidence to offer nothing but praise for our victory and so self protection for his loss. I knew right then that this man was going to be a formidable adversary in every positive sense.

Our victories against him in Winnipeg in July of 1990 were followed by two losses a year later to him in late August/early September of 1991, just before we began our residency program for the first world championship. For us the 1991 world championship was a wonderful run where, after surviving a hair raising opening game against Sweden, we got better every match, culminating with an extraordinary performance to beat Germany 5-2 in the semifinal. This set the stage for the championship match against Norway.

In the final, the United States defeated Norway but it was against the run of play. The incomparable Michelle Akers on two balls from Shannon Higgins gave the United States a 2-1 victory. In the press conference I gave Even and Norway full credit for a game I thought we stole and then just like in 1990 when we first met, but this time before the world press, he again demonstrated his class by saying regardless of the game that day, we had had the best tournament and deserved to be the first women's soccer world champions. I have never forgotten how wonderful that gracious remark made me feel.

For the next World Cup in Sweden in 1995, Even and Norway triumphed. The biggest issue for all of us that competed with Norway was solving the issues of cracking their extraordinarily tough flat back four. It was now a model for all of us that coached at this level. I was a technical advisor for FIFA during this World Cup, responsible for the Karlstad venue, and like all great teams and all reigning world champions, Even's ideas on the game were given a platform for all of us to imitate. Tony DiCicco, my successor as U.S. national coach, made an astute decision to change the United States from the two marking back and sweeper that I have used in a combination man to man and zone in the 3-4-3 in China in 1991 and he introduced the next direction for the United States. One of the new wrinkles for the United States was a back four like Norway's.

Tony wrestled a world championship back with a gold in the 1996 Olympics and the greatest heart stopper in that U.S. run was not China in the final but an overtime victory over a gritty Norway in the semi's. How could this country, without our player population and player development, not only consistently compete with us, but maintain against us (at least while Even was there) a better win/loss percentage? It is an extraordinary credit to his powerful leadership but also his ideas on how to win consistently in this game.

Almost to prove this point but certainly to have a litmus test of his coaching prowess is to see the remarkable transformation in the Canadian National Team since he was hired. Their ascension has been breathtaking. From results on the field for the full team to a clear cut impact on player development with the youth teams he has made his mark again. And there will be more success, judging by the appearance of Canada in the first U-19 youth world cup final in 2002 and as recently as the past fall seeing the best players in a U.S. college soccer final four being Canadian (two superb Canadians delivered Notre Dame to the 2004 Collegiate Championship and one Princeton player in the middle of midfield may have been the best player in the tournament).

The final measure in coaching greatness is to see a powerful leadership force measured over three areas. First, there is the fight against the human tendency to want to be more comfortable and this is the fight the coach has with his own team to stay motivated. Second, there is the design of a system and playing style to make every opponent uncomfortable because of the difficulty of playing against it. And third there is the extraordinary challenge to distill the details that impact on victory because understanding and seeing these elements save the coach from being beaten too often by the greatest opponent: the game itself. If you solve this problem you become consistent, you never beat yourself, you are rarely upset and the game beats you less often. I have coached against many fine coaches and all of them have wonderful strengths, but Even has been the most complete. His teams always bring a motivated, difficult and consistent challenge. I have cherished any victory over him because they have been rare. But for all my enormous respect for Even as a coach, his thoughtfulness and kindnesses in public as well as private forums, show a deeper side that have won my admiration for him even more as a man.

Author's Foreword

I first met Even Pellerud when he was scouting some players in Ottawa in the summer of 2000. The CSA (Canadian Soccer Association) had arranged a reception and I had my first opportunity to meet the man the CSA had pinned the hopes of our Women's program on.

The man I met was frank, forthright, charming, and humorous. More importantly, he was open and interested in the state of the game in Canada.

In the intervening years that Even has shepherded our Women's National Team it is safe to add to that list of characteristics the term controversial. There is never a discussion of Canadian Soccer without some heavily energized conversation on the style of play Coach Pellerud has brought to the Canadian game.

He plays the game the way he lives his life and that is directly, always moving forward.

I hope you enjoy this insight into the man who created one of the greatest women's teams of all time, the 1995 Norwegian Women's World Cup Champions, and the man who is moving the Canadian Team firmly on the road to the winner's circle in China in the 2007 Women's World Cup.

Sam Kucey

In the last couple of years Even Pellerud has put together a team of young (very young!) players and balanced them with his Canadian National Team veterans. It became clear to me during this time that Pellerud was internationally well respected in the coaching ranks. In contact with some of the game's most accomplished coaches, Egil Olsen, Tony DiCicco, Anson Dorrance, Lauren Gregg, Pia Sundahage, Tina Theune-Meyer, it was remarkable how they all had positive interactions with Even Pellerud and particularly his very favorable influence on the women's game. I asked Even Pellerud in 2003 if he thought he had a book in him, as I was sure coaches in the women's game would be interested in his philosophy. He assured me he had and two years and countless hours later, here it is!

Prologue

What does it take to be a World Champion?

The Canadian Soccer Association (CSA) summarizes their Head Coach's career with the following media notes:

- Pellerud was named head coach of Canada's Women's World Cup Team in the fall of 1999 and hosted his first training camp in early February 2000. He earned his first victory with Canada on March 16, with a 2-1 win over Finland at the Algarve Cup in Portugal.

- On November 6, 2002, Pellerud led Canada to their third consecutive Women's World Cup berth with a 2-0 win over Mexico in the Gold Cup Semi-final. The win gave Canada an automatic berth in the 2003 World Cup in the USA. Canada would place fourth at the 2003 Women's World Cup after losing 3-1 to the United States in the third place match on October 11, 2003.

- Pellerud brings with him a vast amount of international experience. He was a professional player in his native Norway from 1973-1986 and was capped once by his country. He played with Norwegian clubs Valerenga, Grue and Kongsvinger.

- He served as head coach of the Norwegian women's national team from 1991-1996, enjoying tremendous success. Some of his highlights include winning Silver at the 1991 World Cup and the 1991 European Cup and Bronze at the 1996 Olympic Games. He led Norway to Gold at the European Cup Championship in 1993 and in 1995 capped his accomplishments by winning the World Cup.

- In July 2003, he had his contract extended to the end of 2008.

That is the official (CSA) biography of Even Pellerud. Hopefully, this book will help us, as coaches and players, to understand the women's game with a little more depth through the experiences of one of the most innovative and successful coaches, Even Pellerud.

Canada Hopes

In the case of women's soccer in Canada, in 1999 our country was hopeful in that, hiring a coach who had been there before, Canada would finally see a World Championship. The game of soccer or international football had become Canada's team sport in the '90s, surpassing even ice hockey with close to 900,000 registered players (male and female). Women crept towards the 500,000 mark and the high exposure for the game in print and visual began to peak with the Women's World Cup in the U.S. in 1999.

Following on the huge success of the 1994 Men's World Cup, definitely the most well-attended and highest profile television event that FIFA had ever participated in, Canada qualified for the '99 Women's World Cup in the United States and were hopeful to make a name for themselves in women's football. Canada's hopes crashed once again when they came up winless at the '99 World Championships, repeating their 1995 performance.

The Canadian Soccer Association (CSA) acted quickly, showing a serious and clear intent to improve the team and Canada's performance when they let long-time coach Neil Turnbull go and shortly after hired Even Pellerud. This bold step, hiring someone with Pellerud's credentials (1995 World Cup Champion and respected international coach) put a lid on a brewing player revolt. The move restored faith in the program for thousands of Canadian club and provincial program players whose dreams were to play for their country.

So who was this guy? Could a coach really make that much of a difference?

Even Pellerud's credentials and experience in a soccer-hungry country with only one-seventh the population of Canada was impressive. Norway was a country with a successful professional men's league and where a semi-professional women's league also thrived. The men's National team continued to over-achieve in the 1990's and Norway also boasted a magnificent women's team, winners of a silver medal in the first Women's World Cup in 1991 and defending WWC Champions in 1999. Pellerud was the architect of that Norwegian women's team and it made him the perfect choice to try to lead Canada's women to their first World Cup Championship. His 1995 WWC team was widely acknowledged to be one of the best women's teams ever assembled in football.

The CSA was to import a little of Pellerud's Northern Magic to Canada.

A new era in Canadian soccer began with Pellerud coming to Canada in October of 1999. The CSA had made its aspirations clear. They had intended to make it as far as the quarterfinals and make it into the top 10 in the FIFA World Rankings. (Those FIFA rankings released for the first time in the women's game in 2003 based on a history of all women's games from 1971 and placed Canada in the 11th spot in the world.) Even Pellerud came to Canada with some challenging work in front of him.

Chapter I

Pellerud: From Player to Coach

The Early Years

There is rarely a moment that Even Pellerud can recall from his childhood when he didn't have a soccer ball at his feet. Born on July 5th, 1953 third into a family of nine (with two younger twin sisters bringing up the rear), young Even Pellerud spent a lot of time with his older brother, Terje, who played soccer, frequently joined by their father, Ingvar.

A great fan of the game of football, Even's father's favorite team was Kongsvinger the club of the largest local town and a team that would figure very large in young Even's future. Ingvar had played as a child and at the club level. A truck driver/fruit and vegetable salesman by trade, nine children kept he and Even's mother, Liv, busy year round. The younger Pellerud saw his first game with his dad in 1955. Even Pellerud recalls his active childhood as a happy time. He feels it has been a significant positive influence on who he is as a person.

His community, the town of Roverud, was a hamlet of 500, a typical Scandinavian village in the 50's and 60's. One hundred kilometers east of Oslo in south-east Norway, Pellerud was outdoors constantly, and activities all winter long-skiing, skating. In the summer, games in the woods, back yards, in the streets, a soccer ball at his feet year round. It was heaven for a young boy. There were few cars in the village and being active was the only way of life. The soccer club was also a great part of the community.

His first club was the local Brane. The players on that senior men's team were the young Pellerud's heroes and the club played a large part in village life. Besides being in the formal soccer community, it very much involved Pellerud and the youngsters of the village because they played soccer all day long and their dream was to make it to the local club where their heroes played. It was not unusual for young Even to fail to show up for dinner on time and even miss it altogether because he was busy playing soccer. Fortunately, there were enough bodies around the table (see picture) that he could sneak in late. Impromptu goals in the back yards, in the streets, teams comprised of neighbors and classmates, this was where the football teeth of Even Pellerud were cut.

Pellerud's childhood friends and neighbors, Rune Sonsterudbraten and Kjell Torp were constant companions. They honed their skills on the ball duplicating what they saw from the older players. They joined their first club together. (Sonsterudbraten coincidentally is presently assistant at the professional club in Konsvinger.)

When Even Pellerud was nine years old he became a part of the Brane club, playing his first organized game: *"I still remember that game. We played in all the age groups of that club and at the local level and actually we had a pretty good team. That first game sticks in my mind. I was happy for the entire hour of play. The club had a progressive structure with all age groups at the local level and when I was 14 years old we won the local and provincial championship and, at that time, that was an amazing achievement for a small club like ours."*

Pellerud's experience at the Brane club was also a great learning experience. He grew up quickly, recalling: *"Maturity was forced on the players because there was no organized leadership behind the teams. The players were responsible for sorting out a lot of the arrangements around the games. If you had a coach he only showed up occasionally and we were happy when he did but we couldn't count on it. So we held a lot of our practices ourselves and we organized a lot of home games. We even had to organize several away games where we had to go by train. I became a bit of a leader maybe because of my enthusiasm. I was one of the most eager players and it wasn't uncommon for me to be the one to make sure we made it to all of the games. I was desperately looking to play and to miss a game because of too few players or because of lack of travel arrangements was something we just didn't want to accept. We as young boys bought tickets for the trains and we went to the away games as a team. If we didn't do it there would be no game. That's certainly something we don't see today, even back home. That independence is gone to some extent."*

When Even Pellerud was 16 years old he moved to the senior team. He had been training with this team since the age of 13 and that played a large part in his development as a player because he continued to play with his own age group, but trained with the senior side. This was a coaching concept he used throughout the rest of his career, always pushing the players, challenging them with greater competition, faster, superior teams, and forcing them to play faster. Pellerud's own personal skills improved rapidly. He was introduced to the politics of football early, as well. The club tried several times to get the soccer governing body to accept Pellerud playing as an underage, but the rules held firm and Even was 16 before he was officially able to play in the league with the senior team. His father, at that time, had been asked to coach the club. Even Pellerud remembers, as a typical teenager, he thought that was a very bad idea. He didn't want to be coached by his father and when he voiced that opinion the players turned to him and said, "then you'll train the team". Pellerud recalls, *"So, I was 16 years old when I had this first offer to begin my coaching career."* He wisely declined as a rookie, intuitively knowing it was a little beyond him yet. A year later he was hired by the larger club team in neighboring Kongsvinger as a player and a budding coach.

At the time Kongsvinger was the highest ranked local team in the next highest division, Brane being in the fifth division and Kongsvinger in the fourth. It was to be home for Even Pellerud for many of the following years.

"Over the years when I played with Kongsvinger we were promoted, won the fourth division, moved to the third, won that, moved to the second, and finally into the premier league. A large part of my career was as a player and coach with the team and I'm very proud that we went into the premier league in 1982 and the team stayed there for 17 years."

The brothers as sportsmen.

The brothers Even and Terje with a young sister - 1958

A typical Pellerud family table - easy to hide!

The young player and his dad Ingvar

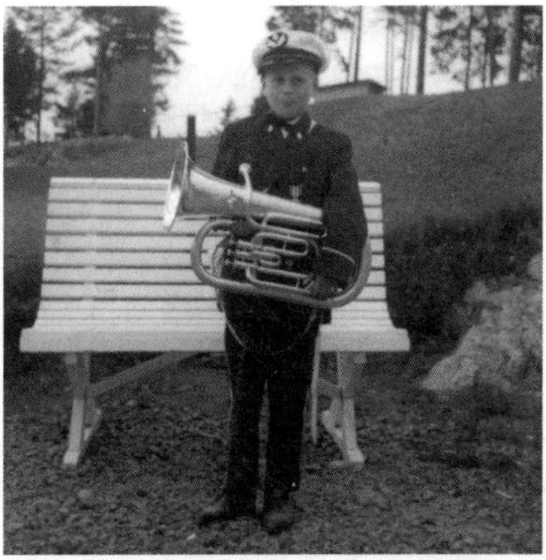

The Euphonium and Even - long since parted

The ball was always present.

Norway Day

The long Norwegian winter

Even's next club was Valerenga in Oslo. Continuing his schooling in the pursuit of a teaching degree, he played there from 1973-1974. His subjects of interest were history and social studies. He then attended the University of Teaching in Elverum and at the same time improved his playing and coaching experience.

He left Oslo for Grue, a third division club north of Kongsvinger, continuing his coaching path. At Grue he was hired as a playing coach and stayed from 1975-1977 until they were promoted to the second league. He went back to university in Oslo at the University of Sports and Physical Education (NUSPE) for further teaching certification and played for Valerenga in 1978. This experience at NUSPE proved to be a very important time in Even Pellerud's life. It was after this time at NUSPE that Pellerud began the most serious portion of his playing and coaching career in Kongsvinger. Those were busy years.

Pellerud: The Coach

Pellerud relished the player/coach role and he immersed himself in the coaching even while he worked as a teacher. He never doubted that his future was in coaching. It was something that he just felt was part of who he was going to be in soccer. While studying at NUSPE and playing with Valerenga, he married and the couple had their first child (Marius) in 1979.

This was an important time for Even Pellerud as a coach. One of his professors was Egil Olsen and many of his future colleagues in sport both on the Olympic Committee and the Norges Fotball Forbund studied at NUSPE. This cauldron of sports intellectuals was a perfect stimulus for a young man intent on being a professional coach.

Child number two (Marte) was born in 1982 and the Pelleruds built a house in Kongsvinger in 1983 where they lived until 1995. Even finished his playing career and signed as the club head coach at Kongsvinger in 1987. He was on his way as a full-time professional coach.

Arvild Sandven, a noted soccer journalist with the Aftenposten in Oslo, recalls that Pellerud as a player was appreciated on the field as a technical and well-playing midfielder. *"He was considered small and fancy and good to watch both at Kongsvinger and Valerenga, Oslo's most popular team. He was Kongsvinger's number one profile on the field for many years, with the years 1982-1985 being the peak of his career as a Kongsvinger player and playing coach."*

Pellerud maintained his contacts at NUSPE especially with Olsen who became a significant influence as Even Pellerud continued to develop his philosophy as a coach. No longer on a conventional career path of a teacher, it was natural for Pellerud to move to full-time coaching.

Pellerud received his first, and only, cap as an international player for Norway at the age of 30, and finished out his on-and-off 10-year playing career with Kongsvinger finally in the Premier League. His success as a player and a coach with that team moving into the premier division was not lost on the Norwegian Football Association. Karen Espelund, presently General Secretary of the NFF recounts why the Association wanted Pellerud aboard: *"The NFF was looking for a highly qualified coach and this meant from the men's football side because, at that time, our women's football was still in the developing stages and coaches hadn't been in women's football for long. Even was educated with the highest coaching level and he had, himself, been a good player and that was the type we also considered strongly.*

At that time the National Team for Women was still not high profile. But Even was in his approach very open to women's football. This was the first time we were hiring a full-time women's coach and we looked carefully. With his formal education in basics and then the right type of approach the NFF knew who they wanted in that position and Pellerud was at the top of the list."

In Norway this was an unusual offer for a men's professional coach. Pellerud was flattered by the NFF's proposal and decided he was ready to join the National organization. He was a little surprised when he was informed that they wanted him to take over the National Women's Team program as their first full-time head coach.

Pellerud was 36 years old. He had never seen a women's soccer game. Indeed, he had never contemplated the concept of women in soccer, but he was intrigued. Pellerud knew after teaching full-time that he wanted to spend the rest of his life in the game of soccer. To accept the position of Women's National Team Head Coach, the Pelleruds would have to move to Oslo, but it was a step forward in his career.

Typical Pellerud effort on the field

Celebrating his joy for the game at Kongsvinger.

The player/coach, 1984, at Kongsvinger

Wrong-footing the defender

Pellerud and Egil Olsen at the NFF, 1991

The well-playing midfielder in the 70's

Celebrating a goal at Kongsvinger
with teammate Olav Andersen

Chapter II

Football in Norway

Norway is a country of 4.4 million souls lying entirely north of the latitude of Edmonton, Alberta, Canada. Canada has a population of 31 million. Approximately 30 Norways would fit into the landmass of Canada (see picture).

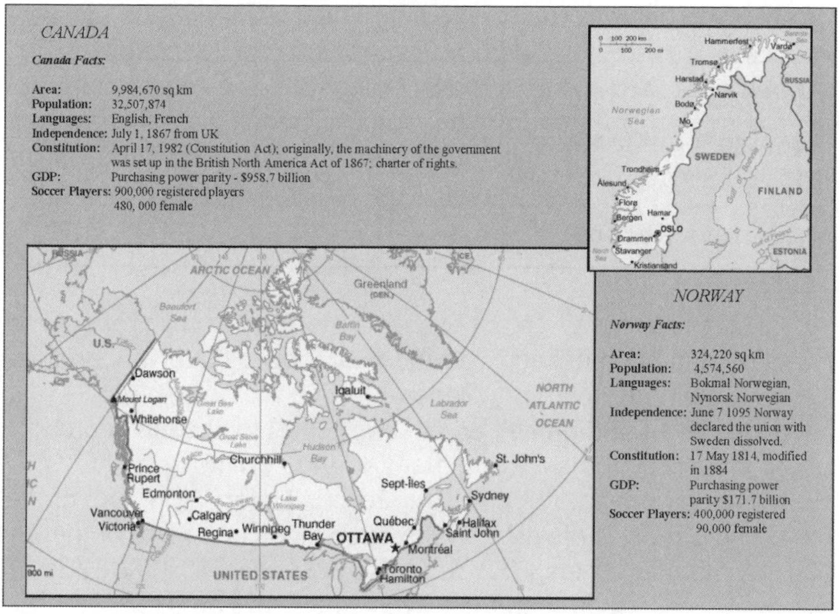

While both countries share similar geographies and heavier leanings towards social consciousness in their governments, they also share, as so many developed countries in the world do, a very common culture-a necessity to win in sports.

Norway has had tremendous success in winter sports (hosting a successful Winter Olympics in 1952 and again as recently as 1994 in Lillehammer). While the most recognized national sports may continue to be cross-country skiing, biathlon and ski jumping, soccer has been a huge part of the national fabric of Norway for years. Handball and ice hockey remain strong sports in the country but there is no doubt that football (soccer), particularly on the men's side, has been a large part of the fabric of Norwegian life for over a century. If there can be a golden age of football in Norway it would have had to have been the last 15 years. The successes in the men's and women's game have been unprecedented.

Norway Men's and Women's Records

Team	Played	W	D	L
Men's Senior Team (1908-2004)	691	235	163	293
Olsen's Record	88	46	26	16
Women's Senior Team (1978-2004)	292	185	48	59
Pellerud's Record	99	72	12	17

This success has not escaped the eyes of the world. The question has been asked over and over, how did Norway do this? Karen Espelund, Secretary General for the Norges Fotball Forbund (NFF) and herself an accomplished footballer, is proud of the influence of the achievement agenda on the sport in Norway and, indeed, in FIFA. She recalls Helen Wille, one of the first female representatives on the executive committee of the NFF. A member of the FIFA congress in Mexico, in 1986 Wille pointedly challenged then-FIFA President Brazilian Joao Havelange, "When are we going to have a women's world championship?" The FIFA-sanctioned women's world championship was held in 1988 due in large part to the influence of Wille and Espelund, both Norwegians.

While the women's league has existed in Norway since the 70's, the men's professional game is closer to 50 years old-relatively late in the European context. Øyvind Larsen, National Team statistician during Even Pellerud's career with the NFF, has lectured and published extensively on the subject of Norway's apparent overachievement in the world of football. In his presentation in Philadelphia at the National Soccer Coaches Association of America (NSCAA) conference in 2001, Larsen tried to explain the "Norwegian Soccer Fairy Tale". Larsen pointed out that, until the early 1990's, Norway was not taken seriously as a soccer country. The culture of soccer was not perceived to be as strong in this small country dominated by winter sports. He recalls that the women's soccer team winning their first World Championship in 1988 was

Norway's first step forward on the International football stage. They maintained this stability for the past dozen years. The world looked upon this as being a turnaround for the profile of women's sports and correctly perceived that an early women's liberation movement in Norway had a significant influence on the acceptance of women in sport. (See box - Brundtland)

A Role Model for Women's Rights

In 1986, Gro Harlem Brundtland formed a government as prime minister of Norway and, of the 18 ministers in her cabinet, eight were women.

"Norwegian women like to tell the story of a young boy who grew up in the 1980s during the term of female Prime Minister Gro Harlem Brundtland. According to the tale, the boy asked his mother whether it might be possible for a man one day to become prime minister of Norway.

In a country where women make up close to 40 percent of politicians and 60 percent of university students, where they have held titles from prime minister to Supreme Court justice to minister of defense and where 80 percent of women have jobs, it is no surprise that Norwegians pride themselves on their international reputation as a role model for women's rights." (by: Carrie Seim, Medill News Service, newsofnorway, 3.03, Page 8)

The men's team provided an even more stunning turnaround. After over 45 years of losing seasons (1945-1992), the National Men's program turned it around in the 1990s by qualifying first for the European Championship and then the World Cup for the first time since 1938.

These results, both on the men's and women's side, have not been lost on the world. Øyvind recollected that many countries had inquired and, indeed traveled to Norway to see what it was they were doing. In trying to explain the reasons for the success, Larsen utilized internal and external explanatory models. Larsen first offers an external explanation.

The Introduction of Professional Soccer in Norway

Professional soccer came late to Norway. And, although the first league was formed in 1914, Larsen indicated that the professional approach over the past 50 years has had a "knock on" effect with respect to skills. He also pointed out that this approach provided benefits that were not just wages or financial or business benefits, but also skills, organization, management, education and administration and an increase in the depth of knowledge about the game itself. Professionalism became a far-reaching concept in Norway and this positively affected the rest of the development of the game.

Player Development in Norway

The second factor Larsen looked at was player development. The successes in the '90's led to a number of Norwegian international stars, such as Tore Andre Flo (Chelsea 1997-2000), Ole Gunnar Solskjar (Manchester United), Rune Bratseth (Werder Bremen), Erik Thorstvedt (Tottenham and Norwegian Men's National Team 1994). Measuring success by the number of talents who were able to establish successful careers with European teams, international stars also emerged on the women's side-Heidi Støre, Linda Medalen, Hege Riise, Gro Espeseth.

Linda Medalen

Linda Medalen was a genuine star in Norway, beginning her playing career with the National Team in 1987. When Even Pellerud took over the team in 1989 he liked what he saw in the midfielder/defender. A gifted aggressive footballer she possessed potential for speed and he converted her to a forward almost immediately on his taking over the team.

Medalen recalls: "Even told me what he saw in me was my desire to win the game and my willingness to get out there and work hard, my efforts for success. It was what he needed in that team. I was happy when he put me in that position permanently. I had played it on my club team, but I learned a lot from Even.

"Our greatest experience was winning the World Cup with Even. But how we got there was how I learned my game. The overall experience of having Even Pellerud as a coach was really a highlight for my career. He was definitely the best coach I have ever had. Very distinguished and a good technical trainer. A complete trainer. He worked with our minds, with our attitudes, with our physical side, and our technical abilities. He was a master.

"I think I improved my fitness under Even's guidance more than anything. He was always letting us know what our strengths and weaknesses were and we practiced trying to improve our weaknesses, but also improving on our strengths. He was very clear in letting me know the skills I needed as a forward and those few skills I practiced constantly. '

"I think what Even Pellerud was most excellent at was picking the right players for the right positions. He didn't always pick the best 16 players in Norway, but he picked the 16 best to make our team. He knew what it meant to have a complete team and he picked the right players for that.

"He also picked the right staff. He would bring in experts and a doctor who fit in with the team and got along with the team. That was important for him. I remember he fought very hard with the Norwegian Federation to bring in Pensgaard as our Sports Psychologist. She fit in so well with the team, but they didn't want to spend the money and now, even over the years, they have finally recognized the importance of having a sports psychologist and I think it's all because of the work that Even did.

"We when look at how we play today and I look back at how Even played it's hard to put an exact statement on it, but I think everybody might be technically better today, but the will to win, the desire, the playing hard and tough and skilled at the same time, having an interest and all-consuming desire to win and putting those players in the right position on the field so you can dominate everywhere, that is missing now.

"The other thing that Even brought to the team was making sure we knew what we needed to do. If I compare him to all the other coaches I have had over the years before and after, when we went onto the field as his team to play a game we knew exactly what to do. We were never running out there because we always practiced a lot of the technical things and we knew tactically what the game plan was. He even went so far to let us know individually what he wanted us to do in the game plan. He would tell me: 'You do this, you do that, and you will score a goal.' He had a game plan for each player and he wanted you to stay with it.

Now it seems to be different. Everyone goes out and tries individually, maybe, but not so much with a single plan in mind."

Linda Medalen's career ended with a lower extremity injury right before the Olympic Games in Sydney. She's recovered and played on her club team and is managing Asker in Norway. She presently works as a police officer with the Drug/Narcotics squad. Always outspoken, Medalen continues to participate and comment on the women's game.

As far as the future, she states that she is a little worried because the National Team does not push as hard as they used to and she would like to see a return to more thorough basic training. She is still a very strong player who spent a lot of time on individual training (she constantly maintained her VO2 max in the 65 range). She is a great believer that physical strength and running capacity (endurance) will give teams the edge to win. She is not sure that the current Norwegian National Women's Team can go a full 90 minutes.

"Under Even, we could run 120 minutes because that's what he expected us to do. I'm not so sure the National Team today can run a full 90 under full power."

Medalen at the end of her career had been capped 152 times and was Norway's leading scorer with 64 goals.

Larsen credits the Norges Fotball Forbund's change in the development model with a further emphasis on training, education, and family and career planning and less of a focus on match results. This model, dubbed the "24-hour performer model", had definitely gained an international reputation. In 1997, the English FA hierarchy ("the masters") traveled to Norway for a week to study player development, looking for successful models as they tweaked their national program.

Things had come full circle as Scandinavian product Sven Goran Ericsson was selected English National Team Coach and the influence of the British, who had brought the game to Norway and Sweden, were about to take parts of it back home again.

The Import of Professional Players Abroad

Larsen also pointed out that by October 1998 there were 70 Norwegian professional players with foreign clubs in 16 countries. As these extremely talented players moved abroad, opportunities arose for younger Norwegian players to make earlier debuts in the Norwegian premier league. With the players at foreign clubs able to compare their professionalism to that in the Norwegian system, what they had come through was obvious and confidence grew. As Larsen stated: *"It was no longer necessary to take a camera when playing internationals at Wembley-winning was a real possibility now."*

Lack of Tradition

In Norway, Larsen points out that there was no "grand ol' man of soccer". There was no Helmut Schon or Franz Beckenbaur or Cesar Luis Menotti to speak with authority how the game should be played. There was an open book so to speak. Even more importantly, there was no press corps or supporters who expected success either. That meant that everyone was happy when results were achieved regardless of how the match was played. This lack of tradition, at least a winning tradition-often noted as critical to success-paradoxically worked to Norway's advantage.

Academics and Practitioners

Larsen also noted that the relationship between academics and practitioners was immensely successful in Norway. Having a sports university such as NUSPE allowed cross-fertilization of ideas and also helped set the required standards and, consequently, a higher level of expertise needed to work as a coach. This educational approach has lessened the opposition to analytical and scientific approaches to the game than would be permitted from an in-the-heart passionate hot bed of soccer, such as South America.

Internal Explanations

Larsen in his paper then looked at the internal explanations for the success of the Norwegian program. This really had to do with what was happening on the field. Larsen keyed on: i) performance analysis (see Chapter XII - Breaking it Down), ii) theory development, iii) the pattern of play, and iv) the systematic use of video in the way of providing feedback as critical internal factors.

Performance Analysis

Larsen in his lecture defined the importance of performance analysis as: "In order to be able to influence a team in the right way, it is crucial that performance is evaluated in an appropriate and reliable manner." He went on to highlight the conventional coaching process. *(See Figure 1)*

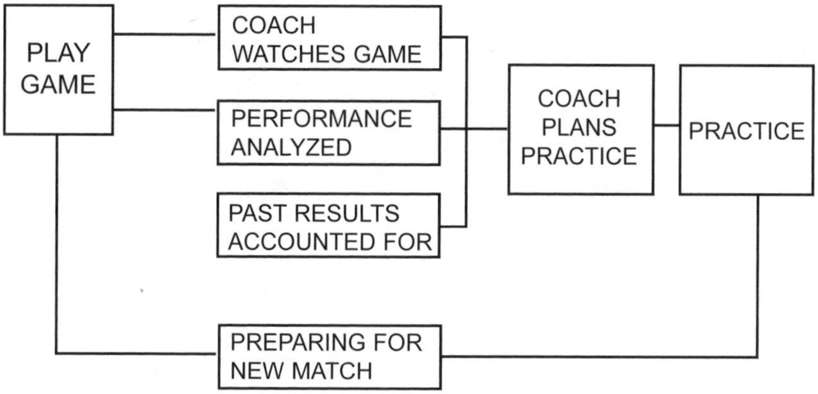

Fig. 1

The Coaching Process

Larsen pointed out that when matches are played, coaches evaluate both individual play and the team as a whole and this analysis acts as a guide in planning further training and choosing tactics for forthcoming matches. If the analysis part of this cycle does not provide the correct conclusion with regards to effectiveness it is highly probable that the potential of the team will not be realized. Several factors indicate that subjective, direct observation is not reliable. Larsen reviewed problems, such as:

1) The complexity of play;
2) The coach's physical and emotional condition;
3) Position of the coach on the field

and noted this made it difficult for a coach, alone, to observe all the appropriate aspects of performance for analysis to produce effective feedback.

Larsen next reviewed theory development as a critical success factor in the Norwegian program. He states, *"In Norway there has been a preoccupation for identifying the syntax, structure, and tactical grammar of the way soccer is played using objective notation analysis for almost 25 years. This method has many names. The most frequently used are notational analysis, performance analysis, and player and match analysis. Whatever you want to the name the process, this analysis consists of systematically gathering actual and/or video information for selective elements of game performance, live or hand recorded statistics, or from video tape and then collecting and analyzing it is valuable. This information serves two fundamental functions. First, it provides the coach and players with information and, secondly, data for particular model development."*

Development of Theory

It was Egil Olsen, one of Pellerud's teachers and admitted mentors, who was responsible for much of the success of the Norwegian Men's National Team in the '90's. By far the most successful men's coach before or since, Egil Olsen was also a student and then, later, a teacher at NUSPE. He defended his Master's thesis in 1973-a dissertation on soccer. The principle interesting features Olsen identified in his work included:

1) Possession of the ball changes very frequently - It is very rare that teams score after they have had the ball for a long period of time;
2) More than half of all goals follow either two touches or fewer;
3) Results also provided the basis for certain reflections associated with-"THE BREAKDOWN PERIOD". The exploitation of this phase seems to be very important;
4) The probability of scoring is no greater when your team's goalkeeper initiates play than when the opposing goal keeper is the initiator. He concludes that, in soccer, the

position of the ball is often more important than who is in possession.

As Larsen points out, Olsen's work is a distinct contradiction to Wade's principles of play as developed in the English FA. Wade's publication, An FA Guide for Coaches, really looks at possession and not goal scoring or attack as being the secret to successful soccer. Olsen's and Pellerud's approach really involved penetration and movement as essential principles in scoring goals. Later, after Wade, Charles Hughes in the English FA adapted a similar approach.

Egil "Drillo" Olsen

Even Pellerud's friend Egil ("Drillo") Olsen remains the most successful Norwegian National Coach in the history of the game. Born in 1942, Olsen played professionally from 1958 to 1975 including 16 games for the Norwegian National Team. As a coach he was in charge of the U-20 National Team from 1979 to 1989. As an NFF coach he continued with the Olympic National Team in 1990 and was appointed to the full National Team in 1990-1998. He took the Norwegian team out of a 50-year history of 30% success to an over 70% success during his tenure. Since he left the Norwegian team in 1998, Olsen went on to coach in the English Premier League with Wimbledon and then back to the Norges Fotball Forbund with the U-21 National Team in 2004 and made a move back to the professional Norwegian league.

The brilliant success with the Norwegian program qualifying for two European Cup finals, qualifying twice for the World Cup, and recently voted the most memorable game ever, defeating Brazil 2-1 in the 1998 World Cup in the first round in France, has stamped Olsen's influence forever on the Norwegian game. His approach to direct penetrating play and strict zonal defense is shared to a large extent in Even Pellerud's philosophy.

Larsen has authored an excellent insight into the history of notational analysis or performance analysis in Frank Cass Journal Soccer In Society (Volume 2 No. 3, Autumn 2001, Page 58-78)-on "Charles Reep, a major influence on British and Norwegian football." Reep had carried on, for close to 40 years, a very exhaustive statistical review of goals and goal chances. His analysis of over 12,000 goals wrought the same conclusions as Olsen. Coincidentally, Olsen was first introduced to Reep's work in an historical context at the first Science in Football conference in Liverpool in 1987. He did not meet Reep at that point, but was fascinated by his work and was buoyed by the fact that the conclusions in Reep's work were much in line with his own philosophy. Olsen began corresponding with Reep in the '90's, and indeed, Charles Reep visited Norway on two occasions before his death in 2002.

Even Pellerud was also familiar with Reep's work and recalls hosting Reep at a Norwegian National Team match when the father of notational analysis was over 92 years old.

Random Chance

Larsen lists some of the points gleaned from the analysis from both Olsen's and Reep's work. The first-that random chance often decides soccer matches-is well understood by all soccer coaches and players. Despite the factual analysis of over 9,175 consecutive goals and every ball and player movement event in the match where goals were scored, Reep's work pointed out that a single match can be decided to a great extent by random chance. "Anything can happen at any time in any one match." Larsen observes that in knock out competitions an inferior team can beat a superior team and league tables can look very surprising after five matches but over an entire season comparative strength tends to win out over luck.

As Larsen notes here, Olsen found documentary proof that the "in off the post/out off the post" effect is real. Larsen continued looking at Olsen's work on theory development.

Seeing Beyond the Results

Larsen points out the method of "seeing beyond results" developed from Reep's study of goal attempts. Reep was able to statistically sort out when a team was unlucky, when a team got a fair result, and when a team got a very fortunate result. Olsen went on to refine goal attempts to scoring opportunities and this method has been used in Norway for many years. Larsen used the example of a Norway draw against Finland in 1997 when Olsen, the coach, scored the result 9-2 in scoring opportunities. Using pure statistical probability it's less than 5% likely that you would lose and more than 80% probable that you would win a match with that advantage in scoring opportunities. In that match that team was unlucky. On the return match in Finland a few months later, Norway won 4-0. But, Olsen had scored the match 7-5 in Norway's favor. He knew that Norway had been lucky.

Larsen adds that the entire country has taken to looking at the games that way and points out that Olsen has allowed many people to see beyond the result. There may be more to correct after a win than after a defeat.

Choice of Style

Finally, Larsen in his Internal Factors points out that the analyses and statistics reinforced Olsen and indeed Pellerud's, belief in intensive, penetrative style of play. The research consistently showed that 80% of goals came from three passes or fewer and, adding to that Reep's meticulous recording of ball and player movements, indicated the importance of frequently reaching the space behind the last line of defense and closest to the opponent's goal. According to Reep, *"This allows a team to influence chance to go their way".*

Larsen listed the various methods used to collect, store, analyze, and present data that the NFF have worked on. Since 1991, just after Pellerud came to the program, all the National men's, women's, and U-21 teams, as well as their opponents, have been analyzed (see Chapter XI on Match Analysis).

The purpose of applying these statistics is as a tool to support and modify the team tactics. The data gathered is used to support one of the cornerstones of the NFF's principle and that is feedback. This method continues to be employed in Norway to this day.

When analyzing the Norwegian pattern of play, Larsen also credits the roots of Norwegian soccer, particularly on the side of defense. Notational analysis is least effective in deciding defensive tactics and immediately when taking over the program in 1989, Pellerud introduced the Women's National Team to an extreme form of zonal defense, in which no man-marking takes place.

As Larsen points out, the position of the player is almost completely defined by the teammates, not the opponents, and in many ways this was unique to Norway, particularly on the women's side in the early 1990's.

Statistics work more to support Norway's method of attacking as they have moved more and more towards a penetrative style of play. The NFF principle of fitness and speed works into the Norwegian attacking style. In identifying an unbalanced situation (see Chapter V-Principles of Play) the entire team should go forward with great mobility after the ball. Though loss of possession may occur, it is further up field and the object is then to regain possession immediately after the loss.

Larsen notes that the debate on this style of play was, and remains, the focus of the media's and the public's attention. He admits: *"Many members of the soccer community dislike this style of play and consider it to be simple and primitive. However, the overall aim of play is to win matches, so we are willing to sacrifice the fleeting beauty of aesthetic style in the name of efficiency."*

It was into this cauldron of exciting innovation in the NFF that Even Pellerud entered and indeed contributed to. As Larsen had elucidated, match analysis, professionalism linked to knowledge, education and organization, plus choices of playing style have been key elements of the *"Norwegian Soccer Fairytale"*.

Chapter III

The Norwegian Women's 1995 World Cup Team

The Norges Fotball Forbund (NFF) was in the midst of redefining itself and the program it delivered when Pellerud was asked to take over the Women's National Team. The federation had decided to move forward and Pellerud had become a high-profile coach. With the success of the women's team at the unofficial World Championships in 1988, the NFF recognized the future of women's football and wanted to move forward in that direction. This forward thinking was not as common in the coaching ranks and, indeed, in the soccer-mad public.

As stated previously, Pellerud was 36 years old and had never seen a women's game. He was surprised at the offer, but excited as well. He wanted to be a part of the Norges Fotball Forbund, which was working on the science and theory of the game, as well as the practical application of programs on a daily basis. Despite admonitions from his male coaching confreres that he would be taking a blind path in his soccer career, Even Pellerud made the decision to take over the Women's National Team in 1989. He felt he had a significant advantage over other coaches in that he had been raised in what he considered to be a politically radical family, with a very liberal approach to life and what he termed "an updated attitude". He truly felt he came to the women's game with an open mind. Even candidly states: *"I was raised in a left-wing family. Definitely a working-class family. We were used to being open-minded. Even the kids could speak their minds and, yes, we had very strong women in our family. It's a Norwegian trait, but maybe more so in my house."*

He recalls watching his first practice and rather than being disappointed at the technical level, was pleasantly surprised at both the technical and physical level of play and, importantly, became extremely excited when he saw the opportunities for developing tactical play, as very little seemed to exist at the time. It was a job he was to jump into for the next 7½ years.

The famous 1995 celebration proved an inspiration for the US

Champions!

Store was dominant in the midfield

Winning the Gold, 1995 WWC Sweden

A tearful/joyful Nina Nymark Andersen

Espeseth celebrating

The champions of WWC95

The story

The winning goal, WWC95

In addition to his duties as National Team Coach, Even Pellerud was very involved with the Olympic Committee. Olympic High Performance Director Bjørge Stensbol, who coincidentally was born in the same village as Pellerud, was involved in challenging the Norges Fotball Forbund to improve their elite programs. Preparing the world showcase for the '94 Olympics, Pellerud participated on several of the Olympic sports committees and was intimately involved with the NFF's redrafting of its principles.

Karen Espelund, the General Secretary for the NFF, recalls: *"Pellerud was intrinsic to development of NFF model for player development and national programs".* (See Chapter VIII on Player Development) On the field, Pellerud was identifying some of the young talent in the country.

One of the first trips he took with the Norwegian National Team was to Canada. Traveling to Winnipeg with Karen Espelund as manager in the delegation, this was an international tournament and Pellerud's first trip to Canada. Canada, the U.S., and Norway played a three-team tournament. With Pellerud was 19-year-old Hege Riise, a standout from a local club. Pellerud was impressed with her vision on the field. She played her first international game against Canada and Norway won 3-0. The next game was against their archrivals, the U.S., who they had been very successful against for the previous three years. They were stunned when they lost 4-0. This was a setback for the players and for Pellerud. He recalled: *"They were better than Norway in all the specialty games. They had more endurance and stamina. They were faster, more skillful and even smarter. We had no chance. We were outplayed for the entire 90 minutes. We met them again two days later and we lost again, but this time 4-2. We had narrowed the gap a bit. Going home to Norway after that tournament, I met with the players in the airport and I told them, 'we have one year left to the World Cup and we have one year to close the gap on the U.S.A. Can we do it?' And I outlined for them very briefly what had to improve, from individual players and as a team, and they responded, 'we can do it.'"*

The importance of international friendlies paid in the fact that it was the only way Pellerud's team could gauge where they stood. Coming off the 1988 (unofficial) win in the World Championship in China, the cockiness was knocked out of them and they knew what they had to do. This was a classical wake-up call for the team and the coach.

Karen Espelund, now the General Secretary of the NFF, also remembered that 1990 tournament with the U.S. and Canada. It was noteworthy because the future all-time best Norwegian female soccer player, Hege Riise, played her first match. It was also the first time the team saw Mia Hamm, and the new dominant 1v1 U.S. play under Anson Dorrance. Espelund recalls discussing what the next approach with the team would be with Even Pellerud on the way home. The edge that the U.S. had in the tournament was not only the 1v1 skills, but also speed and physicality. The one thing Pellerud thought they could do was to train the Norwegian women for speed and fitness. That was a turning point for the team and Espelund recalls that they have often discussed it since. When they went back to Norway they had to introduce the concept of a strong, fit team, the most fit in the world. Programs were put in place to work on the speed and skill of the game. This physical fitness approach was also one of the foundations of the NFF's program for revival.

The NFF helped by introducing scholarships to National Team players to allow funding for more opportunities to train- more than once a day was encouraged. Slowly the women of those teams in the '90's emerged as some of the best trained athletes in the world. It wasn't unusual to train 10-12 times a week. And, as an indication of their dedication, most of them were also students and working.

Pellerud was chiefly responsible for the physical training program. He brought in specialists when possible, but he was the overall program manager.

Hege Riise was a shy young player when she was brought to the National Team in 1990 at the age of 19. She was not a large player, but she had outstanding talent and energy. She recalls first coming to the team and her new coach: *"Before I met Even I hadn't really heard too much about him. He was already the coach when I came to the National Team in 1990. They had won in 1988 and he seemed to be successful in continuing that work. One thing Even was good at was keeping us on our toes, calling us to make sure we did our job, followed his training or even just to cheer you up if you were injured. He really believed so hard that we could beat everyone so we could not find ourselves thinking otherwise. He pushed us to get better and I think that might be something we miss. We took one step down after he left the program. The new coaches don't know how hard we had pushed then and if you put your goal one step down, you still mentally push to get to that goal, but it's a lower goal than what we were used to. Even had the ability to make us strive for something more. There is no doubt that he created an atmosphere around our National Team that was 100% professional and he never tried to do everything himself. If there was an area that someone knew more than him about, he would bring in another professional.*

"Even gave me support from the start. I was shy and didn't speak too much, but I felt I had trust from him from the start. He gave me room. I know I had many less-than-good skills, such as my individual defensive work, which I worked very hard on. My heading also had to be improved. But, he gave me room to be creative and with that he pushed me to train harder and more.

"The club team I played on wasn't the best so he had to keep an eye on me to make sure I was pushing myself. I had to send my training diary in for every month so he could follow very closely what we did. I sat down with him and made a plan. He did this with all the players-what we all needed to work on. We had many camps together. Lots of weekends and week camps. When we weren't in national training camp he would call, e-mail, speak with our club coaches and find out how our training week was so we always knew he was interested and was keeping an eye on us.

"Our league in Norway was from April through October and every team started training in January, so we were training on skills and the physical side of the game just about all year round, and Even followed up with our diary. One day I remember I played what I felt could have been my worst game ever and I felt terrible. Instead of telling me what a bad game I had, Even just asked what was on my mind. He knew there was something else other than a bad game. And that was good because he was right. There was something happening in my personal life that was on my mind. It was great to play for a coach who understood you as a person and I played almost every game with Even as a coach.

"His style, his zone defense, and his penetrating attacking style were new for our team, but he picked players that he saw in every place on the field. He could see in each of the players what they needed for that position and that way we had a good result against almost every team. We never thought that we played 'different' soccer. He believed so strongly in that direct game of soccer he had us believing in it, too, just as strong. After he initially picked the team we played with almost the same players all the time and that made us a very strong team. He also had us playing against boy's teams regularly and always striving to be better. We won with him as a coach. We scored goals. We won games. We really felt like we could take every team. We wanted to score goals and the faster we got there to score them, the better it was for us.

"Norway has a reputation as a physical team. This is something that we always heard in the press from other countries, from other teams. I think that was true then, but now I think there are teams that play more physically than we did. We still may have that reputation, but I'm not sure the Norway team today (2004) is as physical as we were before. I think that reputation grew for us because of the direct play soccer. The long ball, the use of the heading and the running to the ball-that style forces you to play physical, to be fast and long.

"He also understood how important it was for us to be mentally strong. He brought in Anne-Marte Pensgaard as a men-

tal coach to help us work harder to get stronger mentally, to believe in ourselves no matter what happens.

"I think our best year ever was winning the World Championships in 1995. I don't think anything could have made us not believe we were going to win the Worlds. We were just there. We wanted to play more and more. Even had to stop practice some days because we wanted to play so much and he was afraid we might burn up all of our energy in practice.

"I think practice and right before games is where leadership is very important. It's not so important in the games or during the games, but I think having a coach that is enthusiastic and very clear in how he wants you to play, you can do much more than you ever thought possible. We had a strong leader in Heidi Støre as our captain and she was a natural leader both on and off the field. I believe you have to have good leadership from your coach and your teammates always to set an example. Even and Heidi had very good communication. She played behind me in a defensive midfield and I felt safe with her. I could be creative on offense because I knew that Heidi was there if I missed. We had a system that we played and we knew what would happen if the ball was over here or over there or on the other side. We knew exactly where to be, how to position ourselves. We knew we wanted to get forward when we had the smallest of chances and there was only one reason to get forward and that was to score goals. We worked very hard to have three or four players in the box when we had a goal scoring opportunity.

"For me, personally, soccer is important. I played on the National Team for over half of my life and invested those years to get better, to be as good as I could be and it has taken me to many good places in this time. I was lucky to be selected and spent three good years with the Carolina Courage. It was nice to have that attention to the league and the game in the U.S. It was also very sad to have that professional league shut down.

"Women's soccer is growing in Norway now. More young girls are playing and it is important to give every kid a chance to do what she wants most. I would say that the women still don't

get enough publicity, here, in Norway, playing club soccer. It is more noticeable in the media when the National Team plays.
"As a kid I played all sports. I wanted to try everything: ski jumping, team handball, cross-country skiing, but after a few years I know that soccer was where I wanted to be. Everything I learned from soccer I use now in my daily life. I set goals. I use the mental training to keep strong mental health. I use the teamwork. I'm not the shy person I used to be. I use what I've learned from soccer to meet people, media, fans. Everything I learned over these years made me strong. I was shy when I first made the National Team, but after a few years of learning of how to handle things I feel more natural now with people. It is interesting that not many of our older players are so much involved with soccer when they stop playing here. Most of them have good jobs and I'm sure playing soccer on the National Team helps there, but it also helps them in business: setting goals, working together.
"My advice to anyone trying out for a national team is try your hardest, do your best, talk to the coach, make sure you know what he wants from you. Know you're there for a reason, that you are a part of the team, whether you play only one game, or one hundred. Respect what everyone is working hard to accomplish and be enthusiastic about it. I certainly think that watching goals scored is fun. I like that direct style, but maybe not only the long ball. I think a little of both styles is good depending on the team. I know I am direct in my way of play. I want to score goals as fast as I can and to watch the possession game to me is the boring game to watch. I want to see these teams go forward to get goals."

Hege Riise by 2004 had over 180 caps with the Norwegian National Team. She was the FIFA Player of the Tournament in the Women's World Cup in 1995 (and Silver Boot Winner, as well). She was named Norway's Best Female Soccer Player four times and in 2003 received the honor of being the Best Female Soccer Player ever in Norway. She played with the Carolina Courage in the WUSA where she was the captain from 2000-2003.

A natural offensive midfielder, her greatest enjoyment came from the '95 World Cup and her favorite memories include playing together with her teammates for a long period of time, pushing each other in training, and having a coach who reminded them that there isn't anything they can't do.

She has since gone on to be one of the most dominant and well-respected mid-field players in the world.

On the trip to Winnipeg, the shy Riise ended up in the local police station with the whole team when the Scandinavian custom of sunbathing topless at the beach confounded the locals and the team was brought to task for indecent exposure. Pellerud still chuckles at the memory of the culture clash as the team had to button up and were sent on their way. This was just one of the many cultural differences he was to see in his Canada/Norway future.

Ninety ninety-one (1991) was a busy year for the team. The European Championships were held and the Norwegian team made it to the finals. They lost to Germany in overtime at the Denmark tournament but Pellerud was happy with their progress.

The next challenge was the first official FIFA World Cup in China. Norway had an excellent tournament, making it to the final against the U.S. They pushed the final into overtime but lost in front of over 63,000 fans at Guangzhou Taiyang Stadium in China. But they knew they had closed the gap and Pellerud had begun to use his coaching method of layering his defensive tactics followed by his offensive tactics. They were back on an even keel against the U.S.-a great improvement in two years. It is noteworthy that both U.S. Coach Anson Dorrance and assistant Tony DiCicco recall an evenly fought game with a great physical performance by the Norwegian team at that 1991 World Cup game in China. It was a game where Norway arguably had the run of play.

Exiting 1991 with two silver medals and one citation from the beach in Canada, Pellerud re-signed with the NFF for four years and began his preparations for the 1995 World Cup. He was now fully involved in the women's game.

Not dissatisfied with the team's progress, Pellerud had come as close as possible to winning both championships and now he had a goal. He knew what he wanted to change and how he needed to improve. The coaching staff and players were committed and they all felt strongly that they should be able to win in 1995.

Pellerud was impressed with the development. He recalls: *"We worked hard on the technical priorities, basically zonal defense, pressure on the ball holder. We wanted it to be tough to play against us not only from a physical standpoint, but also from a tactical standpoint. Goalkeepers had been our Achilles' heel in the past, but now we had Bente Nordby, a great young goalkeeper who subsequently developed into one of the best players in the world. She steadily improved during those years with coaching from Jerry Knutssen (team goalkeeper coach). We looked and found quicker, stronger players and, slowly but surely, from an attacking standpoint we focused again on our playing style and the philosophy of play. We built quick penetrating attacks, as opposed to possession, spending all of our practice time on that. We went to the 1993 European Championships with a stronger team. We made it through to the final, a very difficult game against the host, Italy, and won."*

One of those great players Even Pellerud added to the team was Anne Kristen Aarones. Aarones was another of Pellerud's outstanding forwards. In recalling her years with Pellerud as her coach and the current state of the game, Aarones states: *"the team is still (2004) trying to work with the same playing philosophy that Even had introduced, but in many ways, other nations have changed. They have adjusted. They're better organized and they've upped their training so the physical or fitness edge isn't there the way it was before for Norway."*

From a personality standpoint, Aarones felt that, *"the newer coaches have a different personality. Pellerud knew what he wanted and didn't ask the players as much for advice. He did what he believed was correct and he stood by that. The coaches I worked with later seemed to be a little bit more uncertain as to how to play. They weren't as definite in their beliefs."*

Aarones felt that she was influenced significantly by Pellerud because he picked her as a 17-year-old. This was a big step for her and she considered herself a trainee that first year and she recalls he told her to *"hurry; slowly"*. This was great advice for the young Aarones who learned from the very best players and she knew what she had to do to become as good as them. Aarones recalls that Pellerud was always directly talking to players. *"He made it quite clear what was expected from you, but he also made it known that the team was more important than one player."*

She also recalls that: *"It was his great skill to put a team together that wasn't necessarily the best players, but it was the best team. He knew how to get the best out of each player."*

Aarones notes, as Hege Riise did, that they had to deliver an honest training diary. Pellerud, as their coach, was always on top of what they were doing in the way of practices with their club teams and when they were on their own. He would make suggestions and comments on their training, sometimes in writing and sometimes in conversation. *"We practiced hard to learn to play the way Even Pellerud wanted us to. We practiced both on and off the field, because it took time for us to learn and understand. Many of us had never played zone before. Many of our drills were just moving slowly across the field according to where the ball was and talking about the game. What do you do if this player does that? Or if she does this? And so on. How do you move if your teammate has the ball over here? Where do you go? I would say, even though I joined the team before 1990, I don't think we really felt that we had learned the style until 1995.*

"We were always known as a fit team and think that is simply because we trained much more than any of the other nations. To play the way that Even wanted us to, we had to run a lot (and if you ask Even, he will tell you that I couldn't run!). His style of play was dependant on that.

"Our peak year was definitely 1995 and we worked hard to get to that point.

"I think the leadership Pellerud gave us was important. I can't say I always agreed with the way that he coached the team, but he was very confident in what he was coaching and that goes a lot towards making it work and instilling us with confidence. It helped a lot too that we had good results. When you win you don't ask questions about the way you're playing.

"There were also a lot of very strong personalities on our team with Heidi Store, Gro Espeseth, Linda Medalen, and Hege Riise being some of the most important. That leadership made us all believe even more than that-we knew that we could win.

"Soccer has really meant a lot to me. It's a lifestyle. I started when I was 8 and played for 20 years, finishing when I was 28. I was a National Team player for 10 years and I wish it was more popular even in Norway. Even though it is the biggest sport, we as women's teams still struggle. There aren't a lot of spectators at our games and the media don't include us in the soccer talk as much. Because the sport doesn't make a lot of money, it is impossible to pay the players, so being a professional over here is difficult. I think our National Team has a good profile and being a World Cup winning team made us popular and many people followed us. And, I can honestly say it helped me later being a known soccer player. I got my first job through soccer and it is often an advantage if people have watched you on television.

"It also helped me grow as a person. I learned a lot about working with other people. That's what team sports are about and you can use that later in life, in school and in your job.
"One thing I would like pass on to any young player trying to get ahead in the game is to have fun. You really have to enjoy it because if you don't you'll never reach the National Team level. Practicing by yourself and with others and with the ball all the time, I think that's important. It's not enough just to practice with your team. At the youngest ages working on your technical skills is most important. The physical, tactical, and mental areas can come later.

"The concept of playing style in Norway remains controversial especially recently with the men's team who haven't played too well. They play a direct style and a lot of people in Norway want them to change the way they play. I think the way we played under Even was attractive soccer. We used a lot of long passes. It might be more exciting to watch someone dribble past 10 people or play a lot of short passes, but I think everyone wants to watch your team win and the best way to do that is to play directly."

Aarones was capped 110 times on the National Team and scored 60 goals in her career. She was the leading goalscorer in the 1995 WWC. She returned to Norway after playing for the New York Power in the WUSA.

With the 1993 European gold medal in hand, the team began to build towards the '95 World Cup.

To maintain the winning record, Pellerud continued working with the core of his team, slowly but surely improving all aspects of play. They had been physically outworked by the U.S. in 1990 and 1991 and the U.S. 1v1-play was superior. Pellerud was sure a properly played zone defense would negate a lot of the 1v1 U.S. advantage.

During the build up to the 1995 tournament, Pellerud took the team to the Chiquita Cup in the U.S.. Working new defenders into his team he faced the new U.S. Head Coach, Tony DiCicco. In that tournament, Norway narrowly lost to China, to Germany, and then a disastrous game to the U.S. 4-1. However, Pellerud fully understood the random chance theory in soccer, and was satisfied with the progress in play of his team.

When Tony DiCicco attended a press conference after the game, in a gracious moment indicative of his personality, he commented that the score was 4-1, but could easily have been reversed if Norway had made the most of its chances in the first 30 minutes. Norway was all over the U.S. in the opening half and DiCicco wanted the relative rookie soccer press in the U.S. to understand that the final score was not the only thing to look at in a soccer game. Even Pellerud, an equally gracious coach in the international scene, made sure that he sought Tony DiCicco out afterwards and thanked him for his honest assessment of the outcome.

In a testimony to the team's cohesiveness, this pre-World Cup test in '94 proved to be a wake-up call for the team coming off strings of continual successes. They refocused to enter the '95 World Cup. Norway went into the Tournament, played six games, scored 23 goals and conceded only one goal against in the Quarterfinals against Denmark. As Pellerud recalls: "This was an amazing peak for our team. I was feeling confident. You can never be over confident in winning but we had a short week-end camp in Norway only one and a half months before the start of the World Cup and at that time, as I always do, I match my team against boys teams. We beat a strong, big, physical junior men's team (18 year olds) 4-2 in a scrimmage. I said to my coaches, 'We're ready to win because that was just an amazing performance' and it confirmed that the confidence we had was justified.

"We came into the World Cup in Sweden very well prepared, only one starter was out with an injury, the rest were fit and ready and we defeated Nigeria solidly 8-0 in the opening game. We went on to defeat England 2-0, Denmark in the quarter-final 4-1, and the U.S.A. in the semi-final 1-0. We ran into our first problem in the U.S. game when we lost Heidi Støre on a red card. She was out for the final game. Normally, that may take a lot of focus off the team, but we were there to win. I still remember the day before the game. I went for a walk in a park and I saw the players in the morning. It was raining in Stockholm, but my players were walking around the park singing and joking and very relaxed despite the final game that day. The pressure was on and we had just lost our team captain; there were a lot of reasons to be nervous, but that morning I was confident in the team's disposition. Our game plan was to go out in the rain that day with an extremely high-pressure game, which is risky against a skillful team like Germany. But with our confidence, the rainy conditions, and the fact that Germany likes to play the short pass game, I thought it was a good idea to press them high, win the

ball early, and punish them high up in their own end. It was a very successful game plan. We defeated them 2-0 and it could have been a lot more. We outplayed Germany for both halves. It was an amazing campaign and definitely a highlight of my career."

Pellerud had now amassed two golds, a gold and a silver in both the European Championships and the World Cup.

Lauren Gregg, Vice-President and Director of Player Development for WUSA (Women's United Soccer Association), recalls that Norwegian/U.S. semifinal game in her book The Champion Within: *"The success of that '95 team had a profound effect on the women's game in the world. The strict zonal defense was unique at the tournament and the relentless physical high-pressure game wilted all the opposition."*

1995 Women's World Cup
from <u>The Champion Within: Training for Excellence</u>
by Lauren Gregg

The semifinals placed China against Germany and the United States against rival Norway. Norway came out in a 4-4-2 as we expected. We played our 3-4-3 (still with two marking backs and a sweeper on defense).

Hege Riise and Heidi Store were two dominant midfield personalities for the Norwegians. Hege was extremely tactical in the quality and timing of her runs out of midfield. Because we were in a man-to-man defense in the back, her mobility gave us a lot of trouble. She tended to come off the right center of midfield. Unlike in a zone, where you have players more naturally in the spaces where the opponents like to attack, we had big holes behind our outside midfielders. As a result, they would organize their attack up one side, playing very direct up their left side, for example. But the area they were ultimately going to attack often was the opposite side. Their weak-side runs off the ball were timed perfectly. So while our defenders were tracking their front-runners up one side, they would release a midfielder, often Riise from the other side. This required our outside midfielder, in this case Kristine Lilly, to do a lot of work defensively to track that space. Kristine is so responsible, we didn't have to worry about her commitment to track those runs. In fact, because Kristine Lilly is so tactically smart, she is given free reign on the field. However, the bigger issue was we didn't get Kristine on attack enough, in part because of the man-to-man defensive system we played.

Up front, they played to their target personality, Linda Medalen. Supporting her out of midfield, or at times as a front-runner, was an emerging personality on the international scene, Ann Aarones. Both Medalen and Aarones are tremendous attacking players. Aarones is especially dangerous because of her six-foot-two inch frame. Marianne Pettersen, coming out of the midfield, posed another attacking threat for the Norwegians. In goal, Bente Nordby had shown us another level for goalkeeping in the women's game. Her high starting positions behind her defense and her kicking game were becoming factors in Norway's success and a new marker for the women's game.

In addition, we gave the ball away too much. The more you give it away the more you give your opponent the potential to score. It was hard for us to hold it in the back partly because of our lack of shape, and also because we hadn't demanded it of our defenders before. The ability of our defenders to hold the ball would be critical because other teams started to lower their restraining line, meaning instead of putting pressure on us in our own defensive end (or "high"), they would drop off and let our defenders carry it out and set play. We were still at a point in time where our defenders were mostly defensive players because of their marking responsibilities. Marking was primarily what we had asked of them. Norway drew a patented corner kick less than twenty minutes into the match. They scored to go up 1-0. Aarones, a tremendous personality in the air, headed a ball in from our six. That would be the only score of the game. We had been dethroned as world champions.

While you have heard me recount some tactical concerns exposed by this match, there was also something less tangible, but perhaps as telling to the outcome. There was an air of unease beyond what one would expect going into a world championship semifinal. We played from a place of uncertainty. We played without the USA Mentality. If there is one team you had better show up to play, it's the Norwegians. You must play with complete conviction, with resolve and a sense of abandon. We didn't have it. With fifteen minutes left you could feel our tentativeness lift. We rallied and hit three shots off the crossbar, but it was too late. Norway had just knocked us off the top of the world by a narrow 1-0 margin. They went on to defeat Germany 2-0 in the Cup finals, while we would re-face China for the bonze medal. Although this was a difficult challenge, we were able to re-group, play with pride and defeat China 2-0.

Norwegian results 1995 WWC

Norway	**8**	**0**	**Nigeria**
Norway	**2**	**0**	**England**
Norway	**7**	**0**	**Canada**
Norway	**3**	**1**	**Denmark**
Norway	**1**	**0**	**USA**
Norway	**2**	**0**	**Germany**

1996 Olympics

Pellerud's last year with the team was the Olympic Games in 1996. He ran into some injury problems on the team, but in group play Norway did well, tying Brazil 2-2, defeating Germany 3-2, and advancing against Japan 4-0. The hot conditions and tough physical play took their toll however, and Heidi Støre was lost for the tournament with an ACL injury after 20 minutes of the opening game. It was a lot different losing the team captain in the first game as opposed to the last game, as had occurred in the '95 World Cup. That same game, the co-captain and defensive leader Gro Espeseth was concussed and sustained a head injury. She was out of the game for 10-15 minutes and the team doctor wanted to take her out. But she absolutely refused. Pellerud recalls: *"I'll never forget, she was on the sidelines crying. She had her fist in the doctor's and my face and said, 'you dare not take me out of this game. I'm going to play this game, you cannot take me out. Don't even try. I'm playing. I feel fine.' She played the whole game and we ended up with a tie against Brazil."*

Gro Espeseth was a standout defender and co-captain on Pellerud's Norwegian Team. Coming to the team from the National programs just before Pellerud joined the team, Espeseth was promoted from the Youth National Team in 1990 to play with the Women's National Team prior to the World Cup in 1991. Espeseth in a recent interview recollecting her first impressions of Pellerud and the team recalled: *"I have a lot of respect for Even as a coach and as a person. I knew he had a lot of experience as a player and a coach and I also knew he was a good coach and a teacher. It was very easy to understand what he meant for us to do out on the field, but he was also a nice person and able to get his points across to us in a human way. The first big change he made to the team was for us to all play in zones. This zone defense was new to us, but he worked through a lot of players and was able to put the right players in the right position and we could see that the team was getting as good as possible. We were all committed as a team.*

"Another one of Even's main focuses was that we had to be in good shape. When we were home with our club teams away from the National Team, Even assigned us homework. Not only football but physical training. Even used expert help in physical training that helped us with the right methods to approach the higher levels of our running capacity. My program, for instance, included a lot of long-distance running and short interval training. I was a strong player, but I needed to be faster and increase my speed and needed help for that. Even made sure I had it. Weight lifting, a strong program in the off-season and less so during the season, was also a big part of our strength training.

"My personal role as a leader in the zone defense was to concentrate on what I was good at: to be aggressive, to win duels, to tackle high and low, and be strong in both defense and offense, particularly in dead ball situations. I was expected to be a leader. I had to talk with my teammates and make sure that all four of us on defense were on the same page when we played; that we had good communication between our line, the goalkeeper, and the midfield. I would advise anyone aspiring to be a good defender to watch good international teams and learn from them. We did a lot of that. Be as tough as you can in duels and tackles. Practice with players who are better than you. It is important to be totally concentrated when you play a game. Listening and learning from a good coach is critical, especially for younger players.

"I can't stress enough that if you want to play at the highest level, play a lot with the boys. Don't only practice with your team, but also on your own or with friends. Involve both feet. Don't be just a right-footed player, because it could be a big advantage to your game to add the other side.

"The biggest moment for the team and for myself personally in our career was the 1995 Women's World Cup. I don't think I've ever felt so well prepared for anything. We had practiced our defensive and attacking play so much, and concentrated a lot on defensive and offensive dead ball situations. Every player knew her role on the team.

"By this time Even had also brought in Anne-Marte Pensgaard and we were all very well mentally prepared. Anne Pensgaard taught us how to focus on the right things. How to make your teammates play better by how you acted yourself. Be a leader by your actions. She taught us how to visualize different situations and figure out how to play those situations. Another very important thing she taught was how to control and achieve the right level of stress before and during the game."

Espeseth has stated that when she started playing for the National Team at the age of 18, she knew nothing about zonal defense and had never played it before. She found the feedback and video analyses from all the games extremely useful. She learned a lot from those sessions and the practices where Even showed them how to play.

"One thing I will always remember, Even taught us never to be satisfied with just playing well. We had to play perfect at the back. The consequences were so big if we failed on the defense. My favorite practices as a defender were really practices against men's teams. I enjoyed playing as a unit with the goalkeeper, playing the goalkeeper and the four backs against the midfield and the attackers. The defensive training sessions were my favorite practices. I also liked working on my 1v1 and 2v2 duels.

"One thing I have noticed in the past few years is that the world game remains at a high level. Some new countries, like France and Brazil, are becoming stronger. I know a lot of the players, including the young players we see in Norway, have better technique every year."

Gro Espeseth played for the New York Power in the WUSA and has since retired from football. She has returned as part of the coaching staff in Sandvigen where she played her club football. She is the mother of a 2-year-old son and works as a social worker in Norway.

The last group game against Germany was a difficult one and it was a tough 3-2 win. German coach, Gero Bisanz, coached his last game with the German National Team after 10 years. His long-time assistant (now head coach) was Tina Theune-Meyer: *"He was a great man, a good friend of mine and a terrific champion for women's soccer. It was a sad thing to see him after Germany didn't come out of the early stage of the tournament, and I was feeling for him.*

"We went on to the semi-finals and we went into the Atlanta Olympic village. This was a bit of a disappointment to me. So many crowds and checkpoints. The security was unbelievable. The Olympic Games themselves were terrific. We played our semi-final against the U.S. in Georgia Stadium in front of over 60,000 people. It was a very hot day, a very evenly fought game. We started out with good pressure and scored within the first 30 minutes and seemed to have the game in control. Neither team was playing particularly well but, as usual, there was a lot of tension between the teams. It was a hard-fought, physical game. In the second half we defended our lead and this was when we really noticed the absence of our captain, Heidi Støre. To add more trouble to our team one of our midfielders, Agnete Carlsen, received a red card and she had also played Heidi Støre's position. This left us in a difficult position. At the 30-second mark, an always contentious penalty kick allowed the U.S. to tie the game. We defended relentlessly, but went into overtime and lost in sudden-death overtime."

Pellerud then recalls his last game as National Team Coach: *"We came back to play the bronze medal game against Brazil and we beat Brazil comfortably 2-0 and played a very strong game. That was my last game with the team. At that point I went more and more with the Norwegian men's side and I then helped in the transition to the new coach, Hans Knudson."*

Pellerud ended his six-year stint with the Women's National Team with an amazing 75 wins, 12 losses and 17 draws. Pellerud had guided his team to a silver in the '91 European Championships, a silver in the '91 World Cup, a gold in the '93 European Championship, a gold in the '95 Women's World Cup, and a bronze medal in the '96 Olympics. In an astounding run under Pellerud, the Norwegian Women's National Team went into six international play-offs, out of six possible, and won medals in all six of the play-offs. Pellerud was ready to move on.

Moving On

During this period of time, Pellerud had continued to work with the Norges Fotball Forbund on some Olympic Committee work. He returned to the men's side of the game at the National level and he accepted an offer from Lillestrom to coach the men's premier team in the Tippeliga. He remained at that position for the 1996-1998 seasons during a tumultuous period in the men's game with the recent advent of the Bosman rule. Leaving Lillestrom under difficult circumstances, Pellerud moved to Ikast in Denmark in 1998 then back to Valerenga in Norway before he received the call from Canada...a call that would change the life of Pellerud and his new family.

Remarried to Anne, Even was busy with the new twins, Tora and Hedvig, born in December 1996. It wasn't an easy period of time for Even Pellerud. Coming off the significant level of success he achieved with the women's team he was back in the spotlight in the Tippeliga. With an acrimonious parting of the ways with Lillestrom and a new family, Even Pellerud was seriously contemplating his football future.

Chapter IV

Coming to Canada

"It is hopeless that Norwegian football let him go abroad. We are saying bye-bye to one of the best coaches in Norway, a coach both the Federation (NFF) and the best clubs should need."

Linda Medalen, 1995 Norwegian Women's National Team

The Call

Canada had never enjoyed much success against the Norwegian women's team. Their international record, however, had been improving and they had some bone fide internationals led by Charmaine Hooper, widely acknowledged to be one of the best players in the game, and Silvana Burtini. Hooper and the team under the care of Head Coach Neil Turnbull qualified for the '99 Women's World Cup in spectacular fashion. After winning the 1998 CONCACAF tournament in Toronto, the Canadian Soccer Association (CSA) was looking forward to a significant performance from their team in the '99 World Cup. In their previous World Cup participation in 1995 they failed to win a game in their pool. The CSA under Executive Director Kevan Pipe and President Jim Fleming, were encouraged by the performance of the Canadian Women's Team since the 1995 World Cup and, although they were not yet competitive with the U.S., China, or Norway, they were certainly considered close to a top-10 team. The goal of the CSA for the National Team was to come out of their pool to the quarter-finals in the 1999 WWC. Unofficial FIFA world rankings at the time saw Canada ranked in 14th position. A modest goal set by the CSA was to see Canada in the official top 10 for the new Millenium.

Before Pellerud arrived in Canada in late 1999, the Canadian Women's National Team had come off a very disappointing Women's World Cup. Once again failing to win a game and not advancing beyond their pool. The program had taken a step backwards. The CSA began a rapid "find-a-coach" process, approaching several international associations looking for somebody to change the direction of the Canadian program.

Just prior to this (1998), the Canadian Soccer Association made one of their biggest changes in history. After an international search headed by Jim Fleming, the CSA identified German National Coach Holger Osieck as the Men's National Team Coach and Technical Director for the country and had instituted some changes, particularly in the coaching certification area. The Canadian Soccer Association had begun to change its financial structure, augmenting income through registration fees in order to support a more significant National Team program. Expanding from three National teams to 13 within a period of four years, the CSA was busy with initiatives on many fronts. It was not lost on them that the future of football throughout the world was sharply tilting towards the women's side.

After the problems in 1999, CSA President Jim Fleming began making contact with various coaching associations. His good friend Per Omdal, President of the Norges Fotball Forbund and long-time FIFA committee-man, suggested that the CSA contact Even Pellerud. With their short list of three candidates, Fleming met briefly with Pellerud in Norway, provided him some basic background and asked for an expression of his interest. Even Pellerud was interested.

The next step was the Interview Committee of Holger Osieck, Kevan Pipe (Executive Director of the CSA), and in-coming President, Andy Sharpe. The Canadian development team was at the training center of the sports school in Dusenburg, Germany and they met with Pellerud and two others in late summer. The committee members recall the favorable impression Pellerud made at the interview. Andy Sharpe comments: *"It was refreshing to hear someone talk about football and not just money. It was exciting to know what this man had done and the very clear ideas he had about how he wanted to take the team forward."*

Kevan Pipe also remembers: *"It was clearly apparent during the interview that this was the man we wanted so the interview discussion became very concise. It was very direct. We had done our homework and we consulted many who had worked with Even and there were no ifs, ands or buts about it. This was the man we wanted for the job. I had the job of trying to negotiate a contract that both sides could live with-that would work for the Association from a financial perspective and Even and his family, from a family perspective, as well. We had a prolonged series of discussions, which led to Even coming to Canada for a very quiet visit with no media publicity on Thanksgiving Weekend 1999. He made a quiet unannounced appearance at the Senior Championships in Etobicoke and the Women's U-18 Championships in Ottawa. He had a look at some players and, in essence, he was already scouting for the National Team.*

"Besides seeing the players we began our negotiations on contractual issues, one of them being location. Toronto, the site of our largest National Training Centre, was our first choice and we showed him Toronto. About a month later we finalized the contract. I can say that nothing with Even is ever simple and there was a very complicated series of discussions. He knows what he wants and we were finally able to bring that contract to a close and I don't think we have looked back since."

The Women's National Team program had been completely competitive with the United States in the late '80's. Lauren Gregg, the assistant coach of the National Team from '86-'96, recalls: *"I remember a Can/Am tournament we had played in 1989, I believe. Canada was one of our great competitors. It was always even play. I think we won that one with golden goals. And then there seemed to be a separation. I think a lot of it has to do with the commitment of the Association, money and resources. Canada's program seemed to stay still while the U.S. moved forward."*

Sylvie Beliveau, the first coach of the Canadian National Team, recalls some of the early days: *"When I was asked to take over the team I let them know I had to get to the Women's World*

Cup in China. We hadn't qualified, but I needed to see the level of play we needed to get to in order for us to begin to compete again."

Beliveau's time with the team was a struggle initially in that it was a part-time position and budgets were limited and, indeed, preparation games and camps were limited due to the financial restrictions. Canada did progress, however, and qualified for the '95 Women's World Cup under Beliveau. She was appointed the first (although short-lived) full-time coach. They reverted the position back to part-time with Coach Neil Turnbull.

For whatever reason, the commitment of the CSA to the women's side, as was so common in most countries, was not as significant at it was to the men's side.

Even Pellerud in his early interviews made it abundantly clear what he felt was necessary for Canada's team to become competitive. His list of demands included:

1) The opportunity to play at least 12 games a year (actual matches with the squad)
2) The squad had to be together a minimum of 90 days per year

The CSA did indeed meet this challenge. As is typical of Even's approach to the game, he wanted to challenge the game by playing the most difficult and competitive teams. Winning and losing wasn't important in the early stages of the team development.

To-date, Canada has gone from an average of five to six games to sixteen or seventeen games a year since Pellerud arrived just five years ago. Pellerud's demands weren't without promises, however. A consummate goal-setter, he let the executive know that if he had the players for that number of games and that length of time consistently every year, that he would improve the overall technical and tactical performance of the team.

Pellerud's position in the CSA grew as he gained the respect of coaches and technical departments. He re-signed in 2003 for five years, expanding his duties throughout the entire women's side of the Association, including taking charge of all of the six National Women's Teams from U-15 through the Olympic National Team and all of the National Training Centres. He also has full responsibility for choosing coaches for all of the women's teams.

The Association was impressed with Pellerud's work and President Andy Sharpe points out that the U-19 Canadian Team lost 11-0 to Minnesota just one year prior to the FIFA U-19. Pellerud working with Ian Bridge reassembled the team and the coaching staff and put together an extremely competitive U-19 Team, the team who ultimately defeated the U.S. U-19 in 2003 and were seeded number one at the U-19 FIFA second World Championships in Thailand 2004.

With a lot of the training centers and coaching and new financial initiatives in place, the CSA was going through a change not unlike the one the Norwegian Federation had been going through when Even first joined in the early '90's. A little reminder of the fragile realities of a National Team Coaching position came when Osieck was let go from his position in 2004, primarily based on the results of the Men's National Team.

Kevan Pipe, long-time CEO of the Canadian Soccer Association, had been impressed with Pellerud's approach to improving the team and has observed some of Pellerud's extraordinary coaching abilities: *"I can attest to his feedback with the players. He's a tremendous motivator and he gives tremendous information back to his players after every single project. He's also very concerned with two things. One, I think he's always looking for every possible angle to improve the team. He's brought in a sports psychologist, nutritionists, physiologists. Two, he's always looking for every possible angle to increase performance from a scientific viewpoint and he's open-minded. He uses some techniques that are out there. Some of them he discards. But, he always has an open mind to explore the unknown, which I think is what you're really looking for in terms of trying to ensure that you've left no stone unturned in your mission to succeed."*

Pipe and the Board of Directors have also been impressed with Pellerud's goal setting and confidence. When the Women's 2007 World Cup was still up for bidding, Even came in front of the Board of Directors in April 2002 and petitioned: *"If you can get me the proper resources with this team, not only will we host and compete, but we will win the 2007 World Cup."*

Pipe comments: *"With SARS things were changed so we couldn't get 2007, so we've gone for the Men's 2007 U-20 (this was awarded to Canada in 2004 contingent on the new stadium in Toronto and had largely come from the huge 2002 U19 Women's FIFA success). I think Even himself would probably say he went out on a limb to be as optimistic as he was considering the way the team was playing in April. By the team's most recent performances (these comments were made just before going into the 2003 Women's World Cup) I think he's feeling even more optimistic now. He just may be able to deliver on that promise to the board in 2007. We've had some injuries, but I think he is happy with the way the team is shaping up and the quality of some of the leaders we have on the team."*

Pellerud's hiring could be called the result of a well-publicized player revolt following the 1999 WWC. While the CSA may effectively argue they were committed to the women's game, there is no denying that the approach to the women's game changed with the hiring of Even Pellerud and followed closely on the heels of outspoken comments from the then team defacto leader, Charmaine Hooper.

Hooper is the most well-known female soccer player ever produced in Canada. Hooper had developed with the women's game beginning in Canada then moving on to semi-professional and professional tours in Japan, Norway, and the U.S. (see Hooper in the International Game Chapter). It was Hooper's outspoken criticism of the lack of funding and support of the Women's National Team after a decade of disappointments that led to a significant split between the CSA and several veteran players.

National program funding was withdrawn for several athletes. After Hooper's public lambasting of their organization's commitment, the CSA fired back, releasing Hooper from the team in 1999, citing declining personal performance, contribution to poor team chemistry and advancing age. Two years later Hooper was named Most Valuable Player in the world. Hooper, to this day, is unrepentant about her CSA comments, firm in her conviction that the calculated risk of going against the CSA was due to her devotion to the National Program. Certainly the situation Pellerud found himself in when he came to Canada was not an enviable one from a political point of view.

Not one to miss an opportunity, however, Pellerud in his first press conferences made it clear that the slate was wiped clean. He was beginning anew with the National Team Program and all players past and present were going to be invited to camp. They were beginning with him without a history and it proved to be one of the wisest decisions Pellerud and the CSA have ever made. In fairness to the CSA board, they agreed to Pellerud's request without much opposition.

Charmaine Hooper's dedication to the National Team Program became readily apparent in the early training. Hooper, who was named to the All-World FIFA Team following the '99 World Cup and went on to be MVP of the All-Star Game in California, was a proven commodity and Pellerud needed her leadership.

A player who had first played the game of football in Zambia with her diplomatic corps parents and brothers, Charmaine Hooper was born in Guyana in 1968. She moved to Canada's capital, Ottawa, Ontario, with her parents when she was eight years old and lived and played her club soccer in Nepean, Ontario (a suburb of Ottawa).

Prior to that time Hooper had been a very active pick-up player in boys' games with her brother's and school teams. To this day she credits her playing with boys' teams to a large degree as responsible for her ability to play the game at a high speed and in a physical fashion. Her mainstay of training remains games and workouts with male teams. It is an automatic way to push herself with respect to speed and physicality.

Canada's most capped and prolific goal scorer, Hooper played a major part in Pellerud's emergency strategy to shore up the back line when the now legendary series of injuries decimated Canada's back four in the 2003 World Cup. A striker in the outdoor game her whole life, Hooper had been a tremendous student of the game and had very respectable individual defending skills. When WUSA player Brianna Boyd's concussion kept her out of the training camp, Pellerud quietly asked Charmaine to consider the role of a central back. Possessor of a great amount of respect on the team for her work ethic and responsibility, the move proved to be an excellent one for the Canadian team.

In the preparation games against Australia and Mexico prior to the World Cup, Hooper was outstanding. She played beside fellow WUSA Atlanta Beat teammate Sharolta Nonen. When Canada's other outstanding young defender Candace Chapman went down with an ACL injury one week before the World Cup, Pellerud's decision to give Hooper the time at the back proved to be very important. Hooper never came off the field for the entire World Cup event. (see Chapter X: Women's World Cup, p 295)

The importance of veteran leadership was not lost on Pellerud and his early decision to stick with Hooper and many of the other veteran players (Silvana Burtini, Isabelle Morneau, Andrea Neil) proved to be extremely important for team development. His team was collectively one of the youngest at the tournament and the mix was critical.

Canada possessed an abundance of young talent, but the experience and the maturity necessary to play the women's game at the National Team level has been proven over and over again to significantly depend on age and experience.

It was into this situation that Even Pellerud arrived. Pellerud's philosophy and his ability to instill that not only in his players but in the coaching staff and the training centers throughout the country was going to determine the success or failure of this undertaking.

Perhaps one of the most telling statements from Norway and an indication of the coach Canada had selected was Linda Medalen's statement to Aftenposten in 1999 when Pellerud was selected as Canadian head coach: *"It is hopeless that Norwegian football let him go abroad. We are saying bye-bye to one of the best coaches in Norway, a coach both the Federation (NFF) and the best clubs should need. He is the best coach I have ever had, and his results show it. When Even has worked with Canada for two or three years, they will be dangerous. They have so many players to pick. In five years they can beat Norway. It is perhaps nice to have more good teams internationally in women's soccer, but they should be able to grow up themselves."* (Aftenposten, October 1999)

In the next few chapters we will look at Pellerud's philosophy of play developed in Norway, his approach to player development and talent identification, as well as his and his player's views on positional play. It is hoped that these principles of play and how Even Pellerud has applied them to his team will be helpful to players and coaches in the game. Even Pellerud has brought the women's program to levels of success it has never achieved before, starting with the 2002 U-19 Championships and ending with Canada's strong fourth-place finish in the 2003 Women's World Cup.

Chapter V
Even Pellerud's Coaching Philosophy

Principles of Play

Preparation

Even Pellerud, when organizing the World Cup team in 2002, very clearly outlined his technical and tactical approach to the game. The foundations had to be laid in his first two years with the squad. In the one-year run up to the 2002 qualifications, he used his direct approach to the game as the starting point in the Canadian National Women's World Cup preparations.

The Challenge

In one of his earliest addresses to the WWC team, he indicated the following factors as necessary goals for success: *"I would like to remind you of factors necessary for success for Canada's National Women's Soccer Team. We need to be the fittest team in the World or, at the very least, equal to the best. Our work rate and team dedication has to be second to none. Our playing style has to be distinct and based around the following principles: a) pressure on the ball; b) play the ball forward and, as offensively as possible, create problems in the opponent's box as soon as possible. Be prepared as a team and as an individual. Take advantage of your individual talents and prepare them to their utmost."*

Pellerud used his extensive international experience to motivate the players. Drawing on his assessment of the team's strengths and weaknesses over his first two years, his first concern was the poor fitness level at the last winter full team camp. His approach was, as it had been in Norway, to address the team as a whole and then address the individuals about deficiencies and what they should be working on. Individual fitness and technical programs were created for the players.

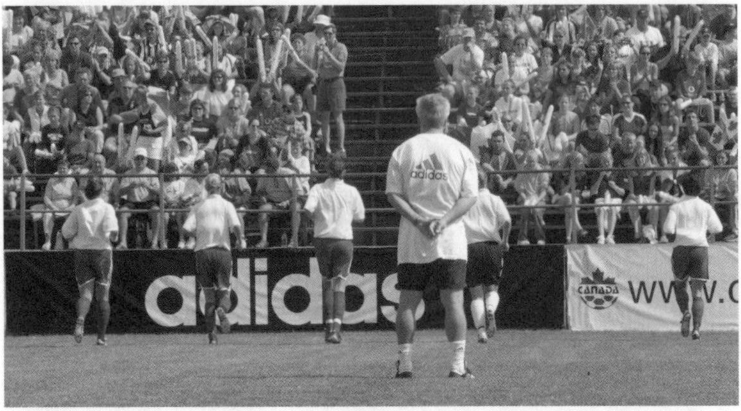

The pre-game routine is important to focus the coach as well.

Pellerud keeps his eye on the starters 5v5 in pre-game.

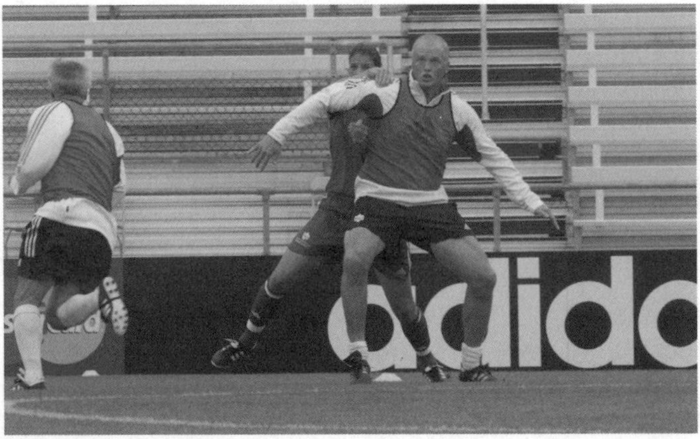

If a defender can handle Ian Bridge, then she is heading for prime time.

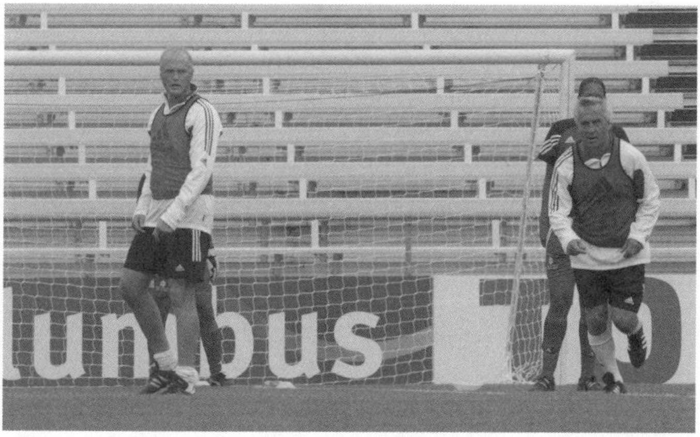
Pellerud and his coaches actively participate to emphasize points.

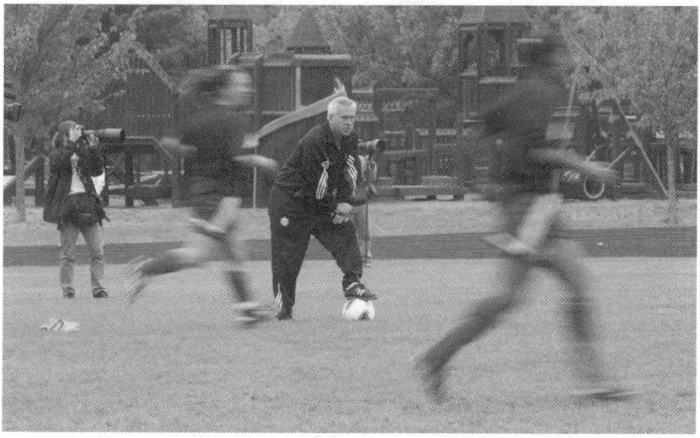
Practice: where the coach makes a difference

A pre-game coaching point

Directing traffic

The technical (skill) level of the team was an area the coaching staff was more pleased about. Although Pellerud's official goal included getting into the medals at the 2007 World Cup, he was becoming excited about more immediate prospects, as he uncovered more and more talent in the Canadian player development system. Kara Lang, Amber Allen, Christine Sinclair, Candace Chapman and Diana Matheson were all U-20's who had a lot of the attributes he felt were necessary to play the type of game he wanted from the team. While as a coach he was quick to point out the deficiencies such as lack of physical preparation, he also recognized individual and team efforts when they were exceptional.

Realizing the restrictions of a country the size of Canada and the disparate locations of many of the players, he very carefully worked to make sure the players maintained individual programs. As in Norway, calls, e-mails, and fax reports to and from players and club teams were part of Pellerud's approach to preparation-keeping a hands-on approach from the coach.

While other nations who were more compact geographically had year-round programs with fitness monitoring as a key, he stressed the importance of physical preparation. Pellerud used the University of Montreal to test fitness levels (such as: VO2 max-see Chapter on Physical Factor). These early results for the Canadian team were, on average, below those of his previous team in Norway. Even used this to motivate the team--he knew what players at this level were capable of and trusted the players would be able to pay the individual price to get there.

By this time, it had become apparent to Pellerud that the Canadian team had the talent, had the equivalent technical tools and he was convinced that he had the more intelligent playing style. The players were optimistic as they saw the team forming and their tactical awareness grew.

The goal they set for the team was not merely to qualify for the World Cup but to fight for a medal. Little did they realize how close they would come.

His final parting notes to the team at the 2002 camp included reiteration of his maxim: RESULTS IN SOCCER REFLECT THE LEVEL OF PREPARATION. His last words to the team before the two-month lead up to the training camp: NOW IT IS PREPARATION TIME.....

The Response

The response from the players to Pellerud's challenge was excellent within a few short weeks. It was a great indicator of the team's unison as they responded to the coach's requirements with fitness levels significantly improved. Prior to the full-out pre-World Cup schedule, Pellerud sent a note to all of the team players letting them know that he had increased his level of optimism about the team's chance because of the new fitness results and the competitive attitude at the last training camp in Saskatoon: *"Those days made me very happy and I was very impressed by the intensity and quality of the team overall. I was especially impressed by the older players who had proven dedication to the program and led the team in the fitness categories. That type of leadership is critical for our team to move to the next level of play in the world. I look forward to the next training camp."* The team had responded to his challenge and the leadership was coming from within. The physical and technical levels were on track. Now it was time to hammer home the team style.

It was time for Pellerud to reinforce his tactical approach to play. The Principles that they, the players, were absorbing were developed over the many years Even Pellerud had spent as a player, a student and a coach. They were the keys to the success of Pellerud teams in the game of soccer.

He laid out his principles in meetings on the field and in both group and individual dynamics.

The Keys to Success

BALANCE: Balance is the key to success in soccer: When our team is in balance it should be next to impossible to create goal scoring opportunities against us.

We must be in balance and as well organized as possible throughout the game. When your team is in defensive balance it is extremely difficult for the opponent to penetrate.

Therefore, when we are in attack this requires us:

- To find a tactical way to break down the opponent's balance;
- We must regain possession and then attack during the "breaking down" period.

One of the most common failures in the game of soccer is losing the ball by trying to do the most difficult maneuver when in possession. For example, attempting to turn and dribble with the ball while double-teamed or playing passes into the pressure on the field. It is critical that all players be aware of tactical situations or circumstances on the field that dictate decision-making. Keep the play simple and avoid the difficult move/play.

Recognizing State of Balance

Recognizing problems with balance in your opponent's game is very important. An unbalanced team may demonstrate:

- **Numerical imbalance:** The defending team has too few players between the ball and it's own goal (eg: midfielders caught up field on a transition)

- **Positional imbalance:** The defending players are in incorrect positions and could be penetrated if the attackers are conscious or aware of the imbalance quickly enough (eg: the center and full-backs are too spread apart and gaps are created).

In order to exploit an unbalanced situation you have to recognize it first. When winning the ball always look for the unbalanced situations:

1. Look for the fast attack/transition;
2. Seek a forward direction as soon as possible;
3. Look for penetration, look for areas susceptible to immediate penetration;
4. Look for space behind the defenders

What to do when you recognize the unbalanced situation:

5. Initiatives without the ball (runs behind the defenders or across the defenders) should be stimulated
6. Run through the defenders' line
7. Challenge the space between the goalkeeper and the defenders with the ball and with runs
    - Most of all be brave...do not worry about failing
    - Try again...use the same principles even when teammates make incorrect tactical decisions with the ball.

This penetrative thinking and this offensive philosophy simply means that we should accept a higher number of technical failures by our players, because it will stimulate risky solutions in the attacking 1/3 of the field and force a further imbalance in the defense.

If we do implement the above principles at every opportunity as a team we will definitely create more goal scoring opportunities and ultimately more goals. The principle to preserve is that most goal scoring opportunities are created when a team is in a numerical or positional imbalance. Your ability as a team and as a player to recognize these periods of vulnerability will produce the optimal chances for goals. These unbalanced situations will remain for only short periods of time. By definition, hesitation (short support passes and dribbling and late runs) means that you give opponents time to regain balance. It is important to play quickly and directly into the unbalanced area of the field.

The Strike Zone

We are ultimately trying to exploit the most exciting space in soccer-THE PENALTY BOX. Use the space behind the defensive line! Pellerud, as he did in Norway, worked to get the ball and numbers with it into this scoring zone as soon as possible.

As indicated in Chapter 3, Pellerud's approach to the game and his playing principles have been unwavering from the earliest time in his career as a player and coach. When he came to Canada, he made no changes to his approach to the principles of the game that he felt would optimize a team's success.

In relaying them to his team in 1999, and as he has reiterated countless times in coaching forums and interviews, he laid out the following principles:

- Playing Principles
- The Defending System/Zonal Defense
- The Offensive System/Penetrating emphasis first

Pellerud has made it clear in all his coaching communication that he plays with the same principles-the same systems of play. The formations may vary, that is the number of players he may have in any one line, but the principles are always to exploit a team's imbalance with penetration as quickly as possible.

The principles of defense are strict zonal defense with maintenance of balance and compact defending. Pellerud is very quick to point out that a coach has to have a full and comfortable understanding of what a zonal defense is to coach it and play it.

The Principles of Zonal Defense

Zonal Defense: About defending with a zonal flat back four (or three or five)

When Pellerud changes his formations he does not change his principles:

- ❑ Covering Space: Covering or defending space is more important than covering/defending players.
- ❑ The first defender is the most important defender (1D).
- ❑ A player closest to the ball in any situation should apply intense pressure on the player with the ball if in our tactically decided area (the danger of the area will determine whether we utilize high pressure, medium pressure, or low pressure)
- ❑ The player next to 1D (the second defender 2D) supports or covers 1D, creating problems for the ball possessor, limiting the options. 2D also defines the support line for other players on the team.
- ❑ Third defenders (3D = all the other players) are covering important space. They are all "in balance".

- ❑ Our defensive line should read the play and have the ability to change the height of the line. They should push up and draw back according to the threat from the opponent and maintain the ability to play the offside trap.
- ❑ Read the pressure on the ball.
  - If our team has good pressure on the ball, as a back line shorten the distance to our own midfield by playing a little tighter on their forwards, minimizing the space between their players and our players.
  - With loose pressure or no pressure on the ball, cover the dangerous space to avoid a penetrating pass behind. Loosen up and be prepared to drop and maintain a little more space between the attacking players and yourself in your zone.

What are the functions of a good defense?

1) Having the skills to win the ball to avoid goal scoring opportunities and goals against. Preventing the other team from effectively attacking;

2) Winning the ball in order to create fast effective attacks in the "break down" period. This transition play should be the first link up in sending the ball forward to our attacking players.

If we as a team can achieve quick and intense pressure on the ball, our opponents will lose control of the situation and be more prone to making incorrect tactical and technical decisions.

Summary of Zonal Defense

To summarize, the characteristics of a team which plays an effective zonal defense include the following:

1) Players are not being marked man-to-man;
2) There is intense pressure on the ball, a ball-oriented type of defense;
3) Team and team parts move smoothly and have effective positioning related to each other;

4) Midfield does not allow players into defenders' areas when the defender is present;
5) There is less running, it is more rational work. It is easy to see what's happening on the field. You're not blindly following the player around the field.
6) The team parts are working in lines. We are denying playing space to our opponents. You are defending the space they want to utilize. Be aware of the dangerous space. Once again, covering space is more important than covering players in an effective zonal defensive system.

Since Pellerud introduced his strict zonal defense to Women's International football with the Norwegian team it has become the dominant system of defensive play in the Women's World Cup. His philosophy on the offensive side, while not as widely embraced, has proven effective and is a foundation of his playing philosophy.

The Principles of Attacking

Attacking with a Penetrating Style

The priority of moving forward is to penetrate. The individuals involved must be mentally in tune with each other. The teams must be highly organized and at maximum efficiency in attacking. There are three attacking types that are outlined below:

1) Our long-lasting attacks, which involve more than six seconds, or more than six passes.

When would this occur? When the opponent is defensively in complete balance it may be necessary to possess or pass the ball to unbalance them.

How should this be played? The risk taking should be at a minimum. My preference as a coach is a long pass behind the defense, take the fight to them and aim to regain possession near their goal line.

Effectiveness of Game Analysis: Statistics have proven time and time again, that approximately 5% of goal scoring opportunities are created by a slow build up or by these types of attacks (more than six seconds). Remember, however, that a clever regaining tactic makes it impossible to take advantage of this situation-give up the ball deep to win it, but in an organized fashion.

This will be given a low priority in practice and in games.

2) Breakdowns (Transition Play)

When do we play this? When the opponent is defensively unbalanced and vulnerable.

How should this be played? Play direct/forward/fast/penetrating. This is risk taking of forward play

Effectiveness of game analysis: 60% of goal scoring opportunities are created through breakdowns or transition. The consequence is it becomes the highest focus in my training in any soccer practice and match. The ability to exploit a quick turnover after a breakdown of the other team is critical to the success in any game.

3) Dead ball situations

When do we play this? When the ball is out of play, the way of playing is fast-quickly and efficiently. The defenders are sleeping/unorganized. Precise positioning as the defenders organize.

How should this be played?
1) Fast if the defenders are sleeping or unorganized
2) Precise positioning when the defenders are organized and quick to do it.

- ❑ Use the competence of the individual players (sort out your specialists or free kick artists)
- ❑ Good service of the ball: throw-ins, corner kicks, free kicks. Identify the players that are most proficient and practice at least 2-3 set pieces for each situation.

- ❑ Headers in the box: 1) ball; work on: 2) ball; Keep your defensive brains at home (balanced!) Make sure that those remaining back know they are doing. Good, efficient organization.

Effectiveness in Game Analysis: 35% of goal scoring opportunities are created through set pieces. Consequences should be high emphasis on training and restarts should be a high priority in practices.

Characteristics of a team that plays an effective high-level penetrating attack:

1) A low number of dribbling situations;
2) The team is not pre-occupied with short passing plays;
3) Passes, for the most part, are played in a forward direction;
4) Early crosses to catch the team out of balance are a big part of play;
5) Many moves off the ball as frequently as possible (effective runs);
6) Runs off the ball from the midfield trying to beat the defensive line;
7) Be very occupied and organized to regain control in non-control situations.

The players on my team should be offensive-minded, eager to attack and create problems for their opponents. This is the scenario I want to see in all of my practices and games.

Once Pellerud had laid out his golden rules and guidelines for playing a zonal defense and penetrating attack to the team, the players warmed to it quickly as they began to have success. The world saw it in the 2002 FIFA U-19 World Cup in Canada when Canada took the U.S. to the final. His assistant staff, primarily Ian Bridge the U-19 coach, and Shel Brødsgaard, goalkeeping coach, shared the philosophy of direct play. On a daily basis, the players became believers as the system and principle were applied in layers during training.

Technical Do's and Don'ts

Pellerud's advice to the players on the technical side generally came forth after observation and analysis. In 2002 after observing players at the training camp in Vancouver and the Algarve Cup, he recommended high priority on the following objectives. (This is consistent with the findings of both Pellerud and DiCicco and the FIFA technical committees on the women's game. These three technical areas, as well as goalkeeping, were identified as areas requiring improvement in the women's game.) i) Long ball service and crossing; ii) heading, and; iii) receiving were areas requiring improvement.

1) Long ball passing techniques: Prefer a flat and hard pass (maintain all around quality in direction and speed); Half high without underspin (This type of ball is ideal for central midfielders and full backs); the bending pass from the sidelines (from fullbacks and midfielders)

2) Heading techniques:
   a. For clearing defenders, practice effective direction and distance
   b. For flicking the ball in a forward direction (midfielders and strikers)

   Be conscious of the most important principles of heading:
   a. Follow through the ball
   b. Central move/core move through the hips
   c. Where to hit the ball on the forehead (at the hard bone)
   d. Aggressiveness
   e. Jump early: You should attack the ball instead of being attacked.
   f. One foot take-off and take the ball at the highest point

3) Receiving the ball:
   a. Remain relaxed in the body part receiving the ball; optimize the first touch;
   b. Deliver first touch away from defender or pressure;
   c. Open your eyes, body, or neck prior to the first touch
   d. At the highest level you have to make earlier decisions and act faster

Practice Philosophy

Pellerud and his staff felt that to effectively employ the principles of exploiting the breakdown period the players had to be trained and coached to act and react at the maximum speed possible. They needed to perfect execution under pressure. He undertook to provide the proper environment to train the team. Pellerud felt that the team had the talent and the coaches, but he had some concerns about the lack of high quality league games and practice situations where the ability to improve reaction speed could be challenged.

The players in Norway unanimously felt that their frequent practice with male teams effectively improved their speed of play. Pellerud recommended that his players seek to play with high-level mens' or boys' teams, a minimum of twice a week to push themselves to a higher level.

This had been Charmaine Hooper's approach to off-season training for years. And it is a testimony to the effectiveness of this approach to be able to maintain her level of play at the highest level in the world for so many years.

Pellerud is a great believer in year-round training. Being "completely off" for more than two weeks was not something he believed in. He never felt there was an "off season" for a Women's National Team player. Recognizing the importance of periodization and peaking, he set plans and suggestions for his team's players between camps.

Pellerud on Tactical and Technical Training

Even Pellerud on Practice

Defending

Tactical practice for us will generally be in four different team parts: 1) midfielders and backs; 2) midfielders and forwards; 3) backs, midfielders and forwards, and; 4) goalkeepers and back four (could also be back three or back five). In zonal defense, positioning is the main thing. Individual and team positioning is critical. The coach has to be thoroughly comfortable with zonal defending principles because you are teaching them at every practice.

<u>Zonal Defense</u>

If you want to implement zonal defense in a team, first of all, remember rule number one: if the coach doesn't have confidence in his/her knowledge of zonal defense, he/she shouldn't coach it, because a poorly coached zone will be worse for your team. The less knowledge and confidence a coach has about defending zonally, the more reason to avoid it. It's not just about the players. It is easier to coach marking and sweeping. In order to be prepared when coaching zonal defense you have to spend a lot of time coaching exercises for strikers and midfielders, midfielders and defenders, and defenders and goalkeepers to go through that time and time again. In reality it takes years, not weeks, to implement an effective zonal defending technique into a team. All positions have to understand how to act and react to each other and to the other team. Have sound principles in place and coach them continuously.

As Pellerud's great defender Gro Espeseth pointed out: *"We really didn't know how to play the zone defense after only one year in 1991 in China. By 1995 we had begun to understand it. We knew what Even wanted and began to communicate with our goalkeeper, with our midfielders and our back four.*

I like to tell my back four, "you have to think together, you have to act together, you have to breathe together". I always compare them to synchronized swimming.

Very often we isolate the back four with the keeper in the defensive training by putting a lot of pressure on them. When we do that it is typical tactical training with a lot of emphasis on stopping, demonstrating, and correcting.

- ❑ It's about 2m up, 2m back, 2m left, 2m right. Think about a half meter here or there. It's all about specific spacing, communication, and everyone together to make them understand and move together, not unlike synchronized swimming.

- ❑ It's about relating to the pressure on the ball and all is related to how a team mate pulls up the line, the off-side trap, the distances between the back line and the goalkeeper.

- ❑ A high goalkeeper will always act as the sweeper.

- ❑ We constantly work on understanding the importance of aggressive pressure on the ball.

- ❑ We work on understanding the importance of solid, effective clearing of the ball.

- ❑ We have to understand, first and foremost, the priority of the back four defending the box. This is my defenders' main priority. If my defenders can to that as a team (defend fiercely) and also clear the ball when they have to, pass the ball when they can, then we can say we have a good back four and, at the same time they are able to create good attacks for us.

Very often we will practice an 8v4 or an 8vback 4 plus one midfielder. 7v4, 7v4+2. We will vary the number depending on what we want to see. We will also practice the back four plus midfield three or midfield four to have the two teams practice together to diminish the distances between the team parts. Now two of the units on the field have to work defensively in unison.

The next thing we do is to coach the strikers' defensive work plus the midfielders together in defensive shape and all these link together towards the game. High pressure on the ball and organized in front of the ball is worked on.

These are typical examples of a tactical defensive practice where we have the main emphasis on coaching instructions and principles and sometimes that is very insensitive. The coach has to be demanding, the players have to be put under some pressure. There are a lot of times, however, where we go slowly through things and we repeat and repeat and take out some more fragments of the defense. As an example, when we are going to be playing against the U.S.A. we always go through the American habit of going to the end line and cutting the ball back 45degrees. That is how they want to attack and so we coach on dealing with that. We take out that little segment of the attack and we design a prevent practice. Normally, all defenders drop down too quickly to the goalkeeper instead of staying tight to the strikers coming into the box. We are seeing dramatic improvement in that area in the last couple of years by eliminating those open players for the cut-back ball.

When we train defense we never isolate defense as defense alone, both for motivational purposes and to teach the players to appreciate and understand the offensive part of the defense and the importance of the counter attack. We always implement the attacking part so when defenders or midfielders or strikers win the ball they are always allowed to attack. So we will always put up attacking lines and attack the goal so they can counterattack after winning the ball. That is good for motivation. It's more fun and it lets them see the relationship between a good defense and a good attack.

Attacking-Technical Practice

I believe that the philosophy you as a coach elect to follow will have some implications on the training sessions you have and also what kind of skills you want to work on in practices as opposed to others that are not as important. In the penetrating style, you are using fewer touches on the ball. You are using fewer passes in the team, you are flicking the ball more, you are playing forward passes as opposed to backward passes and square passes, which means you are losing the ball more because passes are complicated and difficult. At the same time, penetrating play will create more chances and produce more goals because it is harder to defend against.

Flick headers, flick passes, quick passes looking to see where your team is early, hard passing on the ground or in the air, runs on the ball...those things are more important in the penetrating style than in the possession style. You have to break the game down to exercises for different team parts and make it be a part of their thinking and attitude among the play group.

That doesn't mean that general skills are unimportant, of course. For younger players I think general skills are extremely important when they are 14, 15, and 16 years old. Players have to master the techniques of dribbling, 1v1, first touch, striking and receiving. That is best worked on more at earlier ages and tactics/principles of play more at our level. I think you should train more in groups where you are more focused on the skills you need in your position, because when you are 16 or older as a female soccer player, once you have a good idea of where you are going to play there is not doubt that you need some skills in some positions and other skills for other positions. For example, why spend unnecessary time teaching defenders to dribble the ball or your stopper to challenge 1v1. They don't do that in games, you don't want them to do it, so why devote significant practice to it. But, they will need to be good in the air. They will need to: i) pass the ball well; ii) clear the ball properly, and; iii) talk and communicate well. That is what you should practice. Outside midfielders should cross the ball and practice that to perfect it. Make it a point of excellence to cross balls based on where the space is, where the target is. Strikers should practice finishing as much as possible in as many ways and in as many positions in the box as possible.

Attacking-Tactical Practice

In our attacking practices we do a lot of tactical work, of course, on our moves, our technical abilities and our willingness and desire to run forward, to play the ball forward.

We are teaching the players to pass in the right spaces and most importantly to pass early in the right spaces. We have a lot of emphasis on players without the ball willing to move forward, willing to move ahead of the ball. We try to attack both by route 1, which is directed behind the defense and route 2, which is directed between the opponent's back four and the midfield and that is something we will work more on in the next couple of years.

That is the basic frame of our play. Of course there are a lot of details we work on from different skills we need in our attacking patterns and also a lot of finishing work trying to make the players aware of where the defenders are visible. Try to chip balls across the defenders. Try to bend the ball early behind the back running defense before they have established balance. A lot of work we do is to take advantage of imbalance-the defense are not in a position to defend so we have to attack early before they are established and balanced. When they are in balance, we try to find a way to destroy that balance and take advantage of that.

One of my favorite attacking exercises is dividing the field-70m long by 45m wide-with two goals. (Fig. 3) And then I create channels on the sides for free players to cross the ball in. Also to encourage the players to find targets we will have three defenders, for example, in the defensive part and three strikers up front, and one flank player on the left and one on the right in the offensive part of the field. We will vary the rules to direct them how to play. Three defenders will get the ball from the goalkeeper, playing two-touch soccer and they have to link the pass to the striker.

The striker then can choose to turn and finish with open touches or to flick the ball or pass the ball wide to an up-running channel player for a crossed ball. Then the channel player will have one or two touches. We always encourage a maximum of two touches so we can attack before the defense is organized.

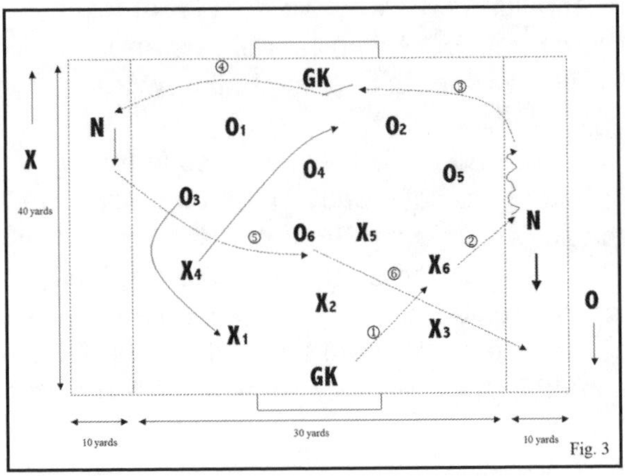

Fig. 3

The objective is to link a pass between defender and striker. One or two defenders can also pass the midway line to join the attack, while the opponent strikers are not allowed to track back so the attackers can outnumber the defenders if they succeed in establishing that link pass.

As a coach, the 4v4 game remains very important in training a team. Much has been written and discussed on the 4v4. Most importantly, the players know the game and they find it fun. It's about using your skills and it's about speed. It's about offense and defense in close spaces under pressure. It can be and should be about shooting, finishing, rebounds, and aggressiveness. It should be intense and there is a lot players can derive from that. As a nice bonus it is also recognized as the best way to develop game fitness in your players.

Developing Your Game Plan

In planning his tactics, Pellerud provided the following information to the team in the training camp. He used a tactical pyramid. Consistent with his rigid approach to the principles of zonal defense and a penetrating attack, Pellerud highlighted his tactical pyramid with expressions or key words that he felt were important in coaching the game of soccer. He reiterates that the philosophy of the team is the main key in any team sport. In his outline principles (how we play the game), the base of the pyramid should be reflected in every single step in preparing for the competition (World Cup).

Pellerud's Tactical Pyramid

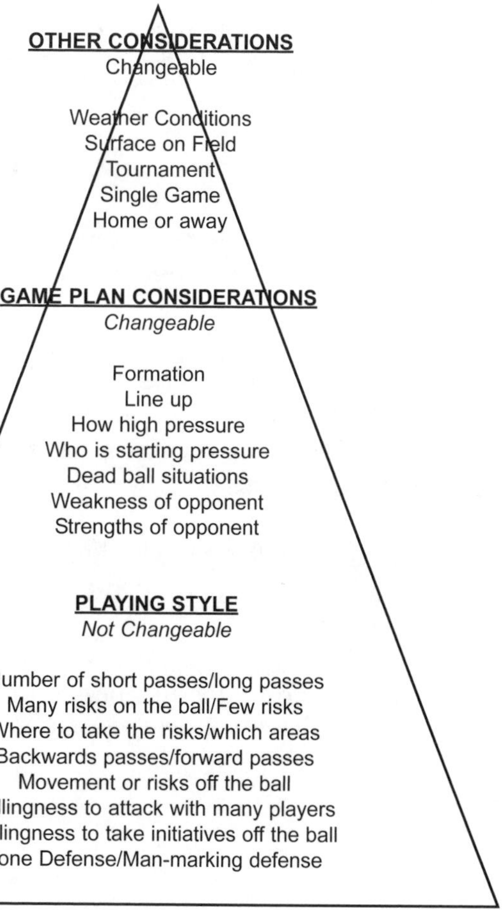

In explaining his tactical pyramid to coaches, Pellerud included:

Tactical Pyramid

I have listed some key words/expressions that I feel are among the most important factors while coaching a soccer team. Reading from the bottom upwards, remember the fundamental principle in a pyramid is that it is wider at the bottom and this is what gives the structure its greatest strength. You will learn that having a philosophy is the main key in a team sport, and that how we play principally should be reflected in every single step preparing for our competitions.

Whatever philosophic standpoint, without distinct coaching leadership in these areas a team will fail in the long run. We have chosen our way to play, and that is going to become the major success factor for us.

It is of greatest importance to realize that playing style is the most important factor for a team, though most people (soccer people and the media) tend to believe that formation is the main choice for a coach. That is not the case, although formation is important:

- ❑ First of all to take advantage of the skills and qualities you have available in own team; exploit your strengths
- ❑ Secondly to hide your own weaknesses and exploit the opponent's weaknesses

Playing style is not something to change between games or within a game; it is a consistent part of your overall approach as a focused player and coach.

Game plan factors - for instance formations - are changeable; and this is actually the coaching part of a game.

Playing Style Versus Formations

Pellerud explains that it is of great importance to recognize that playing style or principles of play are the most important factors of forming a team's success. Pellerud, the soccer fanatic, is frustrated that most people around the game including the media, tend to believe that formation is your system of play. He states firmly: "Although formation is important in the playing of an individual game, the principles of play or playing style are what make a team work. Formation routine is important because it first allows us to take advantage of the skills and qualities we have available in our team, exploiting our strengths. It allows us to hide our weaknesses and exploit our opponents because this playing style is not going to change between games or within a game. It is part of your overall educated approach and it has to be the engine that drives the team.

"Formations are simply just moves designed to optimize the outcome of your playing style. Whether you are 4:4:2, 5:3:2, or 5:4:1, the principles are the same."

Game plan factors, for instance, formations, are changeable and that is where the coach has to perform.

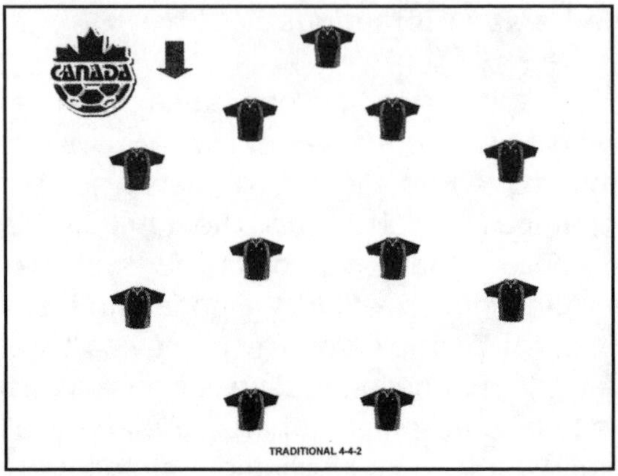

Traditional 4-4-2

FORMATION

- Medium to high wide players in midfield.
- Two balancing central midfielders.
- Two central strikers with equal tasks.

GAME PLAN CHALLENGES

- How high do we pressure?
- How wide are strikers as first pressure?
- Is the first pressure from strikers or wide midfielders?
- How and where to lead the player in possession of ball?
- One striker as a 1st defender what is the position of the other striker?
- Do we lead the pass inside or outside?
- Should wide midfielders be traditional midfield players?
- Do we have even tasks for both wide or one higher position?
- The two central midfielders must be able to cover a lot of space, read the play well and support the central stoppers

FORMATION STRENGTHS

- Easy to understand; 2 flat fours
- Easy to execute; clean roles
- Very basic pattern
- Familiar to most players
- Always 2 balancing midfielders
- 2 strikers with a lot of offensive freedom to improvise
- Allows us to play with one typical target striker and a fast striker using the speed in the room behind defenders

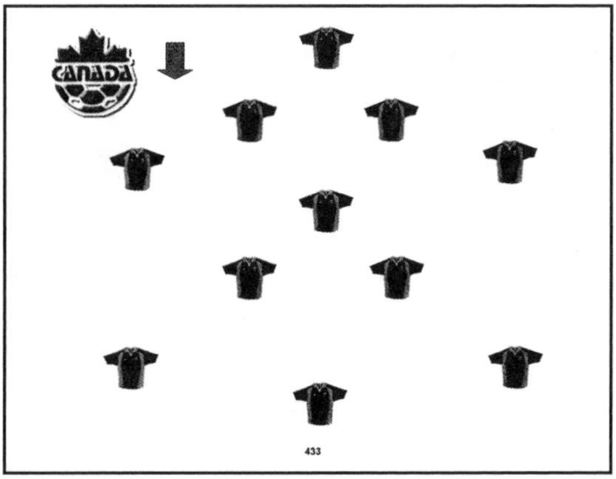

4-4-3

FORMATION

- Play with left and right-wingers and a central striker.
- Use 3 central midfielders where the middle one is the anchor and the two others giving support to strikers.
- As least one (at a time) of the inner midfielders should have the ability and desire to make penetrating runs, especially when we need a second wave, but also behind the fullback on the ball side.

GAME PLAN CHALLENGES

- What are our pressure heights?
- How do we force the play? Inside or outside?
- How to avoid moving past the wide striker?
- Cover the 2nd defender sport by inner midfielder or by fullback?

FORMATION STRENGTHS

- 3 offensive thinking strikers
- Ability to attack wide both sides and at all times
- Considered an offensive formation, and works well when you are the stronger team.
- Good defensive shape while covering the sidelines well

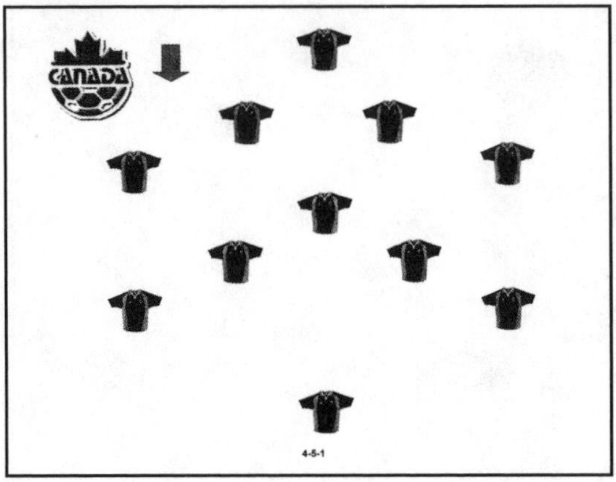

4-5-1

FORMATION

A variation of the 4-3-3 formation is called the 4-5-1

GAME PLAN CHALLENGES

- When to start the pressure? Often deeper in this formation.
- The central striker must pressure 2 defenders
- If the pressure is deep, the counterattack will begin a long way from goal.
- Deep pressure tends to lead to a defensive mental state of mind!
- How much should the inner midfielders attack?
- We must have enough players in the box when the ball is crossed! WE can release the player from opposite side.
- We must cover the defensive spot behind the central striker
- How do we give fast and solid support to lonely striker when our team is deep?
- We need inner midfielders with ability to make long runs; to support striker and/or to penetrate themselves.

FORMATION STRENGTHS

- A very compact midfield
- Hard to penetrate on the ground against us
- Effective, and sometimes necessary, against skillful teams
- Good basis to create counterattacks
- Allows the central midfielder to cover important space in front of the central stoppers.

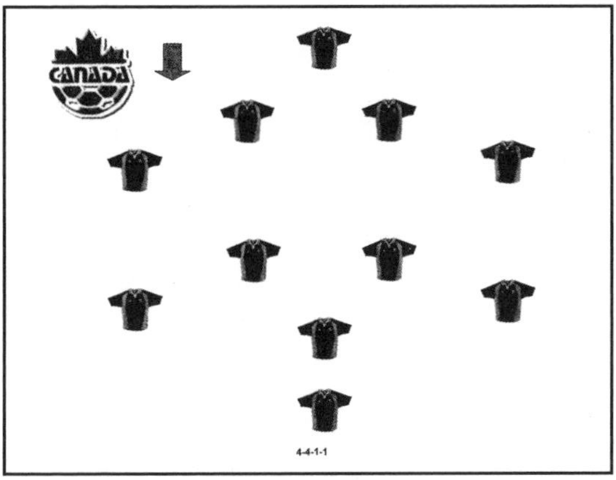

4-4-1-1

FORMATION

The player behind the top striker could:

- Be a midfield type player that basically supports the striker and is a strong passer; not penetrating a lot off the ball, but has a good eye for the penetrating pass and the long range shot.
- Be a hanging striker type, with a desire to do the penetrating runs into the box; needs to possess the desire to score goals and have the endurance and ability to make the longer runs.
- Have a tough job, by combining the penetrating/offensive role as well as dropping back to midfield.
- It allows us to be in good balancing shape with the back 4 and midfield 4.
- We still maintain excellent offensive potential and freedom.
- The game development decides how high/offensive the wide players play!

GAME PLAN CHALLENGES

- What is the position of the player behind striker when defending?
- Ability of player behind striker to move as high as possible at any time
- How to organize the first team pressure phase
- What is the ability of high striker to occupy, and keep busy, the central defenders when there?

FORMATION STRENGTHS

- Great offensive flexibility due to withdrawn striker's role.
- Great defensive flexibility due to withdrawn striker's role.
- Easy to adjust players positioning based on game development

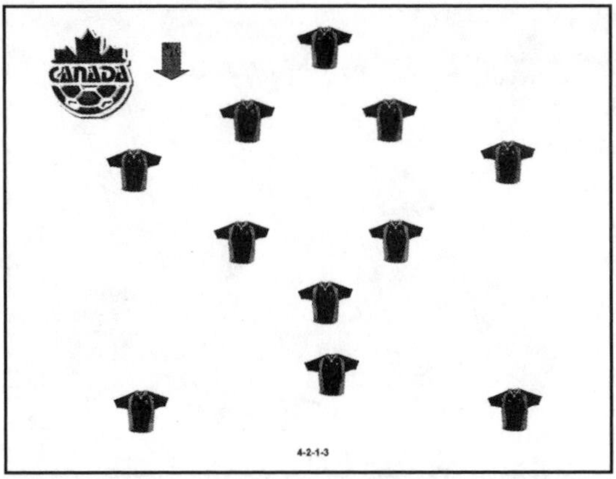

4-2-1-3

FORMATION

This formation is extremely flexible and allows us to make tactical use of every member of the line up.

GAME PLAN CHALLENGES

- With the central striker that much withdrawn (defensively), the two wider strikers have to position as high as possible. That means you must push as far as possible to penetrate all the time to take advantage of every mistake in defense.
- The withdrawn striker has a dual task: To cover a deeper defensive space when not in possession, and to have the attitude and ability to be the 3rd striker immediately when our team wins the ball. This player must resist the temptation to occupy a deeper spot for a longer time.
- The deeper player is a good link for a counterattack because we should already have the other two wider strikers in position.

FORMATION STRENGTHS

- Excellent space coverage in central mid; difficult to penetrate us with short passes.
- Increases our chances to win a lot of balls in midfield.
- The two central strikers can both act as links for counterattacks. The two of them can easily change position in the attack while maintaining the shape.
- The more withdrawn those 2 players are, the more offensive positioning for the wide strikers.
- The two wide players can penetrate without worrying about defensive tasks.
- The positioning flexibility up front will provide an opportunity to get the maximum out of every players' potential

As the depth of preparations and development for the 2003 WWC began to layer, Pellerud continued hammering home the point of playing principles and philosophy of play. As Pellerud has commented: *"Whatever philosophic standpoint, without distinct coaching leadership in these areas, a team will always fail in the long run. We have chosen our way to play and that is going to become the major success factor for us."* - It is critical that the team knows the coach's philosophy. Both Norwegian and Canadian players drew strength from Pellerud's clear view of the game. In a recent insight into how the Canadian team was developing, Andrea Neil stated: *"The team really started to come together after the Gold Cup (2002) in Los Angeles. We saw that the way we played, the style of play had become a fundamental part of the team. We believed in ourselves and we saw that it worked and now, what we did at the practices transferred onto the field. That was the breakthrough for us."*

Pellerud, during his camps, drawing on his background as a teacher and educator, is always layering his coaching philosophy and providing moments of enlightenment for the players. In one of the preparation sessions he reinforced the concepts of defensive play and risk-taking by playing a Manchester United game tape. Pellerud pointed out from the film that ManUnited is not always very well organized at the back. Their right fullback Neville destroys offside traps and has very poor discipline and no clue how to act in a flat back four. The midfield is completely committed to the attack and caught in defensive imbalance frequently. The entire back four struggles with the pace and even an understanding of the game. But, as he also pointed out:

- ❑ The team has a skill level second to none.
- ❑ They are a beautiful team to watch.
- ❑ They have an excellent concentration level and a consistent performance.

He further noted that the most impressive part about the Manchester United team is the work rates of the players (and coaches). As a motivation for his team he summarized the positive points of United's play: *"The next time you watch this team, study the work rate especially in the midfield when attacking, as well as defending. There is never a let up and very few teams can match them.*

"A perfect example of that work rate is David Beckham (when he was playing for Manchester United). He was considered to be a poser with the good fortune of possessing some astonishing free kicks. This is a true soccer media star and a favorite of the fans (to say nothing of being a multi-millionaire). On the average this may lead to a poor attitude, but observe David Beckham playing the game. He's not fast, but he runs for 90 minutes, never letting up. He covers a tremendous amount of space and he wins a very high percentage of second balls. That effort comes from joy within. He still loves to play the game."

Pellerud reminds his midfielders: *"This is the type of work rate that applies to the whole midfield and they never ever give a player in possession time to pass unpressured. I can enjoy just studying that type of midfield running and chasing when defending. They often run together at the same time, sprinting in order to be in position as a first defender or second defender. They play off each other consistently so the opponent will be under pressure immediately.*

"This is a great way to learn a game. Watch this team next time you get a chance. There is a lot to learn from their work ratio and commitment level."

Pellerud also enjoys developing philosophies with the players. Shortly before the World Cup 2003 he chose the topic, "Performance or Luck?". His insight to the players that day was, *"In order to become a winner, producing our peak performances when it counts most, we must practice at our peak level. We have to perform well everyday. That is, do not trust luck on that special day. Trust, instead, your preparation."* The players come to the conclusion: It isn't a coincidence that the most well prepared seem to be the luckiest. In the long term, sports is fair in that performance and results reflect the preparation.

A strong believer in mental coaching or training (see Leadership chapter) Pellerud, as so many modern coaches, loves to employ the motivational quote. At a recent practice Pellerud quoted Alessandro DelPierro, an Italian National Team and Juventus player: *"If we don't run in battle for 90 minutes...we become an average team-and can be beaten. It's all a question of our head."* This was Even's approach to the mental state of mind-the toughness the 100% effort for 90+ minutes that he needed to win.

Pellerud summarized what he wanted to see from his team as they entered the WWC training phase:

a. We will focus on winning every day, even should we face the men's National Team of France.
b. From now on we shall have no respect for any team or any nation, the only focus is on winning

Pellerud went on to emphasize that to some players this competitive take-no-prisoner approach would be a natural part of their personality and wouldn't need reminding. He was targeting the other players, however, those that needed to absorb this approach and adjust to a new state of mind, slowly but surely.

He wanted that attitude of accepting nothing but winning as palpable on the team. He asked the players to refuse to accept a bad work rate from fellow teammates. Address them, if it's necessary. He was particularly concerned, as all National and Provincial team coaches are, that the players be consistent in this approach on their club teams, as well. If you were the only player with that attitude on your team, be creative. Make it contagious. Be sure your coaches create competitive rules. Introduce informal competitions with teammates-count the goals. Make it pay to win or lose even if it is as simple as playing for a coke. Keep that competitive environment around you. Create and maintain good work habits. Pellerud wanted to impress upon the players that this approach would improve their competitiveness and their game and, most importantly, he told them you'll have a lot more fun every day.

Key Principles in Set Pieces

Dead Ball Situations (DB)

Introduction

Pellerud spends a considerable time in practice and preparation working on set pieces and dead ball situations. In explaining his principles to the players and coaches, he recently reviewed the following principles.

- ❑ 35% of all goal-scoring opportunities are created following a Set Piece.
- ❑ A lot of teams have a tendency to say "...they could only score on us on a Dead Ball or set piece situation...", a statement most often used when opponents score on a DB. We need to have the attitude that it does not matter how we (or they) score goals. The only thing that matters is which team scored the most goals, no matter how!
- ❑ Dead ball situations-or set pieces-represent a type of uncontrolled situation, nobody can stop a good service (9.15m/10yds), the rules don't allow us to put realistic pressure on the ball. A lot of players positioned in or close to the box (in most DBs) also means that many uncontrolled actions are involved.
- ❑ On offensive DBs, we must take advantage of these circumstances as much as possible.
- ❑ On defensive DBs, we must eliminate as many of the uncontrolled details as possible.

Key Words

POSITIONING - SERVICE - AGGRESSIVENESS

1) Positioning

- ❑ Choose the most accurate player to do the service (analyze the demands, based on distance/angle/curve)-identify this in practice
- ❑ The best header - either by size and/or pure desire to win the ball - aim at winning the first ball in goal-scoring areas.

If not winning the first ball, these players should ensure a poor clearing of the ball

- ❑ Aggressive players in position to anticipate and fight for second and even third balls. Remember, mental strength/desire is the most important quality in DBs.
- ❑ Two players in rebound areas. Important qualities - anticipate and win the loose balls, and the ability to recover to a defensive task.
- ❑ Two players home in order to cover in case of counterat tack-your defensive brains

2) *Service*

- ❑ Generally spoken, I prefer inswingers-they seem to create more problems for defenders than outswingers. If one player can serve from both sides, I would use this player. This would in particular apply to corner kicks.
- ❑ On free kicks the service desired would vary from situation to situation, based on which space we want to exploit-where they are vulnerable. If they give away a lot of space between the goalie and their own defense, I would prefer an outswinger, so you can run onto the ball with pace and strike/slide or tackle it into the net (if the free kick is from the side corridors).
- ❑ If they position tight to the goalie, I would prefer a hard inswinger served long the 5m-line (can be scored just by tapping the ball in, either our player or their defender).

3) *Aggressiveness/Determination/Anticipation*

- ❑ To get the ball into the net is often a combination of soccer skills and mental skills. I believe with DBs, the mental part means even more and outweighs skills.
- ❑ Determination and aggressiveness and anticipation will be decisive. Some athletes are more or less born with these attributes, others need to develop. This means that every individual athlete involved in DBs must take time and energy to work on this mental part.

Pellerud preparing a set piece in practice

Coaching the set play

Chapter VI
Positional Play

Choosing your Players

When asked about Norway's National Team's success, Egil Olsen had this to say about how Pellerud and himself chose the National Team: *"We didn't always have the best players, but we had the best team. It is the coach's responsibility to make sure the right pieces are in place for the results."*

One of the reasons Pellerud appears to have achieved success is his ability to have a clear plan for his team and, even more importantly, for his players as individuals. He takes it a step further by being able to communicate that plan to the players so they are rarely confused or uncertain of their roles and responsibilities on the field.

Linda Medalen offered the following insight into her years on the Norwegian National Team with Even Pellerud: *"Even didn't always pick the best players...We didn't have the 20 best Norwegian players on the team. What we did have were the players who were best for doing their job. Even had very specific abilities that he wanted to see in each player. Special jobs you had to do on the field. Special roles and responsibilities you had to have and Even chose the players best suited for that and it worked very well for him. One thing that was very important was that we all knew what our job was. We knew what was expected from us in this part of the field or that part of the field. What was expected from us when the ball was here or there. We had a job. We never had to be worried or confused about what we had to do on the field. Even made sure we were well prepared and were the right players for the right position."*

While he has a direct approach to coaching, with respect to his tactics Pellerud also has an acknowledged knack for picking the right players to fit into his system. It's a quality Pellerud feels is critical in a good coach.

The following are some of the attributes that Even looks for in positional players and what some of the Canadian players feel are the qualities players should bring to their positions; which physical, technical, tactical and mental attributes are important for their positions.

Even Pellerud spends a great deal of his time identifying players who will help make the Canadian National Team strong for years to come. While identifying talent is a coaching skill, knowing what to look for in a player's position/role on the team is even more critical.

In this chapter Pellerud outlines his philosophy on positional play. Some of his National Team players also share from a player's perspective what it takes to be an effective positional player. It is recommended that your players look closely at how these individuals see their roles.

Midfield

A good work rate will always be the most important attribute in an effective midfielder. They do not have to necessarily be the most physical or athletic, but all midfield players must have a good work rate and good work ethic. The types of qualities you require in your midfielders also depend on whether you play 4-4-2, 4-5-1, 4-3-3, 3-5-2, etc, and vary from formation to formation.

They need to have good range, vision and understanding of the game. They have to know the defensive concept and be mentally responsible to help out in front of the stoppers. The center-mids need to be able to receive the ball with a good first touch on short and long passes. They should be able to stand physical, mental, technical, tactical pressure as the last midfielder in defending.

If you are playing with a higher midfielder, that player should possess great skills, quick ball treatment and the ability to see the opportunities for penetration. She should possess excellent passing skills to send the ball behind the defenders to strikers running onto the ball. Also important is the timing of the passes and the standing time of the passes with the timing of the runs of the ball. Some qualities in the box for finishing is a big bonus.

They must be mentally brave and willing to take risks on the ball. Physically, they need not necessarily be very athletic, but fast ball treatment is all important-more of a quickness than pure speed.

They must have exceptional work rate and range, preferably able to and willing to recover from high positions to help out in the midfield.

The outside midfielders will require different qualities. They will be more defenders in 4-4-2 as opposed to more attack oriented in 4-5-1, but to treat them in common, outer midfielders have to be good players, not necessarily the quickest players on the team, but good players overall. They must possess sound speed and excellent endurance with an ability to run up and down, up and down, and up and down as a defender and as a striker and as a midfielder covering the line.

Midfielders must be mentally consistent players. Players you can trust to do the job. They have to be able to beat a player and get the ball in from the outside line. They have to cross the ball effectively using their ability to challenge 1v1 on the sides.

Defensively, good midfielders have to be good 1v1. They have to be excellent first defenders, challenging, pressuring the ball and preventing penetration.

Midfielders must be able to cover a big space with a fullback on the other side. At the same time they must work closely together in the midfield when they are under pressure. They have to recognize how to play as second and third defenders, providing second pressure, cover and balance.

Sometimes you as a coach will recognize talent right away and go with her and stick with her. Other times, it may take a little longer. You shouldn't give up because some players are developing right in front of you. The first time I saw Diana Matheson in 2001 at Nationals in Winnipeg she was not having a lot of impact on that game. You could say she was a good player on the flank, but not great. The next time I saw her was with our U-19 team in 2002 just before the World Cup and she played just a little bit with no impact and I didn't rate her very highly. But I saw enough to follow up on her and the next time, almost by coincidence, I saw her practicing in Toronto at the Soccer Centre and she was totally dominant in that role. She played a flank midfielder in that scrimmage and she played great. She almost made the other players look childish. I brought her to camp and she just took all her talents and challenges and grew and grew. She has a lot of work to do from a skills standpoint, but has a great mentality, is very confident and is always willing to learn. Having a coachable athlete is also important.

Midfield Play

Kristina Kiss (KK), veteran midfielder, and Diana Matheson (DM), rookie center midfielder, share their thoughts on what it takes to play their positions.

Physical Attributes

A central midfielder requires good endurance, as well as a good strong core. Maintaining balance as players attack from front and back is important to allow the mid time to get a pass away. Depending on the role of the mid, speed and height can be important attributes to join the attack or win balls in the air. *(KK)*

The physical attributes necessary for a central midfielder are greatly varied, but strong endurance is essential. Personally, I am a small, quick player with a high fitness level. I am always working on strength (core, upper and lower body). *(DM)*

Technical qualities

Accurate passes, both penetrating and short to maintain possession, are very important qualities. One-on-one defending and ball control are also necessary skills to possess. Varying service techniques (outside of foot, chips, etc.), allow for a more dangerous attacking midfielder. *(KK)*

The central midfielder should have good ball control, the ability to turn quickly, and good vision. She should master all types of passing including fist-time passes, chips, and long balls. Personally, I am working to improve my long balls. *(DM)*

Tactical requirements

Realizing the best points of attack and quick decision making are important. When to join the attack and when to balance for the counter are important tactics. Shifting defensively with the play and knowing when to push, when to drop back and be patient is also very helpful. *(KK)*

They should be available at all times to receive the ball from a teammate. They must put pressure on their opponent's attack. Upon winning the ball they must look to go forward and begin an attack. I am working on starting the attack as quickly as possible. *(DM)*

Mental Qualities

As a mid I feel that there is more attention put on a defender after a mistake than a mid. Refocusing after a mistake is key and not letting the same mistake be made twice is very important but many times a defender cleans up for a midfielder, while there is no one to clean up for the defender. Performing at a high level under pressure requires confidence in your abilities and the abilities of your teammates. However, too much confidence or cockiness can lead to silly choices and mistakes. *(KK)*

Like any player on the field, a central midfielder must be intense on defense and creative, composed, but quick on offense. They also must be aware of all other players on the field. *(DM)*

What are you good at?

A couple of my strengths are my set pieces, as well as my vision (although I've had to work on this to accommodate a new playing style). My long balls are okay as well. *(KK)*

1v1 defending, team shape, vision *(DM)*

What are you working on to improve?

I'm working a lot on my physical game, winning balls in the air is a priority. Working on my aggression in defensive situations is also very important. I'm working on improving and maintaining a good fitness level and using my body to shield to allow for more time to make the pass. Although these are my weaknesses I'm working on right now, I have to constantly work on everything else to become a better player. *(KK)*

Long balls, passing quickly and accurately *(DM)*

Coaching advice

The coaching staff lets me know what I'm weak at and what my strengths are. Weaknesses are pointed out in scrimmages, games and video and players are instructed and encouraged to work on them. Coaches also have players constantly work on their strengths to improve as much as possible. *(KK)*

Good team shape and defending, work on passing and shooting *(DM)*

Developing Qualities

Working on fitness and endurance is done individually with the help of coaches and therapists who provide training programs which target personal weaknesses. Aggression is one of the most difficult weaknesses I've had to work on. Sometimes it felt like I was going against my nature, but with a coach pushing you and teammates who don't back down it can be worked on in scrimmages and in games. Once you have a taste it becomes easier. Video analysis is also helpful-it provides both positive and negative feedback. *(KK)*

I practice striking the ball every day. I focus on long balls but also work on bending the ball and hitting low, straight balls. I also plan to practice shooting more. Repetition is the key. *(DM)*

Expectations

First defender responsibilities and shifting in zonal defense are two very important attributes when defending. Doubling up when possible is expected, as well as tough, physical play. Joining the attack and making penetrating passes are key offensive traits. Communication is also stressed in all situations. *(KK)*

I am expected to pressurize the opposition and win balls. Attacking responsibilities lie mainly in transition. Once I win the ball I must immediately push the ball up the field, looking to strikers first. *(DM)*

Kristina Kiss' Favorite Practices

1) 4v4 +Ks and offensive walls

Set-up: 14 players on a 40x20 field; 5v5 on inside & 4 on outside; Inside players have two touches, outsides have 1

Equipment: cones, balls and 2 nets

Objective: Works on touches, decision making and transition play. Focus is on moving forward quickly using walls. The goal is quick attacks, lots of shots on net, defensive pressure.

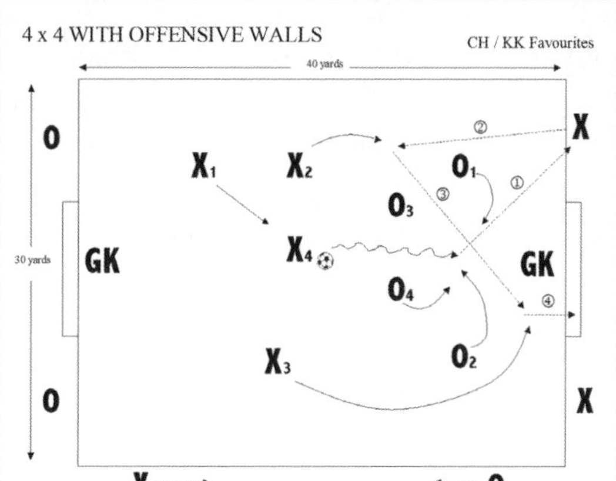

Fig. 1

2) Chipping Game (Soccer Tennis)

Set-up: 12 players on a 40x20/3 grids.

Equipment: Cones and Balls.

Objective: Focus is on touches and movement off the ball. Defensive pressure comes quickly. Good set ups for teammates is stressed.

Goal: Outside team must get five passes with two defenders coming in and then chip to opposite box. If unsuccessful, team becomes defenders.

3) Long Balls

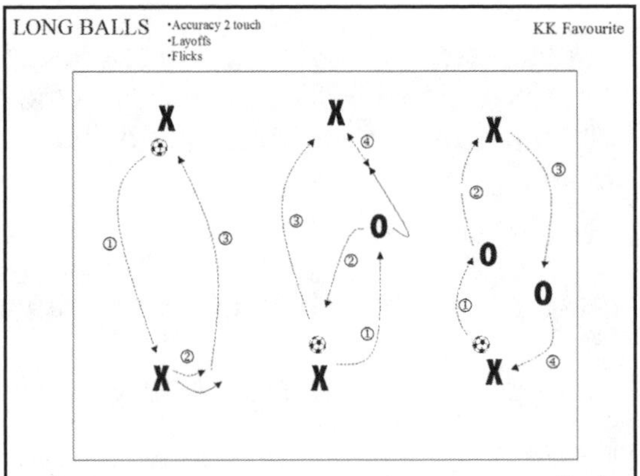

Fig. 2

Set-up: 2 players

Equipment: balls; use full width of field; strike 25 yards and longer

Objective: Players work on receiving with different parts of the body and challenge themselves to hit varying long balls. Can also be done with a player in the middle using one touch to set up outside player, or with four players with inside player flicking to outside players. The goal is to improve long passes-driven, curled, underspin, outside of the foot, etc.

4) Touches - Volleys, Chest, Head

Set-up: 3-18 players.

Equipment: balls

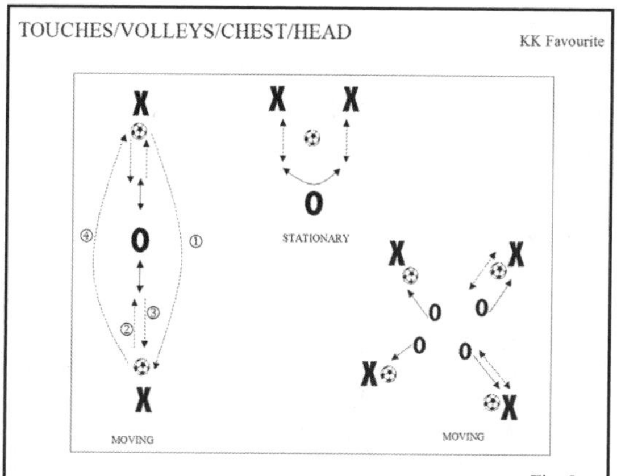

Fig. 3

Objective: Quick feet with stationary work and incorporating fitness with player moving towards passer inside, top of the foot volleys, chest volleys, head, thigh etc. Work on touches with different parts of the body and fitness.

Diana Matheson's Favorite Practices

1) Keep away

Set-up: 7 players on a 15x15 yard field

Objective: The goal is to split the defenders as often as possible. Teaches midfielder vision/decision-making

Game: Can progress to 4v3; can vary ground size

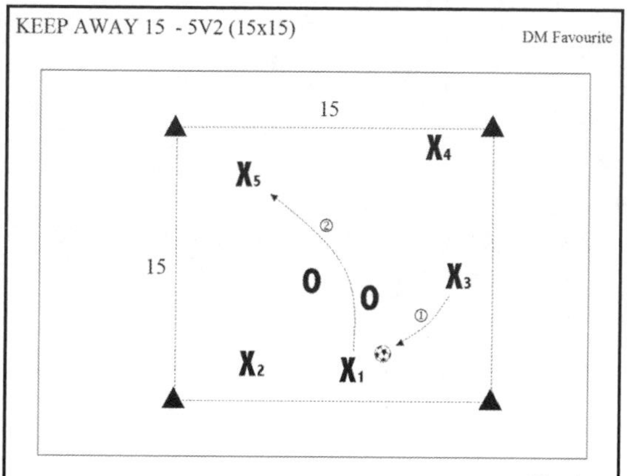

Fig. 1

2) 1v1

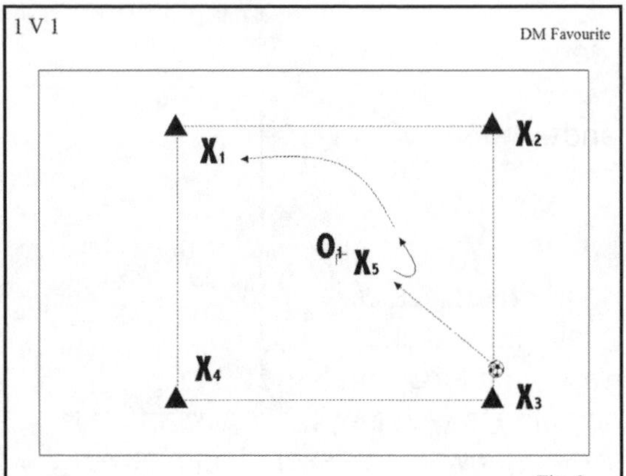

Fig. 2

Set-up: 6 players on a 10x10 field. Players are set up in a square with a defender and mid-fielder in the middle. Objective: The goal is to work on turning and 1v1 attacking and defending. The attacking player receives the ball from one of the outside players and must turn and pass to a player without a ball. Focus is on turning and shielding.

3) 4 Goal Game

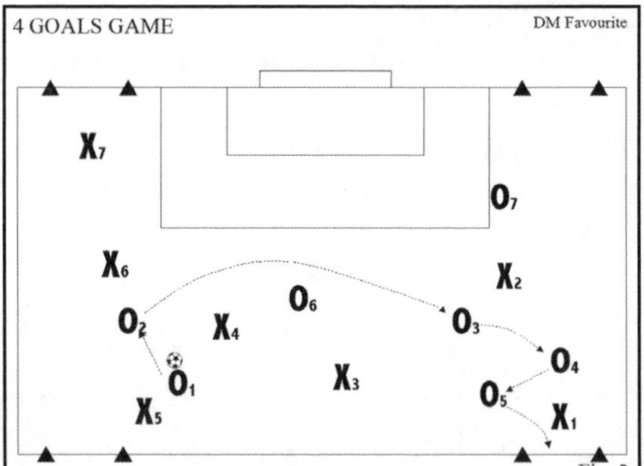

Fig. 2

Set-up: Whole team on a half-field.

Objective: The goal is to work on vision, accurate passing (short and long) and quick attacks, switch the point of attack.

Game: Players are divided into two teams. Each team must try to score on one of the four small or coned goals placed 5 yards in, in each corner, looking to switch the play often.

Forwards or Strikers

Scoring ability is quality number one for a striker. Some strikers just have that ability to look dangerous. Many strikers can be invisible for long periods of time, but then they appear and when they get a ball they are incredibly dangerous. They scare the defenders, they scare the goalkeeper. They create the confidence in your team because they always look to be able to score a goal out of nothing. That is quality number one in a striker. I saw this quality in Christine Sinclair more than any other player when I saw her as a 16-year-old. She had the whole package--size, good speed, excellent in the air, both feet--a true striker. Probably I knew when I first saw her play that she was for the team--no question. Christine Sinclair is an example of a striker that always looks dangerous and always is. That unbalances your opponent.

If you have that quality you should watch that player closely and pick her for that position.

You also have other types of strikers that you need to make a team complete. Very often you need a target with more ability to be visible...for long ball passes and flicks with the head or foot. They have to be able to wrestle and fight the defenders to get attention, to create a space for other strikers or even midfielders to use the space behind the striker. That is another quality you need in the team to have the complimentary qualities that make a team work. They have to have a nose for the goal, they have to have great 1v1 skills and want to shoot. We are fortunate to have at this time some of the biggest, fastest players up front. I call them my monsters: Christine Sinclair, Kara Lang, and Christine Latham have these qualities. Abby Wambach of the U.S. has matured and she has dedicated herself to the game and has become one of the best strikers in the world. Sinclair is getting there, as well. (See box)

Christine Sinclair

When Even Pellerud was asked about the players that made the largest first impression on him in his years in the women's game he stated without hesitation, Christine Sinclair. She had the whole package. She could see things on the field. She made things move at her pace. She had deceptive speed, great size and an incredible knack for putting the ball in the goal. Even knew his first impressions wouldn't let him down.

Sixteen years old when she was first noticed by the new Canadian National Team coach, Sinclair was to play 15 games for the U-19 National Team. Culminating in the gold medal game for the first FIFA U-19 World Championship she played 15 games and scored 22 goals in international competition.

On the full national side since the age of 16, she is second in goals only to Charmaine Hooper. Capped 65 (2005) times she has scored 49 goals for the full women's side. Choosing to attend the University of Portland in 2001 and coached by the legendary Clive Charles (the program boasted U.S. National Team stand-outs Tiffany Milbritt and Shannon MacMillan, as alumni). Sinclair became a leader on Clive Charles' team. As a sophomore she led the Portland Pilots to the National Championship with an outstanding year.

Born on June 12th, 1983 in Burnaby, British Columbia, this superlative striker has been named MVP in every NCAA tournament she has played. In 2002, she broke Mia Hamm's 1993 record of 6 goals and 16 points, with 10 goals and 21 points, scoring both goals in the championship game.

Christine Sinclair has become on of the most popular athletes in Portland, her adopted city. When Sylvia Beliveau, FIFA Technical Director, was in Portland for the 2003 World Cup she was amazed when she asked the local players who they were pulling for and they responded both Canada and the United States, because of Christine. Sinclair banners hung around the Portland field for that Canada/China game.

The three-time All-American took the 2003 college season off for the World Cup. Still recovering from a summer illness during the Women's World Cup she scored Canada's opening goal against Germany and gained strength as the tournament went on. Unfortunately, her coach and very close friend, Clive Charles passed away in the fall 2003 and it was a difficult time for the young athlete.

A brilliant on-field tactician, Sinclair has appreciated the different nuances of the game and understands the differences between the possession-style she played in under Clive Charles and the direct attacking approach of Even Pellerud. Sinclair won both the Golden Boot and MVP award in the 2002 FIFA U-19 World Championships. She was awarded the Hermann Cup Trophy (outstanding NCAA player) in January 2005.

A 21-year-old with a year left in Portland, Sinclair would like to bring another National championship home to her program, but her main goal is to win the 2007 World Cup with the Canadian National team.

Sinclair, who has a knack for scoring timely goals (she led the nation in game winners) is also no slouch academically. She is a three-time academic all-American and enrolled in Life Sciences at the University of Portland.

Canada's program appears to be in excellent hands as Christine Sinclair matures into a leader in all aspects.

Charmaine Hooper, of course, has all the physical and scoring talent of any world player. Her work ethic and desire is second to none. We will move her out of the back in front when we look for a goal. Even in deal ball situations you want those players in the box. (for more on Hooper, see The Physical Factor chapter on page 189))

Center Forward Play

(Charmaine Hooper (CH) {Forward and Center Back} & Christine Latham (CL))

Christine Latham out of the University of Nebraska and WUSA 2003 Rookie of the Year in SanDiego and Charmaine Hooper, all-time leading Canadian scorer, share their thoughts on their positions. Charmaine also provides her insights on the role of the center back (CB)-a position in which she feels having the mind and experience of a forward (FWD) has helped her play.

Physical Attributes

(FWD) Strong, fast, quick; (CB) strong, intimidating, fast, quick - My first few steps are quick and explosive so I am able to gain a little distance on my opponent, enough to make me dangerous in different situations. I am working on my heading to goal by spending 20 minutes after practice with crossing balls. *(CH)*

In order to be any forward there are certain things you need and they are as follows: speed, skills, aggressiveness, and aggressive scoring mentality. I feel I have decent speed, could be better; skills are average, but I am very aggressive and have a good scoring mentality. I am working on my power muscles for an improvement on speed and doing skill drills everyday to work on that area. *(CL)*

Technical Qualities

(FWD) This is a very important aspect of being a good player, simply because a player cannot survive without technical abilities. I believe I hold the ball well, which helps our team move up the field together on attack. (CB) I am able to win balls in the air and anticipate well. *(CH)*

I feel that my volleying techniques are good but different types of volleying like outside of the foot and even laces could be improved so that myself, as a player, can be improved. A player who has an extended technical vocabulary and can do more things makes you more successful because you are more versatile than other players. *(CL)*

Tactical Requirements

(FWD) Knowing when and where to be/run, always being dangerous and creating scoring chances. (CB) Knowing when to step or hold the line with the three other defenders. Also positioning yourself well enough to prevent opponents from being dangerous and creating scoring opportunities. *(CH)*

The tactical requirements are as follows: You must be able to shoot with both feet (ex: driven, curved, lofted, chips), flick and hold balls while pressured, be good in the air for flicking. On the transition side, finding the channels for space, making runs behind your defense and lastly, be able to work off your other forward partners to create mayhem. *(CL)*

Mental Qualities

(FWD) Always focus and have determination to win the ball and score. (CB) Focus at all times because one mental lapse can cost your team the game. A center forward can have lapses in concentration during 90 minutes and still score a goal but a defender can't afford to have one lapse in concentration because that may be the time the forward scores. *(CH)*

Being a forward requires a good focus at all times. The tactical side must be sharp in order to create chances. After making a mistake it is important to regain composure and re-group in order to be successful. Because your job is to score, pressure and work hard, you don't have time for mental breakdowns. *(CL)*

Quality Development

(FWD) My job is scoring goals and I'd like to think I'm good at scoring goals. I am working to improve shooting and heading/flicking the ball with my head. Coaches haven't directly said what my weaknesses are, but it is pretty obvious that my heading and flicking the ball with my head or foot with a defender challenging me from behind is something I'm working on. *(CB)*

Since this is a new position for me I have to work on maintaining good shape in the back and making good decisions. *(CH)*

I feel personally, my strengths are being aggressive and working hard. Those two have gotten me a long way. If you always try and never stop working, eventually you will have success. I am working on improving my speed, touches, and finishing. Canada plays a very aggressive style of soccer, with high pressure and a fast pace, this obviously goes with my strengths and helps me grow even more. As for my weaknesses, I feel I could be a little more patient on the ball, especially around the goal, so during finishing exercises they make me more aware of my mistakes, as well as during drills that need a higher mental focus. Every day in practice I work on finishing, and during drills that need to be thought through more, I'm extra aware of the level that is needed to be successful.

For me, personally, I like to watch the older more experienced players and what they do in the situations that I am weak in. I try to do what they do and learn from them. Besides that, I try to do individual exercises, taking what Even has told me to work on and do it, like my speed for example. Working on speed drills like the ladder in which foot drills are done quickly, help improve quickness. And constantly finishing on goal is another thing I have been working on. I try to do a little of everything so that the things I am good at don't get bad, but the bad things get better. *(CL)*

Expectations

(FWD) As a forward it is most important to score of course. I must also be able to hold the ball, allowing my team to get up the field so as to continue the attack. Making runs across the field for my players is very important in getting the defense to shift and hopefully become unbalanced. I must also try to stay as high as possible and be ready for quick counter attacks. I must also be able to defend as high as possible at times. (CB) I am expected to keep the defensive shape at all times helping to start the attack and, of course, preventing scoring opportunities and helping to stop/prevent goals. *(CH)*

Being a forward involves a lot in the attack phases of the game, my job being the obvious (to score). I am also required to create space for my teammates and get into supporting positions for my other forwards so they have options when we are attacking. On the defensive end, our jobs are simple. Once the ball has gotten into our attacking third, don't let it leave it. We are the first line of defense and we must work hard to fulfill that role. We can be more aggressive with our pressure because we have no line to hold or men to mark. We must, however, work as a team and our pressure must be quick, exact, and hard.

Each game is different and therefore, my role is changing all the time. In one game we may look to exploit the wings, in the next we might play one forward where my job is to hold the ball more.

With Even's philosophy in the Canadian National Team, it is hard not to be successful. His coaching is exact, precise, and to the point. For me, it fits perfectly with my playing style and I have improved tremendously since being with the program and Even. Our team plays with a lot of heart and determination, which makes us successful and motivated. *(CL)*

Charmaine Hooper's Favorite practices

1) 7v7 +GK Scrimmage

Set-up: 16 players (incl GKs); Small field

Objective: Playing long balls, moving into good scoring positions, defending and keeping track of players, and shooting.

2) Flank Zones (See Pellerud's practice, Page 82)

Set-up: 5 or 6 per team; small field

Objective: attack from flanks with crosses and scoring

Game: Players on side have one touch or they can do overlapping runs with each other and cross balls into the box for field players to try to score. Can coach timing of runs, crossing the ball, finishing; Vary field size for different crosses

3) 8v8

Set-up: Almost 3/4 field, a 10x10 square marked in each corner;

Objective: A team has to pass the ball successfully to a teammate into the square and then out again to get a point.

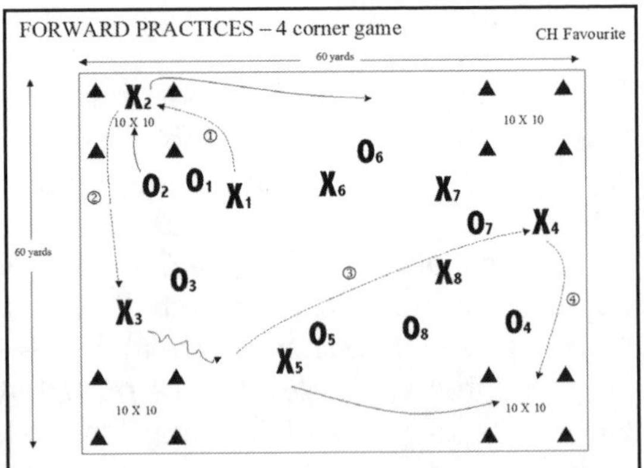

Fig. 3

Game: Once a team has passed into and out of the all four squares (one time each square) that team wins.
(See Diagram)

Christine Latham's Favorite Practices

1) Goal Scoring

Set-up: 3 teams of 6; 40x25 field

Objective: Scoring, possession, movement and communication

Equipment: cones, pinnies, goals; the focus is speed of play, communication and effective movement. The practice works on all of the above as well as touches.

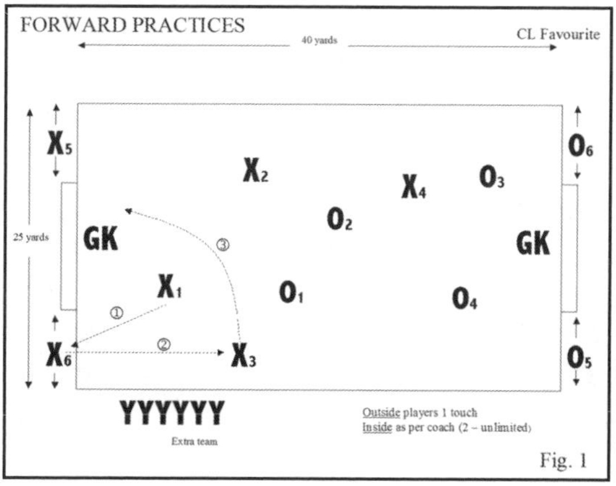

Fig. 1

2) Finishing Drill

Set-up: 6-7 players; ½ field

Objectives: Finishing, touches, movement

Equipment: 1 pinny for defender; balls, cones

Game: The object of this drill is to create space from your defender enough to allow a successful chance at goal. The center mid sends balls to either the left or right mids who then send a lofted cross (early) to the opposite forward who is rounding her run away from the defense into the box. From there they can shoot directly on goal or knock it down to partner forward who is making a direct run into the box. Alternate sides and forwards. Works on forward spacing, communication, working with each other and finishing.

3) Forward Drill

Set-up: 8 players; ½ field

Equipment: 1 pinny for defense, balls.

FORWARD DRILL – LAY OFFS /FLICKS

CL Favourite

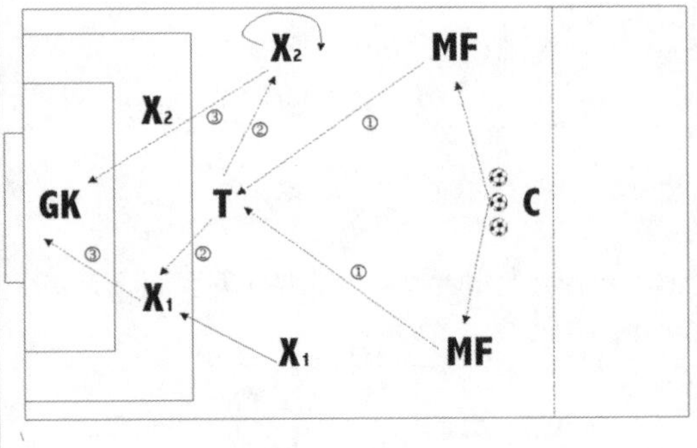

Fig. 2

Objectives: This is forward work. The object is rightly timed runs from the wing forwards and good flicks and layoffs from the target. The mids send lofted balls into the target who then lays them off to on coming forwards who finish on goal. This drill is good for forwards to work together, touches and finishing all in a game-like atmosphere. Make sure speed of play is emphasized for game like conditions.

4) Warm-up

Set-up: 3 teams of 6; 25x15 field

Objective: Works on touches, communication, and transition

Game: There are 3 teams of 6, with one team in the defensive grid and the other 2 in the attacking grids. The passer sends a ball into one of the attacking ends. There is a 2-touch restriction. The defensive grid sends two players in for pressure. The object is to complete a certain number of passes (ex: 4, 5, 6), with your team avoiding the defensive pressure, and then send the ball in the air over the center grid to other attacking grid so they can do the same thing. If the ball is won by the defensive team then they switch with the team they won it from and they become offensive and the other team defensive. Points are awarded to the team after a successful service into the other grid is completed. Games to 10 points.

Qualities of a Defender (Even Pellerud) in Positional Play

Defensive Qualities - When looking for a stopper or a full back I search for an undefined ability to stop an attack. I am not necessarily looking at special skills or even speed, but just this ability to be right there when it matters. A lot of good-looking players are never there in the war for you on the field and have a tendency to fade out and hide. Truly special defensive players stand out when it matters with a long toe or a great tackle or a flicking header to clear the ball away from the danger zone.

Specifically, the defenders have to possess an ability to work in team shape: back four, back three, or back five. They have to be able to adjust to a playing style and formation, and, of course, to teammates. You need some fast defenders, but you don't need to have all defenders very fast. It is more about speed in the brain and reading the play than running speed. I think that this is a common misunderstanding in soccer, that you have to be fast. It is a big advantage, but you can still play soccer at the highest level without being extremely fast, because you can compensate by being even smarter. It is a lot about positioning and reading the play and anticipation, stealing the ball, which is more important than being extremely quick over a longer distance.

Offensive Defenders

Striking the ball is increasingly important in the women's game. The ability to play a nice pass, a constructive pass, a simple pass, a fast pass to a better position (midfielder for example). To understand the reasons why you may have to clear the ball without address in a critical situation where defending is more important than creating. That understanding is also a crucial part of what makes a great defender. The first and foremost duty they have is to stop attacks. Their second job is to create and set up good attacks.

Fullbacks

I want to see defensive thinking, but I also like to see the players go up and down the flank. I want them to have an attacking attitude to support the midfielders and, once in a while even go the whole way up to the endline to cross balls. This requires good runs on and off the ball with good timing. Recognizing the moment, not having too many players together, but one at a time from the back line to support the attack, keep the momentum, regain the ball if your team loses it by being in a good position and conscious about how important positioning is in the rebound area.

The fullback also needs to take advantage of that position to keep the momentum in the attack, to stay in there and either go for a new overlap or cross the ball from a longer distance into the box. That doesn't help you much if you can't strike the ball well. Ball striking is gaining more importance from a fullback position, and also from the stopper position.

Defender Play

Sasha Andrews (SA) & Randee Hermus (RH)

Canadian National Team outside defender Randee Hermus plays with Floya in Norway while center back Sasha Andrews plays at the University of Nebraska.

Physical Attributes

Some of the physical attributes needed for a central defender are great timing for the aerial aspect of the game (strong heading), quickness and speed for 1v1 defending, a good sense of body balance and an ability to hold players off with body strength and not foul.

I have been working on flexibility to maintain a good core and body balance when defending. When working out I work on things that may improve the explosive and quickness part of my game while still being a big and strong defender. Things like plyometrics, ladders, hand clings, and squats. I personally have gone through and am still going through many sets and reps of pushups and sit-ups. The amount asked for was around 300 of each per day and they eventually get done. *(SA)*

As a defender, a physical presence is a must. Both upper and lower body strength are a key to back line success. Power in the legs to get low, tackle hard and distribute accurate long ball passes is very important. The upper body strength to shield an opponent from the ball and get another player off the ball is an asset. Power is probably one of my strongest physical qualities. General fitness is also necessary, especially for a player like myself who is responsible for coming up for free kicks and corners. You must have the endurance to make these quick runs up, as well as recover immediately and still have ample energy to go hard into a tackle.

Another important physical attribute for a defender to have is speed. Unfortunately, this is not my specialty. However, down hill sprints, as well as resistance sprint exercises have helped me a bit in this department. *(RH)*

Technical Qualities

Technical qualities are winning head balls and directing them at the same time to start a new attack. The ability to clear any type of ball by a volley or a BFC (big @*&#% clearance) low body position and balance to be agile when defending 1v1 and recovering from tackles.

The ability to play long and short balls precisely, and to use different techniques to direct the ball. Things like curling it, driving it or passing it. *(SA)*

Passing is definitely key for a back-line player. Precision and accuracy on both short and long balls as well as chipped and driven balls is very important. Although it took me a good 4 years to get this down, with a lot of repetitions and tons of hard work, I am finally comfortable playing all different types of passes although I am still not where I want to be.

Clearances (aka BFC's) are another technical quality that is an asset when under pressure in the back. Using proper techniques and the biggest surface of your foot, the instep, is key. Another quality, especially for a central defender, would be heading. Winning aerial battles is one of my best qualities and I have learned that what it all comes down to is good positioning and even better timing. 1v1 defending is also of utmost importance. *(RH)*

Tactical Requirements

A central defender has to be able to have split vision. She needs to have a ball-oriented defensive mentality. Tactically we need to organize not only the defense, but others surrounding us in the midfield. A central defender must be able to communicate. We must be able to win balls in the air and create transitions with them. We must be able to read the offense and some of this comes with experience. We must know when to hold the line to create an offside, when to stay with a runner, and how close to be on second defender pressure. We must see things and think cynically at all times to avoid surprises or risks. We need to anticipate passes and use open midfielders in transition. We also must sacrifice and do whatever we need to when defending in the box. *(SA)*

The most important requirement of the back four (B4) is understanding the system and defensive shape. In a flat back system it is key to realize the importance of keeping the line, stepping and dropping accordingly, providing adequate support, and achieving great 1st and 2nd defender pressure and positioning. Communication, therefore, is vital. *(RH)*

Mental Qualities

Mentally, after a game, we should be, if not as tired as we are physically, mentally drained. At this level the ability to overcome faults and mishaps is mandatory. We need to be able to refocus quickly after stops in the game. We must come into the game confident in ourselves and believing in our skills and abilities. To be reinforced we need to have the respect from and for our teammates. We need to believe in them as they believe in us. Before games and practices players often visualize and listen to music to focus for field time. It is very important to maintain a strong positive mental status. *(SA)*

For me, soccer is a very mental game. Much thought and a great deal of strategy go into each game and practice. Being able to visualize yourself doing well and having confidence in your abilities is key to your performance. Most often, as players, we are our biggest critics. An elite athlete must be able to mentally refocus after making a mistake. Although it's easier said than done, being able to erase a mistake and override it with a good tackle or a brilliant pass separates a good player from a great player. *(RH)*

What are you good at?

I believe that I am great in the arial aspect of the game defensively. I am good at 1v1 defending, but good is not great so there is always room for improvement. I am good at long ball passing. I have improved my game vision and increased the speed of my decision making. *(SA)*

Personally, I feel my strengths have a lot to do with my physical game. I do well in 50/50 battles going 100% into tackles both on the ground and in the air. I think one of my biggest strengths is my ability to win most aerial battles. With more and more confidence I have become incredibly comfortable with my first touch. I am able to make precise 1st time passes with my feet and my head, adding an attacking dimension to my game. I think one of my best qualities, however, is my ability to communicate. Providing a sense of security and control on the back line is a key element of my game.

My ability to anticipate events in the game is also quite strong. Being not such a speedy player, I am very thankful that I am always thinking ahead of the current situation. *(RH)*

What are you working on?

I am working on quickness, speed, agility and consistency in my game. I take one thing at a time but eventually they all get worked on. I am also working on my mental strength and understanding or seeing things before they happen. *(SA)*

Each and every day is a struggle at this level to be better than your best at as many things as possible. Over the past 4 years my focus has been largely on my passing ability and quality. With tons of practice and even more patience, I have become more and more confident passing with both feet and making all types of different passes. In addition to this, although I need most work on defending rightly turned players coming at me, I have also been working hard to step in or tackle players as they receive balls with their backs to goal.

A component of my game which seems not to improve a whole lot but one that I wish would is my speed. Although I may be on the slower side in a foot race, the minute I can use my body to my advantage I seem to be a lot faster...hmmm. *(RH)*

Coaches' Influence

Coach Pellerud especially out of all the staff responds to our individual performances on a daily basis with constructive criticism. They let you know when you are doing well and push you extra when you're not. All of the staff is very in-tune with each individual's capabilities and collectively they have made all of us take leaps and bounds into better futures. Comments are made throughout practice, and sometimes the coaches hold meetings. In each case the meetings are straightforward and usually positive and encouraging. They let you know what needs to be done and what needs to continue. *(SA)*

Coach Pellerud and the staff coaches make an effort day in and day out to offer constructive criticism both on and off the field. At this level it is so important to be told straight out what it is we need to do as players to be better. I think Even is bang on when it comes to my strengths and weaknesses. He is a very good judge of character, as well, which allows him to get the most out of his players. He encourages me to become world class at those things such as aerial battles, positioning, physical play and communication, which he tells me I am already good at, but I could be great at. Those things I am not so good at or need improvement on like my speed and my consistent passing he is patient with and will push me to practice even harder to make these aspects become stronger parts of my game. *(RH)*

Personal Training Techniques

To improve my individual performances and individual techniques, I will follow programs created by the coaches outside of camp. I go to the gym on a regular basis and work on cardio and core. I go out to local pitches to do ball work with myself or a partner. I try to get involved in as many game-like scenarios as possible. Sometimes it is hard mentally to get up and do things, but that's part of the training. *(SA)*

Favorite Exercises & Drills: keep away, 8v8 with walls, clearance drills (short, short long, or have them served in to clear), soccer tennis, and shooting.

My personal training techniques have been improved by focusing much of my attention on those areas I need most work on. Practice and repetition for me seem to work best.

However, with confidence comes the belief in my own abilities and with that comes success. Much of my improvement over this last year has come with my decision to sign for a team in Norway. The soccer environment there has renewed my mental focus as well as increased my confidence a great deal. In addition, the opportunity to play every day and receive extra sessions to work on my weaknesses has greatly influenced my personal training techniques. *(RH)*

Quality Development

To work on developing my skills and tactics of the game, I need to be persistent and have an open attitude towards learning. I need to not get frustrated and put my own time and work in outside of camp. I need to use older developed players as learning tools for my future. Finally, get feedback from the coaches when possible so I steadily head in the right direction. *(SA)*

- ❑ Passing long balls-repetitive passing
- ❑ 1v1 defending situations-training with boys or lower division men (quickness and tougher tackling)
- ❑ Mental training and visualization on focusing on my strengths before practices and games is key
- ❑ Speed - difficult to change slow twitch to fast twitch fibers, but resistance exercises and down hill spring have helped
- ❑ Heading - both clearances and accurate passing after sessions. *(RH)*

Expectations

The roles and responsibilities of my position are to:
1) Prevent goal-scoring opportunities;
2) Strong hard ball winning;
3) Create offensive transition out of the defense;
4) Create fast attacks;
5) We need to be organized and cynical;
6) We need to apply pressure and have great second defender pressure
7) Defensive parts of the game: we need to stop the ball;
8) Need to have ball-oriented marking (zone);
9) Communication is also huge in the Canadian team philosophy;
10) Split vision.

(SA)

As a central or outside defender playing in a flat back formation, it is of utmost importance for me to communicate and control the line as much as I can. I am responsible for keeping the back line dynamic so we are prepared for both attacking and defensive situations. In the defensive phase it is my responsibility to provide hard 1st defender pressure, tackling hard and preventing goal scoring opportunities. I must also support well as a 2nd defender setting a new line. I must also recognize the importance of stepping out of the line to break up an attack. Splitting up is key for a center back duo. Anticipation is also a great asset to have in order to stop an opponent's entire build up and begin a transition of your own. If I, as a defender, can break up an attack successfully and make a good forward pass, it is possible to catch our opponents in an unbalanced situation and create a scoring opportunity for ourselves.

My main responsibility in the attack phase is distribution. Quality and precise passes from the back directly to the forwards or penetrative passes to the mids can lead to scoring chances and even goals. As one of the taller players it is also my responsibility to get involved in attacking dead ball situations like free kicks and corner kicks. *(RH)*

Sasha Andrews' Favorite Practices

1) 8v8

Set-up: 8v8/goals (+Ks); ½ field

Objective: To score off a wall can be awarded as 2 goals

Game: Play 8v8, four on the field and four walls of players creates fast transition and goalies can score; End players allowed one touch, side players allowed two touches

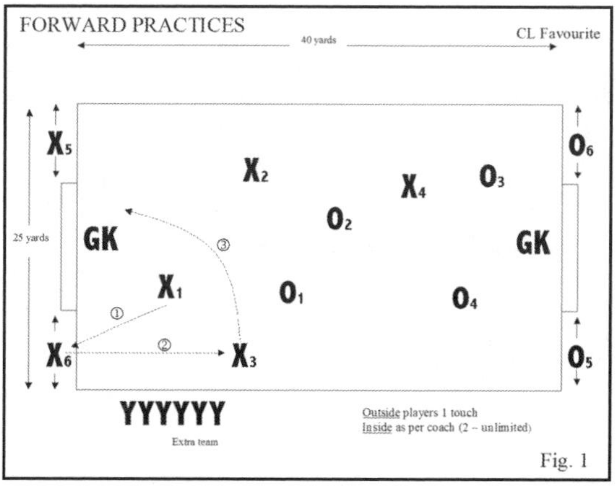

Fig. 1

2) Clearances

Set-up: 4 at a time; 18-yard box

Objective: Work on communication, covering and, of course, clearing.

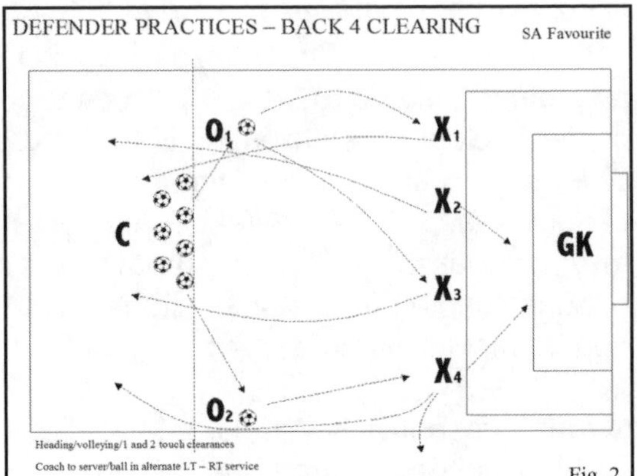

Fig. 2

Game: Two outside players serve random ball into the area for clearing by the back 4 in the air and on the ground. Can add scoring for one time accuracy and distance points

3) Shooting

Set-up: All players; ½ field with goal

Objective: Score using different techniques. Pass ball in, the coaches/players on the 18-yd lay off. Shoot, collect ball and go to the end of the opposite line. Coach varies lay off service, left, right, high/low; Can keep score.

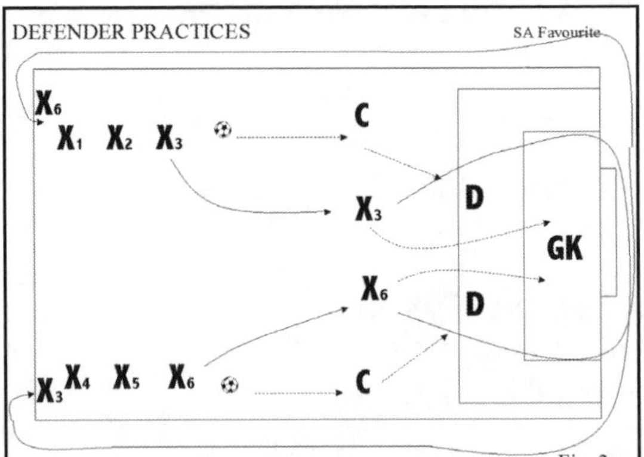

Fig. 3

Randee Hermus' Favorite Practices

1) 4v4 +Ks

Set-up: 16 players w. 2GKs; 40x40 field

Objective: To outscore your opponents

Equipment: Just two goals, cones to mark field, and players; 4v4 with walls.

Goals: Teams on field have two-touch, walls have 1-touch. Object is to create as many goals possible in a three-minute span. Teams rotate through every three minutes. Pressurizing the ball is key in teaching defending. Fast forward direct play and passing quality is key to attacking.

2) 3v2 Defending with Scoring

Set-up: 16 players w. 2GKs; ½ field (20-yards wide) (50x20)

Objective: To have the best goals for and against average

Equipment: 2 goals, cones to line field, all balls at defending team's end; 4 teams of 4.

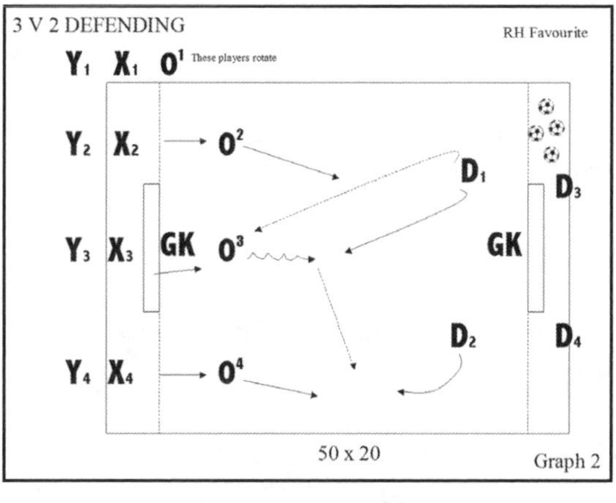

Game: 3 teams start as attackers, 1 team as defender. Set up 3v2 situations one at a time. Fourth player within teams rotates through. One defender plays long ball in to Team 1 attackers and comes out to defend goal in 2's. If defending team regains possession they can counter attack quickly and score on opposing team's goal. Attacking teams attempt to score one at a time, rotating through until 10 separate attacks are made. Points awarded for goals for and against. Switch defensive team until all have defended and tally total points for and against; Can also play 4v3/2v1, etc.; Coach defending principles.

3) Chipping Games

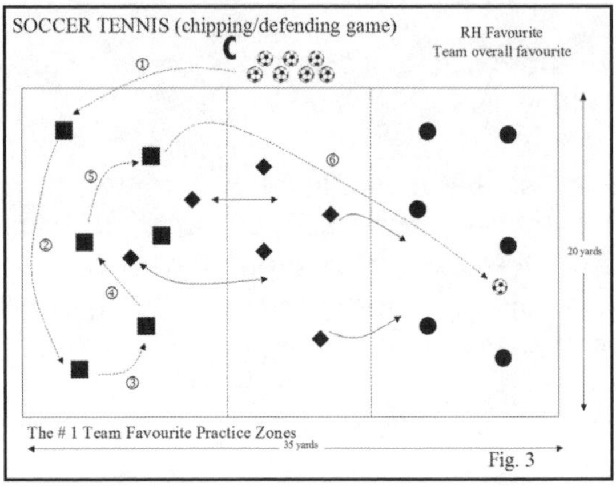

Fig. 3

Set-up: 15 (3 equal teams of 5); 15x30 field

Objectives: To reach 10pts first. Points awarded for 5 consecutive passes within grid and chip over to far grid

Equipment: Cones, players, server, balls;
Make 5 consecutive passes within team while two defenders release from center and try to dispossess ball. If unsuccessful chip team X becomes defender for team O and team C replaced team X and so on.

Center Back Play

Clare Rustad-Also see Charmaine Hooper's comments on page 210

Clare Rustad was on the U-19 2002 National Team and plays with the Vancouver WhiteCaps and at the University of Washington.

Physical Attributes

Overall body strength (so you don't get knocked off the ball), power and speed, tall, good vertical, quickness (balance), and endurance.

Technical Qualities

Leading, 1v2 defending, various types of passing (long especially) good and accurate clearances, safe ball control, ability to direct clearings and headers.

Tactical Requirements

Vision, ability to read game, knowledge of playing style, constant communication with everyone, understanding of spacing and 1st, 2nd, 3rd, etc...defender pressure, ability to mark players or space and to choose when to do either one.

Mental Qualities

Constant focus on game (should be mentally exhausted afterwards), be composed when handling the ball and in organizing the team, be demanding when organizing team shape.

Development of Qualities

I incorporate plyometrics and short sprints with various starts into my workouts. Personally, I need to work on being stronger on tackles, and lifting can help with that, as well as just practicing. Just constantly being around soccer and playing games and practicing with my team (or with boys teams) is probably the best way to improve on the above qualities.

Expectations

With the national team the center backs need to see everything and say everything and have an ability to read the game. Center backs should take no risks, be able to read the pressure on the ball and adjust the line of the back four accordingly. We can often contribute to the attack by directing cleared balls or through set plays.

Clare Rustad's Favorite Practices

1) 4v4 or 3v3 with walls

Set-up: 14 Players; 60x40 field

Objective: Good for defensive pressure, finishing, transition, and speed of play, movement off the ball

Equipment: cones to mark field; pinnies for two teams.

Game: Keepers play as normal, offensive walls have 1 touch. You can vary the touches of the inside players, when the ball goes out it goes to the keeper of the other team, play as normal using walls when needed.

2) Speed Workout

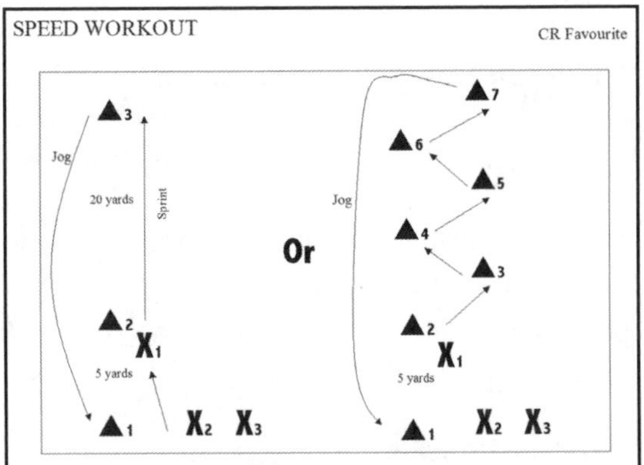

Fig. 1

Set-up: 1 player at a time

Equipment: cones & ball; Sprint should be 100% for the exercise to be effective.

Game: Make up any start that feels good or sets up for what you need to work on. Vary the starts at cone 2, sprint to cone 3 (or alternatively could sprint zig-zag to five cones to end) then jog back to cone 2, walk to cone 1 and start again. Choose sets/reps that work for you. Starts may be jogging, walking, standing; sprint from a lunge or a squat; sprint, hop back and forth on 1 or 2 feet; shuffle backwards (keep low), turn sprint; tuck jump/do a 360 and sprint; start on your front/back, get up and sprint.

3) Also enjoys the tennis/chipping game

Other Qualities to Look for in Your Players

Leadership is important and experience is important in producing leaders. Andrea Neil and I both know that she is not the most talented soccer player in the world, but it depends on how one defines talents. Her talent is leadership and a good team needs leadership. Without her we would not be where we are today.

Peer leadership, communication, personality, makes the other players work and that allows them to do their job more effectively. On a bad day for Andrea, she uses other qualities that make her very consistent from a team standpoint. She always has something to offer on a good day and bad day.

Her qualities in the air and in "double" situations...those are the qualities that have decided many games for us. Seeing her play from the stands, she will not look like a star on the field, but for a coach is a very, very important player. Her leadership and experience cannot be overrated. I would caution that the best players don't have to be the most spectacular.

Charmaine Hooper is both the same as and different than Andrea Neil. The same because she has experience and leadership, but different because her talent is more obvious and her aggressiveness and intensity second to none.

Soccer is a tactical game more than anything else and tactics take time to be learned. You can't base a team on 20-year-olds and teenagers and expect to play the game in a sophisticated way. If you have not been in that role for years, you will not learn the skills that are needed to perform at the highest level. Skills and speed are qualities on he ball that are important on a team. We also need some age, experienced people who have played under pressure in big games before, and wisdom on the field and those are some of the qualities Andrea and Charmaine have.

As a coach, I am always looking more for complimentary qualities, special competence, special qualities to form a team. For example, in midfield, you need the good, clever, smart, calm player, but you also need a creative, skillful, speedy player to create the amazing passes, to see the openings, to be able to deliver that pass at the right time, to be tactically aware and disciplined. You need some players that have the ability to take that risk to thread that very difficult pass because this is about creating goal chances and preventing opposition goal chances than anything else.

I am highly suspicious of midfielders with general qualities that always look good and, if you start studying them closely they aren't producing. This is about consistent production. Production of good passes. Production of goal chances. Production of free kicks and corner kicks. To see that amazing little hole in the defense and exploit it. Those things are more important for me than just looking good, kicking the ball around, and being able to keep the ball in possession, and do a fancy thing here and a fancy thing there, which makes that player look great, but doesn't help the team to produce.

Chapter VII
Goalkeeping

Even on the Goalkeeper

Even Pellerud was fortunate enough to have played against and trained some of the best goalkeepers in the world in Bente Nordby (Norway) and the former Swedish keeper, Elizabeth Leidinge. He notes what he find the most important attribute in a keeper: *"To be a goalkeeper is a very big mental job, not only her own mentality, but the way a good goalkeeper creates respect from opponents and from her own teammates is more important than the saves made. Shot stopping is important, but overall I would rate a goalkeeper by looking at her confidence level, her ability to grow with expectations, to be calm under pressure, to be better under pressure-all those qualities of a mental nature are very important to me as a coach. A psychologically strong goalkeeper positively affects her own team. The confidence a team has in its goalkeeper is one of the most important factors in how they play. This cannot be overstated."*

Pellerud comments on one of his outstanding WWC 2003 keepers: *"Taryn Swiatek, our goalkeeper, was one of our players who took time to develop. I saw her in a scrimmage in Edmonton, and I noticed her right away by her quickness in the box and her willingness to get in there and be aggressive and quick. It took some years for her to excel to the next level, but she is a very exciting goalkeeper. She has started to show those strong mental qualities more and more. I think we have a terrific future for goalkeeping in our National Team in Canada."*

The position of goalkeeper in international women's football has in the past been widely acknowledged as one of the weaker aspects of the female game. The technical reports from the '99 Women's World Cup were unanimous in pointing out the limitations among the tournament's keepers, citing communication, involvement in the game, decision making and distribution as problem areas.

Tony DiCicco, coach of the two-time World Champion U.S. National Team and acknowledged leader in education in goalkeeping development, states: *"When I look for a goalkeeper I look for two things. I look for a very special athleticism and I look for the mental skills. Brianna Scurry has those qualities on our team (U.S.A.). She is incredibly athletic. She's got tremendous mental skills. Late in the game when the game is on the line, you might be leading by a goal and you think you're getting a pounding, and it looks like the other team has got about 15 players on the field, and the game seems to be getting quicker, and quicker, and more frantic. For her it seems like everything slows down and her composure reflects on her teammates. It's a tremendous quality to have. You can always teach your keeper technique and tactics and I did that, but that athleticism and that ability to mentally stay in the game, they have to bring those to you. So those are the two things I look for in a goalkeeper, especially on the women's side of the game. A special athlete. The women's game is different from the men's game and that's important.*

"Your goalkeeper is not always going to have the whole package. Breanna's weakness was her kicking game and we had to play around that. She got better though. She worked on it. And keepers have to do that. They have to work on their game outside of team practice and team training."

Tony DiCicco recently completed a technical report on the World Cup. DiCicco was also of the opinion that goalkeeping was an area in need of improvement. His report on the 2003 Women's World Cup confirmed the findings of the FIFA technical committee that the level of improvement in overall goalkeeping, was one of the largest steps forward for the women's game from 1999 to 2003.

The FIFA technical report for the 2003 Women's World Cup indicates a significant improvement in the goalkeeping levels, both in athleticism and tactics. Former Canadian National

Team Coach Sylvie Beliveau, confirms that-noting in the 1999 WWC the goalkeeper was not at the level of the outfielders. It was a weakness. Beliveau-present at all WWC to-date and on the 2003 WWC and 2004 Olympic FIFA technical panel-and also notes that all participating countries have improved their goal-tending-a ringing endorsement to continue issuing FIFA technical reports.

Even Pellerud has long been a proponent of the keeper as a fifth back, well connected to the team in first appropriate high position to support the backs and the first point of attack in transition. Bente Nordby developed as a young keeper under Even Pellerud's term in Norway, is Norway's National Team keeper and continues to be one of the strongest women's keepers in the world.

Lauren Gregg has commented that Pellerud's use of Nordby as an active sweeper/keeper changed the women's game in the '90's. Pellerud was aware of the need to build a team around a strong goalkeeping philosophy and, when he first came to Canada, brought Jerry Knutsson with him from Norway. Knutsson had trained Bente Nordby and had been with the National team for 10 years. This was important to an incoming National coach, assuring that the same coaching philosophy was being implemented with all positions, none being more important than goal. Knutsson was an acknowledged goalkeeper coach and former international from the NFF and spent 1999-2000 with Pellerud's team in Canada. Knutsson, presently NFF's Women's goalkeeper coach, had the following comments about goalkeeping and Even Pellerud's philosophy: *"Even wants the goalkeepers to master all parts of the goalkeeper job, but especially that they are good at taking the role as an extra sweeper outside 16m when possible. This allows the entire team to move more forward."*

Knutsson and Pellerud shared the thoughts that a goalkeeper's desirable qualities included speed and strength, good concentration and focus and the availability to "get into the game".

LeBlanc setting the wall in practice

Knutsen and Bente Nordby in pre-game preparation for Norway

LeBlanc and McLeod - the role of the sub is even more difficult in the goalkeeper position

German goalkeeper Rottenberg dazzled at the WWC2003

An aggressive Swiatek “owning the box” in the quarter-final vs China

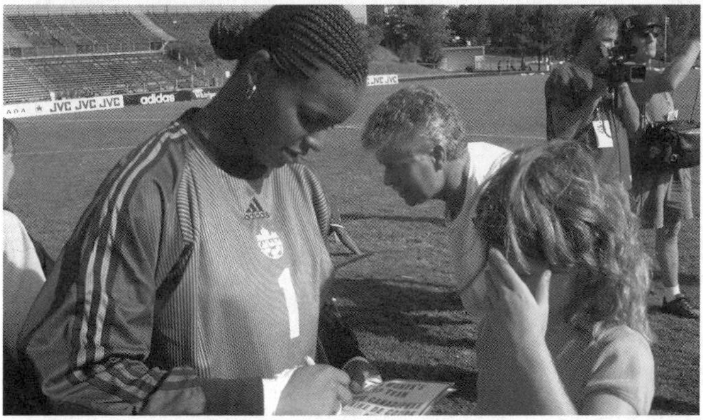

Karina LeBlanc sparkling personality as a popular Canadian player

In general Knutssön found when he began training in Canada that female keepers had both mental and physical limitations: *"The first thing that struck me was the low speed when training and in games and, besides that, they did not think football -- they just thought about stopping the shots! So they really had to learn how to conduct themselves as part of the overall team strategy and tactics. Another very important issue was to build up their physique--physical training in general had to be improved."*

In Canada, Pellerud identified with Shel Brødsgaard, former International/Canadian keeper and provincial goalkeeping coach from British Columbia. Brødsgaard's strong Danish background also struck a chord with his Scandinavian coach. They met and shared a philosophy on goalkeeping athleticism and team connection and Brødsgaard took over the position and has gone on to become the full-time goalkeeping coach for the women's team. In 2003 Brødsgaard was also appointed the CSA's full-time National Goalkeeping coach responsible for Goalkeeping Development. One of Pellerud's main objectives in coming to Canada was to develop a National Team coaching staff that would support the team for years to come. Brødsgaard and Ian Bridge have filled those roles.

With respect to player personnel, Brødsgaard and Bridge took Erin McLeod along to peak for the 2002 U-19 Championships and the vivacious young keeper star of the Canadian soccer scene has moved on to the roster of the fall National team along with Karina Leblanc, a WUSA stand out with the Boston Breakers 2001-2003, and Taryn Swiatek, University of Calgary grad and Ottawa Fury, W-League player. This trio has developed Canada's goalkeeping squad into one of the strongest in the world and Brødsgaard has a terrific group of goalies to practice and challenge. Stacey VanBoxmeer on the U-19 2004 team is also an outstanding talent.

As Pellerud noted, Taryn Swiatek (age 23) has come along over the past three years. Tony DiCicco watched Taryn Swiatek in the 2003 Women's World Cup: *"I was a little surprised and I questioned it a little when Even switched Karina LeBlanc.*

Taryn Swiatek

Karina was playing tremendously well at the end of the season with the Boston Breakers. They won the league championship and she was really the best goalkeeper in the last of the season. So, I sort of wondered what was happening when I saw him switch to Swiatek, but when I saw her play, I liked her a lot. I understood why he made the change. She's that very special type of goalkeeper. Very athletic. Karina's got that athleticism. I don't know her well enough on the mental side, but I know I really like the qualities I saw in Taryn Swiatek immediately. She's fearless. She goes for balls in the penalty area very aggressively and I love that. Because you can always take aggression and back it off a little and teach patience, but sometimes you need to be a little more patient, but it is hard to teach aggressiveness. It is a lot easier to teach patience.

"I think the team now has two outstanding goalkeepers and for them to be able to compete against each other and get better, that's great for the Canadian team. You really want that competition. You want the two of them working hard together, but competing."

Pia Sundahage, outstanding former Swedish National star and coach of the Boston Breakers, coached Karina Leblanc: *"It was nice coaching Karina at Boston because we also played zonal defense. Your Canadian National Team is a little more precise than us, but one of the things we have to work on with the goalkeeper in the zonal defense is that she has to be like a conductor. Before I came, Boston gave up a lot of goals. They needed to match up better in the box and I said to Karina, then you have to tell them, you have to yell at them. You have to find eye contact and tell them that you're pissed off. Because you gave up a goal because of their play and you're not satisfied with the way they're playing.*

"I encourage my players to always be as direct as possible when it comes to communication. For me that's important for a goalkeeper to be a conductor. It's the same for us in attack when we play from the back you have to demand options for the fullback to be there as an option. They have to get back quickly, get wide quicker. Don't always count on a goal kick. The excuse 'I have no one to play to' should not exist. It's your task to make sure they get back and in position to move forward quickly. It's important in the attack.

"I like Karina as a goaltender. I think she's very strong and very athletic. And what I like best is she is a nice person, and she is easy to talk to. I really want them to tell me how they feel. That kind of feedback is important to me so I can understand what they're doing and why they're doing it. Our communication is good and that's important, especially with your goalkeeper."

The Goalkeeper

In 2003, Shel Brødsgaard published his first book Guarding the Goal on basic goalkeeping philosophy. It is an excellent text with a companion video/DVD. The publication has been well received in Canada.

In this chapter, Shel Brødsgaard shares the Canadian National Team's goalkeeping philosophy and some of his experiences with Canada's excellent contingent of young goalkeepers.

Canada's most experienced international goalkeeper, Karina LeBlanc, also shares with us her thoughts on goalkeeping at this level and her approach to training.

<u>Shel Brødsgaard on the Goalkeeper</u>

Philosophy

We need the goalkeeper to be offensive minded, it is essential to release the traditional approach to playing the position, which is defensive minded, and develop new playing habits which are forward and progressive minded. We need the goalkeepers to adopt an attacking style of play and progress beyond their comfort zone.

Implementation of the National Team Goalkeeper Philosophy

During a recent training camp in Fort Lauderdale (December 2003) Even gave a talk regarding attacking priorities for the team. He asserted that our key principle is to penetrate and listed three attacking principles:

a. Play directly into the space in behind the opponent's defense
b. Play into a rightly turned midfielder who has penetrated the defensive midfield line
c. Play forward to a defender who has penetrated the opponent's strikers (the first line of defense)

These guidelines are then transferred to the goalkeeper in the national team. The process is simple-there is a discussion with the use of diagrams (if needed). The topic is also related to the training and/or functional situation (see below).

Discussion Topic: Counterattack situation

When a goalkeeper intercepts a crossed ball or through ball it is critical for the goalkeeper to recognize when and if the opposition is pushed forward deep into our defending zone. If this is the case the goalkeeper exploits the imbalance in the opponent's defense by initiating the counterattack according to the following conditions:

a. *Priority One:* play long, directly in behind the opposition backline (target = strikers).

b. *Priority Two:* release with a throw into a rightly turned midfielder who has penetrated the opponents midfield and/or defensive shape. Case in point, during the FIFA 2002 U19 Women's World Cup in our game against Denmark, Erin

McLeod cut-off a cross from the Danish attack and sent a quick throw to Kara Lang on the right side of the midfield who was on the counterattack. Which led to a lovely goal from Lang that caught the Danish goalkeeper far off her line with her shot/cross and into the far corner of the goal.

c. Priority Three: when neither of the two options listed above are available, the fullbacks release and provide an outlet for the goalkeeper to play out of the back.

d. Priority Four: when the opponent is completely balanced, play the ball long from the hands with a volley or dropkick.

The goalkeeper must be able to react and deal with a counterattack situation- always prepared for a breakdown in the attack and make sure that our defensive line is not imbalanced or outnumbered.

Training or Functional Situation

These guidelines are implemented into a team training session. The set-up is with the backline plus a goalkeeper dealing with attacking passes from the midfield (who will switch to become attacking midfielders for the defensive team at the loss of possession) into one or two target players (passive in the attack- pressure to regain the ball defensively). The aim is for the defenders and the goalkeeper to interact and make decisions to play the best ball forward on the breakdown. It is key for the goalkeeper to release the ball as early as possible, rather than kill" the momentum by studying when and where to play the ball. Importantly, prior to receiving the ball a goalkeeper must take a snapshot of the field and identify the weakness of the opponent and strength of her team to play the counterattack ball into for the greatest success.

Discussion Topic:
GK Start Position Relative to Pressure on the Ball

The defensive line adjusts their position relevant to the amount of pressure applied to a player in possession of the ball. Likewise, the starting position of the goalkeeper is also dependent on the same principles:

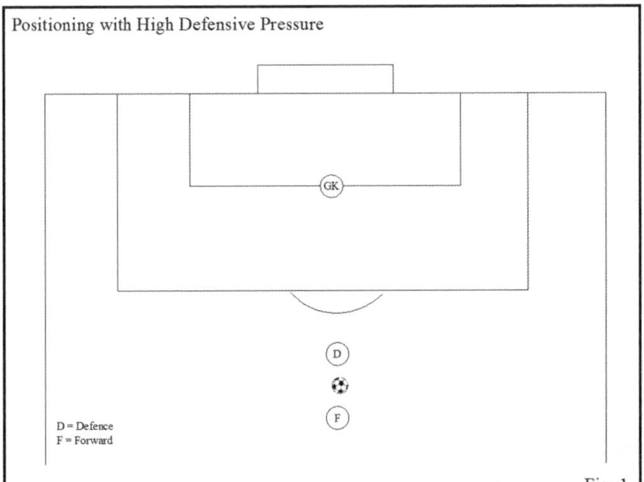

Fig. 1

a. high defensive pressure- see book "Guarding the Goal" (Fig. 1)

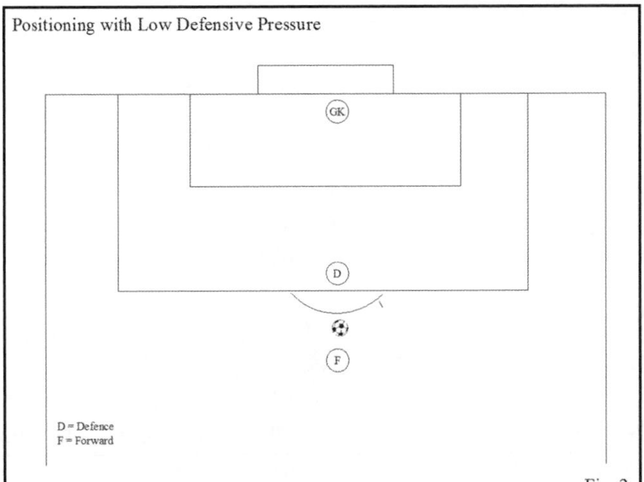

Fig. 2

b. low defensive pressure- see book "Guarding the Goal" (Fig. 2)

Training or Functional Situation

Small-sided games, 6 v 6 in an area 30x 40 (with channels on the outside for neutral players who play for the attacking team) is the ideal venue for the goalkeeper to be studied and/or

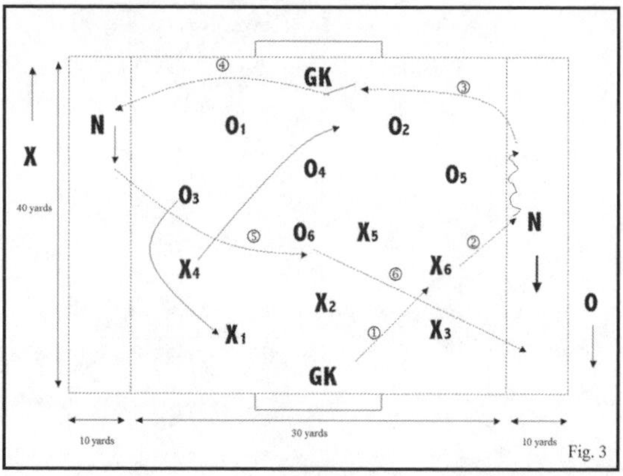

Fig. 3

coached. The goalkeeper's focus for the game is to analyze when to play the ball into the target players, when and where the most dangerous area is located for the opponent to attack. When service is played away from the goal or cut-back to an attacker, the goalkeeper must analyze the amount of pressure applied by the defender(s) and adjust her position accordingly. This is an essential part of the goalkeeper's mental process: read the game; interpret a situation; make a decision and react. The speed at which the goalkeeper processes this information is the difference between a save and a goal.
(Figure 3)

Training

There has to be a combination between team training addressing functional or game related situations, as well as personal training directed to the role of the goalkeeper to address the different areas of focus compared to the rest of the players on the field. The goalkeepers spend about 15- 20% of the time away from the team each training session, some days more, some days less. It is essential that the goalkeepers participate in team warm-up activities, rather than exclude themselves from the group. Activities such as 5v5v5 and 5v2 are excellent ways to work on skills relative to goalkeeping and boost team morale as well.

The aim for the goalkeeper coach is to address individual weaknesses in the goalkeepers, while paying attention to the priorities for the team on any given day, particularly when preparing for competition. The coaching staff takes time to meet to discuss the priorities for the training camp, competition or practice and discuss the focus for the particular event. This information is then applied to the goalkeeper in our preparation or during our time together before they join the team for the remainder of the practice. For example, when the team is going to work on crossing and finishing, the goalkeeper warms-up receiving high numbers of repetitions for crossed balls with a variety of service and pressure. Sometimes, the goalkeeper warm-up is a combination of analysis and practical training. Especially after a game, the best and easiest time to review the performance is when the goalkeeper is relaxed, and available for discussion. The first practice after the match is usually an appropriate time to speak about such matters. However, when the time does not feel right because the goalkeeper is feeling down, wait for another moment and work on their confidence. The talk generally discusses positive and negative situations from the game. Rewind the mind and talk out loud decisions that were made, both good and bad.

In the event that topics are not covered in the training session that the goalkeeper(s) would like to work on, then we either remain after and/or come earlier to the next training session. Often, the last one to leave the field is the goalkeeper.

What work should the goalkeeper be expected to do at this level on her own?

The biggest part of the responsibility for being the best at something is to do a little bit more each day than any of the other athletes, or specifically goalkeepers in the world (for the respective age group). This is a serious commitment with tones of sacrifice. Which means, this step or decision is not for everyone- all of the national team goalkeepers are given this opportunity and must decide for themselves if they can or cannot afford to make the step.

As a goalkeeper trainer, I can only make so much progress with a goalkeeper who has not been able to make this commitment. Once they have decided to pursue this goal, then we can start to progress beyond their comfort zone.

The next step is to develop a routine based on the strengths and weaknesses of the individual. I can help them to understand the areas that need to be worked on, as well as develop a strategy and/or plan of attack. But the goalkeeper needs to invest the time and create space for self-improvement. It may come in the form of distribution; strength training; tactical analysis; mental training; communication and/or leadership skill development. The problem area is identified, a program is developed to evolve the particular area in question and the goalkeeper must find time to improve on the particular task.

One of the nicest situations that we have developed is mentorship training from within the women's program. On any given day, as long as training camps coincide with one another, the world cup team goalkeepers may lead the youth team goalkeepers. Some examples include observation during functional training and games; cool-downs; stretching and strength training; and/or mental training.

This is the key to a successful learning and/or training environment- individuals who are prepared to work and compete with each other. We spend so much time together as a sub-culture within the particular team, or program for that matter, that we come to rely on and trust each other. Establish a network of support from the people who you may spend as many as 100+ days with in a year.

Consider the toll it would take if the relationship between the goalkeepers was sour during an international competition such as the World Cup or Olympics (including preparation, this means 60 out of 64 days together). Realistic. Perhaps this brings me to the most enjoyable part of working together with Even and the feeling between the goalkeepers and myself. Our relationship is based on trust, openness, intimacy and communication. The goalkeepers are encouraged to pursue themselves in all aspects of life, because a healthy, balanced person makes a healthy, balanced goalkeeper. The key to forming a positive environment for the goalkeepers to excel is a positive reinforcement and unconditional support.

Everybody makes mistakes--it's what we take away and learn from our experiences which matters most!

Canadian Keepers

Work ethic

The goalkeepers typically invest 4-5 hours per day training to play at the international level. These qualities include the technical, tactical, physical and mental (which will be discussed later in the chapter). Each of the national team goalkeepers has her own character and each is motivated in her own way. It is important to understand this and appreciate their individual differences as a goalkeeper trainer.

The three current goalkeepers are Taryn Swiatek, Karina LeBlanc and Erin McLeod.

Taryn Swiatek takes a little longer than the others to warm-up or prepare because she needs time to look after her body and mentally prepare for the training and/or game environment. When focused and ready to play, she analyzes and reads the game very well. She asks questions that are well thought out, and does not rest until given an answer that makes sense given a particular situation. She is a thinker.

Karina LeBlanc is the most athletic and powerful of the three goalkeepers. Her ability to handle pressure and remain cool in stressful situations is a quality that helps her compete at the highest level. Take a look at her reaction skills, when the ball is deflected or struck toward goal from short distances she is the fastest with her feet and softest with her hands!

Erin McLeod is the most energetic, aggressive and motivated goalkeeper and she will be tremendously successful due to these qualities. It will take time for her to learn to read the game at the highest level, but she is open and willing to learn. This makes all the difference in the world, enabling her to work hard physically, and remain focused mentally.

The hardest part for the goalkeepers is to realize no matter how hard they work, or how good they feel about their performance in training and recent games they may not be selected to play. Simply because there is only one goalkeeper selected to play at any given time.

In the event that you are a midfielder or defender there is a chance you may be selected to play another position (other than your normal spot on the field). This is not the case of the goalkeeper, which means the role of the back-up or second string, sometimes third string goalkeeper is important.

During the recent world championships in the USA, Erin McLeod visibly became one of the loudest cheerleaders for the team, and for her fellow- goalkeeper Taryn Swiatek. It was a tremendous benefit to the team to see her screaming off the bench when we scored a goal; or to hear her enthusiasm yelling from the sidelines to motivate the players on the field. Likewise, Jessica Hussey was the back-up goalkeeper for the 2002 FIFA World Cup for Canada and never played a minute. The impact of the goalkeeper who is not playing must be positive. In her the team found a friendly face, always smiling, always laughing. Her strength and support enabled the team to release pressure in difficult moments. This is a vital role for the reserve goalkeeper, not to become a distraction for the players and teammates who are focused and directly involved with the competition.

When we select a team for competition, one of the critical questions is how will a player impact the team if she is not selected in the starting eleven or not to play at all. There is a need for support at all times for these athletes, and there is nothing worse than when an unhappy player takes away from the team because she feels neglected. In this way, the role of the goalkeeper coach is obliviously to nurture the individuals according to their mental and emotional frame of mind and help them keep it all in perspective.

What the Coaches Expect

The first time a goalkeeper enters the national team program, extensive technical analysis takes place by myself, with the assistance of the remainder of the coaching staff. It is assumed the individual will have a basic understanding and/or established set of building blocks to work from when they achieve this level.

Definition of Tactical Role for Women's National Team Goalkeepers

1) Recognize that the main principles of the team strategy defensively must also be implemented by the goalkeeper
    a. Cynical defending: when dealing with pass backs, clear the ball for height and distance, make sure to clear the ball early to safety and away from the opponent.

"Absolutely no RISK or creativity by the goalkeeper will be tolerated!"

    b. A goalkeeper who holds a high position of support to the back line must be able to cut balls played in behind the defensive line, which prevents the opponent from progressing further down the field of play and/or in the direction of the goal.

2) Provide support to the defensive line relative to the location of the ball on the field of play (attacking third, neutral third and defensive third), the goalkeeper must actively readjust her position according to the conditions listed below:
    a. High defensive pressure
    b. Low defensive pressure
    c. Lateral or sideways movement

3) Create space between the defender and goalkeeper to receive the ball with time and space in front of oneself to clear away from pressure; or pick-up when headed back by the defender.

4) Communication is essential and a critical part of the organization of the zonal defense, which also keeps the goalkeeper mentally involved in the game. The goalkeeper must also be able to evaluate the position or shape of the defensive line, and adjust their position with verbal commands and nonverbal cues. Be a "proactive communicator," do not be afraid to speak to the defensive line, and make sure to analyze the shape or distance between the individuals in the defensive line.
    a. The further away the defensive line is from the goal, the greater the distance or space between each of the defenders.
    b. The closer the defensive line is to the goal, the shorter the distance or space between each of the defenders.
    c. The goalkeeper must determine the shape or position of the defense on all attacking free-kicks and communicate this to the team.
        i. Corner kick
        ii. 25 meters from goal
        iii. 40 meters from goal
        iv. 60+ meters from goal
    d. The goalkeeper must decide when a defender can allow a bad shot, or well-struck ball to run through to the goalkeeper to be collected in the hands.

"Distinct, precise, early, loud and clear communication is essential!"

5) The goalkeeper must remain mentally active during all training and game situations in order to develop technical, physical, mental and emotional elements in equilibrium.

6) The goalkeeper must learn to differentiate between the areas of mental focus while the ball is in different areas of the field of play.
    a. When the ball is in the attacking third the goalkeeper may relax the level of concentration to mentally recover while holding a high position of support
    b. As the ball approaches the neutral third the goalkeeper begins to evaluate the shape of the defensive line and

positions to be able to intercept balls played in behind the defensive line.

c. While the ball is in the defensive third, the goalkeeper must be "totally" focused on reduced goal scoring opportunities.

Keeping the Keeper Healthy

Common injuries include sprained fingers, scraped knees and hips, and bruising. A goalkeeper must protect herself as much as possible in training situations and ensure that she is healthy to perform on game day. This means: elbow pads, knee pads, hip pads, padded track pants, taped fingers and/or wrists, padded jerseys, and so on. If the ability of the goalkeeper to perform is hindered by a lack of preparation in training- ultimately the team suffers.

Regarding physical injuries, the goalkeeper, as well as the rest of the individuals on the team must take time to warm-up and cool down the body. For all rehabilitation and recovery see the medical staff and/or physiotherapist contributions. Nutritional requirements and intake for keepers is exactly the same as the individual athletes on the team.

Coaching Decisions/Changes

Going into the tournament, we decided Karina LeBlanc was going to be the starting goalkeeper in the World Cup (she was coming off an exceptional season with the Boston Breakers in the WUSA and was capable of dealing with the pressure and demands for the game at the international level). Even had confided in me prior to the tournament that he was considering playing another goalkeeper for the second game against Argentina,

Karina LeBlanc

because the game would be low intensity for the goalkeeper, which means very little action related to shot-stopping and/or interacting with the flat back four. But the game presented a tremendous mental challenge for the goalkeeper to stay "tuned-in" to the game, regardless of the inactivity expected. Swaitek has always been the strongest mentally as far as the three goal-keepers are concerned.

Leblanc is the most athletic and powerful. McLeod is the most motivated and energetic. Swiatek was coming off an exceptional tournament at the Pan-Am Games in Santo Domingo, where she repeated high-level performances to lead the team into the second place finish.

However, the toughest decision for the tournament was who to play against Japan, third game of the round robin. Is it worth the risk to go backwards after replacing LeBlanc following her performance against Germany- a performance that reinforced weaknesses in her decision making/interaction with the back four. Or do we play Swiatek, who was relatively inexperienced at this level but came in to do a very good job, instilling confidence in the team with her decision making and timing.

The job was given to Swiatek and the team never looked back. She raised the level of play for all Canadian goalkeepers to achieve, it was a stunning turn of events. But, in hindsight, the amount of work together with McLeod over the past 5 months had prepared her for this. The confidence and intimacy established between the back line and Swiatek was empowering. The players, the opponent, the fans, the coaches feed off of her. It is a lot like having a player like Christine Sinclair on your team, when she is one on one with the goalkeeper, you can always turn away knowing that she can score. The same can be said of Swiatek during the final portion of the tournament- she was unbeatable against China. The same against Sweden.

The toughest part of this transition was dealing with the disappointment and frustration for both LeBlanc and McLeod. Daily meetings were held individually with each of them to discuss and deal with their feelings. Leblanc had planned to use this tournament as a vehicle to prove that she is one of the top goalkeepers in the world. McLeod was setback. We spent countless hours together, as a group, as individuals, settling nerves and refocusing.

The worst thing that can happen is for a sour goalkeeper (or any other player for that matter) to destroy the unity of the team because she is not happy. McLeod was unreal- she became Swiatek's number one fan (there is a clip immediately after the China game with McLeod and Swiatek walking from the field arm in arm smiling from ear to ear) and the teams loudest celebrator (she was the first one off the bench after every goal- even ahead of Pellerud!)

So, in the end, a lot of time is spent interacting with the goalkeepers and addressing confidence levels.

Karina LeBlanc from British Columbia was a multi-sport athlete in high school. She attended the University of Nebraska under John Walker, and excelled as a keeper for the University of Nebraska. She was selected as the National Team keeper in 2002 and on graduation made the starting team as keeper for the Boston Breakers. In 2003, she was twice named keeper of the week and she led the Breakers into the playoffs. She recently made her National coaching debut with the U-15 Girls National Team as an assistant.

Here, Karina shares with us her thoughts on goalkeeping.

Goalkeeper Play
(Karina Leblanc)

Karina LeBlanc has played with the National Team since 1998. Born in the Dominican Republic she moved to Vancouver, B.C., at the age of eight. A standout scholarship athlete at the University of Nebraska she was a Herman Trophy finalist and an Umbro Select All-star. She was the starting goalkeeper for the Boston Breakers from 2001-2004 and the WUSA Player of the Week on several occasions. Karina shares with us what she feels are the qualities a goalkeeper must possess and some of her favorite practices to get there.

Physical Attributes

Upper body strength, quick foot work, lower body strength for explosion and to enhance your jumping abilities, speed and agility, coordination reaction speed.

Technical qualities

Kicking long balls, punting, catching, punching the ball, being able to control the ball with both feet, clear communication, distribution of the ball with both feet and hands.

Tactical requirements

Reading the game, trying to anticipate instead of simply reacting, positioning so I can make simple saves versus always having to come up and make a big save. Depth positioning also, when to come out and cut down the angle versus staying on the line and making the save.

Mental qualities

Stay positive even after a mistake, learning as game goes on, reading tendencies of what players like to do and how, composure on and off the ball.

Quality Development

I feel that I can improve on all areas of my game. My strengths are probably crosses (balls in the air), shot stopping, communication, punts. But, in saying that, I believe I can improve on these things along with my positioning in different areas depending on where the ball is, the pressure on the ball, where I should be when the ball is in their half, my supporting position when the ball is in our half. I think always in reference to reading and anticipating the play so the easy save can be made instead of having to make a huge play. To improve on this, I watch game tapes and take chances when I can, such as in practice where I am not afraid to make any mistakes. I can also improve on my kicking and to do that it is purely repetition and focusing on my technique that will make me better.

Expectations

Roles and Responsibilities: communicate effectively with teammates because my view is the best, read the play and be in a position to come through for the balls which are sent over defenders, be a leader (confident) so teammates trust my decisions on field. Distribute accurately whether it be on quick counterattack of back pass so that it hits our target players in the air for either a flick or direct attack. Defensively keeping the shape in the back by staying high, as mentioned, but also being able to read the play and drop back to my line so I don't get beaten over the top or through bad position.

Karina Leblanc's Favorite Practices

1) Keeper War

Set-up: 2 Keepers; 18-yard box

Objective: To score as many goals as possible. Usually first to 5 goals.

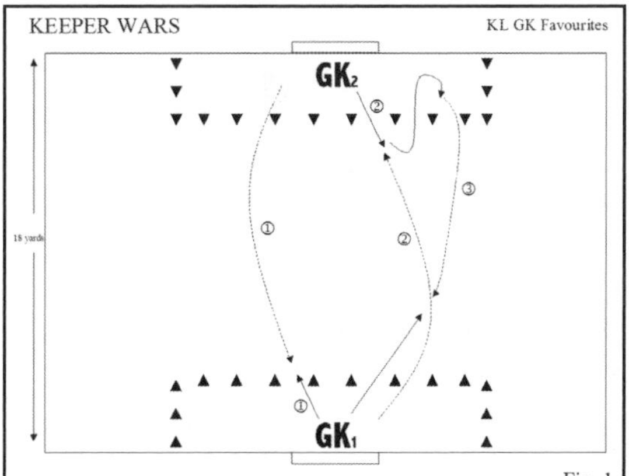

Fig. 1

Equipment: balls & cones;

Game: Keepers hit volleys/throws to score on other keeper. Rebounds are live but if you come out to save it, you still have to return to small box to shoot/throw/score, only the keeper getting to a rebound can shoot again from where the ball is.

2) Shots on Keeper

Set-up: 3 Players (two fielders and keeper); 12 yards

Objective: Work on quickness of getting up and covering area of goal while making challenging saves

Equipment: balls, net

Game: Player X1 shoots rear post GK makes save, gets up quickly while Player X2 shoots just as GK hits middle of net and is in moving motion. The goalkeeper after making first save should get up but run towards player right as she's about to hit it as a way of closing down space and being bigger, making it harder for player to score.

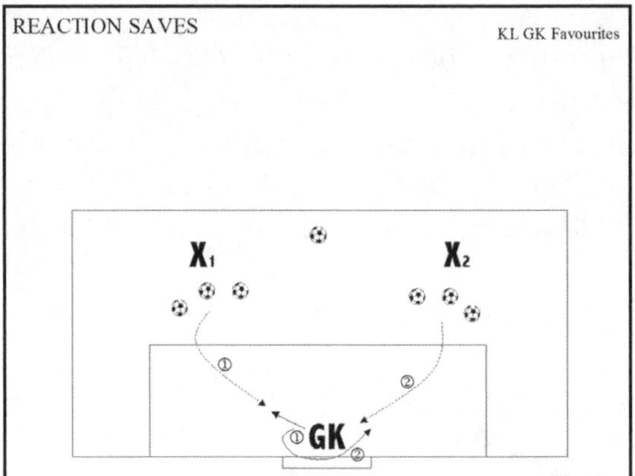

Fig. 2

3) No-Vision Shots

Set-up: 1 coach, 2 or 3 keepers;

Objectives: Working on reaction, dealing with balls when players are in the way and only move at the last second.

Equipment: balls, goal, 18-yd box; Keepers named ABC or colors.

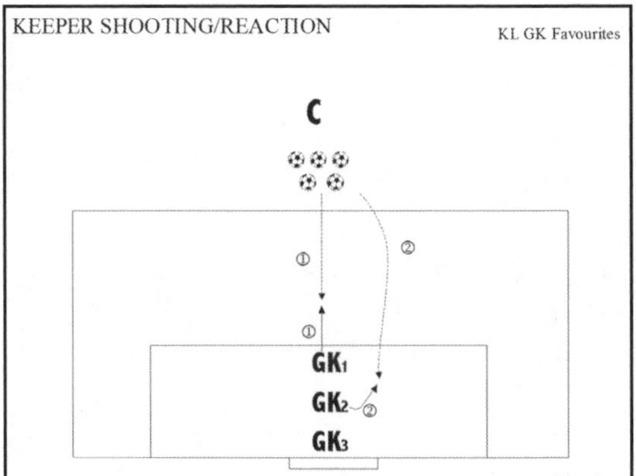

Fig. 3

Game: Standing in front of one another. Coach yells a letter and shoots in area of keepers. Whatever letter yelled that keeper makes the save, others get out of the way. Switch.

4) Cross Ball Saves

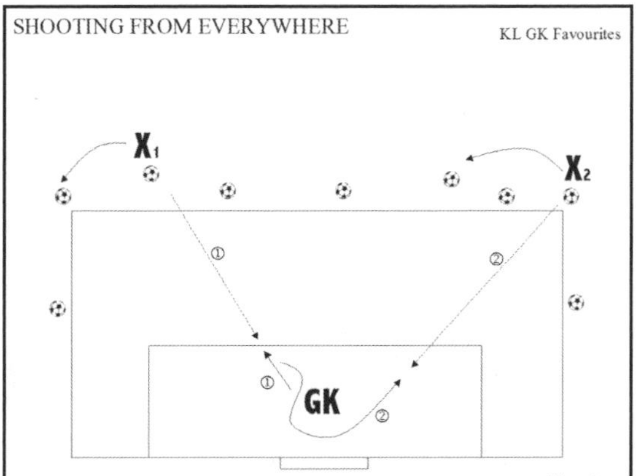

Fig. 4

Set-up: Players - 2 keepers & 2 shooters; Field - 18 yard box

Objective: Save crosses while under pressure

Equipment: balls, goal

Game: Throw/kick in crosses from all over, shooters alternating shots and have keepers fight to win it.

Chapter VIII

Player Development/Talent Identification

Taking Care of the Future

The National Approach: Norway

When Even Pellerud arrived in Canada he brought with him a distillation of years of work on player development and player identification. While in the Norges Fotball Forbund Pellerud participated in a significant redesign of the organization. A strategy put in place in the mid-'90's resulted in a tremendous leap forward in the Norwegian men's and women's programs. The initiative was in cooperation with the Norwegian Olympic Committee and the Norwegian Football Association.

The High Performance Director of the Norwegian Olympic Committee, Bjorge Stensbol, challenged the NFF for the lack of results in International competitions. There was a concern about the stagnation both at the club level and, particularly, on the men's National team. The question was asked, "Is the development model the NFF has in place a truly elite program?"

As a result of years of strategy sessions and over 12 months of meetings to pull it all together, the strengths and weaknesses of the program were identified and solutions or corrections instituted. The NFF's approach to close the gap between the richer, more populous European-neighbor nations and Norway included making some very difficult decisions and attention to specific aspects of the game.

The main areas addressed were fitness, talent development, playing philosophy and the cornerstone of the new program, feedback (which included identifying and analyzing the information and effective return to the players).

Egil Olsen, one of the most significant coaching influences on Pellerud's development as a coach, had always been very clear on feedback: *"The most important thing I have learned as coach of the National team is that people like feedback. I have never met anyone who did not like it. This makes it an obsession for me. Players must receive feedback about what they do. This has been the basis for both player and match analysis. Players must be able to see what they have done in black and white and should talk about it, as well as watch it on video-written, verbal, and visual feedback."*

The strong belief in involving the players based on the Norwegian development model was in the philosophical package Pellerud brought with him to Canada. Interviews with the players from the Norwegian '95 team as well as the current Canadian team have one consistent feature. Whether it is Heidi Støre, Gro Espeseth, Linda Medalen, Hege Riise from Norway or Christine Sinclair, Charmaine Hooper, Andrea Neil, or Karina LeBlanc from Canada, they unanimously identify Even Pellerud's ability to let them know where they stand-this provision of feedback-as critical to their success and comfort level as a player. He identifies what he wants from them, how he wants them to accomplish it, and is clearly able to articulate his philosophy and style of play to the players, why he wants them to play that way, and how they could get better at it. The Norwegians felt this was the essence of development.

Karen Espelund, Secretary General of the NFF, remembers Pellerud's contribution on the implementation of the new NFF player models: *"Even was central in organizing our new model for talent development. After many years of work this was established and implemented in 1994. One of the abiding principles was that the NFF was to be the same organization for the women as for the men. Because of the success we were having I recall the BBC (British Broadcasting Corporation) coming over to interview Even as the National Team coach and to see why the Norwegian program was as strong as it was."*

Establishing and maintaining a consistent approach for over 10 years in the NFF was important and produced early success for Pellerud in Canada. Putting a National philosophy in place-getting the clubs and associations in the country to buy in was no easy task in Norway. Pellerud recalls some of the problems that the Norges Fotball Forbund had to overcome in the early '90's and sees some parallels with what has happened in Canada: *"I really feel that the strategy we had in the Norges Fotball Forbund in the mid-'90's due, in no small part, to some cooperation with the Norwegian Olympic Committee, has led to the strength in the Norwegian program that persists to this day. You look at a team like Rosenberg in a small country like Norway (Rosenberg has made it to the Champions League a record nine consecutive times). We challenged ourselves at the time. We knew there were things we couldn't control. Climate is one. This is similar in Canada. Facilities were another big problem in Canada, as they were in Norway. You can't control that in the long-term, but in the short-term you have some control over that. Finances, as always, are probably development's biggest obstacles in any country.*

"The size of the population, the television and sponsor money available within societies we couldn't do anything about it. We had no advantage in that. We, therefore, concentrated on the things we could do something about."

Fitness

"The first order was fitness. We felt that with the right strategy here we could definitely have an advantage over other countries and we used a very systematic approach to fitness. We trained and modified our training with scientists in endurance, power, and speed. That was the agenda during the entire '90's and it continues to be improved today." (See Chapter X - The Physical Factor)

Technical

Then on the technical side: *"We really concentrated on what we needed to do to develop the kids we had, both male and female. We tried to develop a model with priorities on aspects of the game: striking the ball, receiving the ball, technical aspects, and then introducing tactical aspects at the appropriate age. It began to pay off quickly. Many of our players were exported, both on the male side to premier clubs throughout Europe and on the female side to WUSA. The results were so dramatic so quickly that we had many countries coming to us and asking how we developed this.*

"A big part of it is the pyramid of play or having National teams in place." (Espelund explains over the past 10 years in Norway, they have moved from three National teams to 11-six on the men's and five on the women's side. This and the professional leagues serve as a pyramid of play for the players.)

Playing Philosophy

"Another critical aspect of what makes a National program move forward is having a consistent playing philosophy. I worked together with the Norges Fotball Forbund and, especially our technical guru, Egil "Drillo" Olsen, who at that time was the Men's World Cup Coach. Based on much of Olsen's work and others at the Norwegian University of Sport and Physical Education we analyzed what we knew about the game and what the most effective approach to playing the game would be. The forward development of that model would be applied to the National Teams and the top teams in the country. We tried to produce a consistent approach."

Feedback

Finally, on feedback Pellerud recalls: *"We developed an accurate feedback system to the players based on their performances on the ball. What to do in a game. Technical pluses. Technical minuses. We had to be able to look at the results of our analysis and give players more accurate feedback, and we had to develop a background for that feedback so it was based on good information."* (See Chapter XIV on Match Analysis).

Pellerud and the committees involved in putting this strategy forward in the NFF ran into the same obstacles in Norway that he later found to persist in Canada. He recalls: *"The first step was to sell this product to the Norges Fotball Forbund, but there were strong leagues and strong clubs and strong personalities in the country and the association can't just go out and arbitrarily take initiatives on behalf of all clubs, which have been developing on their own for years. So, for us to go out there and implement new things, new philosophies, new ideas, was quite a challenge and we (a large contingent of technical, marketing, medical, political (board members) personnel) spent a solid two years going out to the clubs and meeting with them. We met the teams where they were and sold all these ideas. It was something the country bought into. It was important to note that these changes and the development model were not an evolution. It really was more about how to approach all of these areas in a more systematic and organized way. We based a lot on what we already did in Norway, but the approach was much more structured.*

"When the clubs began to see this as our attempt to provide more information, share our information, provide player development, that was important. But, what was also important was that the NFF helped out by paying salaries to development coaches linked to the association, but who were also firmly linked to the player development in the clubs. These coaches could then share ideas on how to do our player analysis, provide the feedback and also how to play the game in a more developed and updated way based on knowledge, science, and what we knew, rather than tradition alone."

The National Approach: Canada

The CSA Blueprint

There is no doubt that these were some of the challenges Pellerud saw the CSA facing in Canada.

In an interview with CSA CEO Kevan Pipe in 2003, the subject of the financial health of the Canadian Soccer Association was broached. It is interesting to note that the structure of the NFF and CSA are distinctly different from a financial standpoint.

First, the budget of the NFF is the equivalent of over $55 million Canadian dollars, serving 373, 532 players in 1,814 clubs in a country of 4.5 million (as of January 2004). The CSA has a budget of $13 million serving 900,000+ players in 4,000+ clubs in a country of 31 million people. Adding in Provincial budgets and Canada still only approaches 50% of the Norwegian Program. Clearly, funding of programs is limited in Canada. In Norway, monies are collected through professional clubs, and television contracts and sponsorships. This money then flows back to the clubs and players through the NFF. Due to the limited sponsorship structure-primarily because of complete lack of television revenue from any professional Canadian teams, the Canadian Soccer Association's budget is primarily harvested from competitive players. The CSA, which was struggling tremendously with its programs due to lack of funds was prompted, when the new Technical Director, Holger Osieck, came into the Association in 1998, to address the issue of funding short falls. Under President Jim Fleming and Vice-President Andy Sharpe, the Canadian Association made very rapid changes in the organization beginning with budget and coach development. Income to the Association from player registrations increased tremendously, going up five-fold in a short period of time. These funds primarily support the National Teams and the National Training Centres and player identification. As the CSA continues to implement its blue print for success the plan is for more programs and more contact to flow from the CSA downwards to the players and clubs, but there remained a lack of a cohesive vision for the Canadian game. When Pellerud arrived, the poor international performances of the National Teams in the '90's remained a priority that needed to be addressed early. Hiring Even Pellerud was part of that plan.

When he first came to Canada, Pellerud was aware of the type of athlete Canada produced at the highest level of the game, but he was unsure and curious about the foundation that was in place to promote player development.

One of Pellerud's great loves is history, particularly social history, and he was eager to both discover his new home geographically, as well as develop a good insight as to what was going on across the country soccer-wise. He spent the better part of his first year criss-crossing the country visiting the National Training Centres in the various provinces, showing up at club championships, tracking down every lead he could get on exciting new players and just taking the pulse of where club and player development was in the country. His observations from these early trips were significant in deciding what he felt needed to be put in place for the future of the women's game.

He noted: *"I was happy with the athletic level of the Canadian girls. I felt that they were technically sound for the most part. One of the technical weaknesses that I noticed most in the Canadian youth game, both on the women's and men's side, was poor striking of the ball."* The service of an accurate long pass was intrinsic to the game that Pellerud coached and believed in. While he found the Canadian team a reasonable collection of athletes, he also found them tactically without direction.

If there was a CSA philosophy or coaching approach it was that of a possession/indirect play game. Pellerud came in with the intention of continuing to develop his direct-play with emphasis on strong physical forwards, constant attacking technique, and an absolute belief in strict zonal defense.

Even Pellerud may have missed the notoriety and constant spotlight on the professional soccer coach and National Team positions in Norway, but he didn't evade the media's attention in Canada. He clearly understood that they had to be allies in developing the game of soccer in Canada. Jerry Dobson, Canada's face of soccer on Sportsnet, gave an insight into the media's take on Pellerud and what he brought to the program in an interview in 2003. Dobson, who has been involved in the television media aspect of the game for over a decade, gave a frank comparison of pre- and post-Pellerud women's program: *"I think it begins with a simple concept-professionalism. Before Pellerud, the women's program was inadequate and amateurish. Scouting and development of players was poor. Pellerud has scoured the country looking for players, sends scouts in advance to look at the opposition, prepares his players for big events. Under Pellerud, the team has played far more games than ever before.*

The program used to go almost dormant between World Cups. He brings an even temperament to the job, but is a straight shooter. The players always know where they stand with him. His dealings with the media are always up front. He understands the role the media plays in helping to develop the sport in Canada. He seems to know that the easier he makes our job the better our product will be, which in turn will be a good reflection on the sport. It seems to me he is also a consensus builder, which is vital in this sport in a country where there are so many stakeholders with a wide range of agendas."

These comments were consistent with a strong commitment that Pellerud had to developing the Canadian National Women's Program.

Identifying Talent in Young Players

Even Pellerud stated in the past how important it is for a coach looking for talent to "hide in the stands" to be able to watch players play naturally. Pellerud's job when he came to Canada-to assess the talent in the country and assemble the best team possible-was a daunting one, but he embraced it heartily. It gave him a chance to get out and see Canada as a complete country. As a teacher, educator and an admitted product of a "left-wing" family he enjoyed the strong social structures in Canada. His priority in his soccer job was to assess the existing talent and delve into that pool of over 850,000 competitive soccer players (450,000+ of these on the women's side) spread over one the largest nations on earth. Putting this team together was a significant task. It was obvious that he couldn't do this alone.

One of his first approaches was to assemble coaches from the previous programs and assess coaches from across the country that he felt might be useful along the development system. Pellerud was delighted with the quality of coaches he found at the National level. Assistant coach from the previous World Cup, Ian Bridge and he were on the same page with respect to playing philosophy and that was a big step forward for Pellerud. He needed close advice and Ian Bridge was his man.

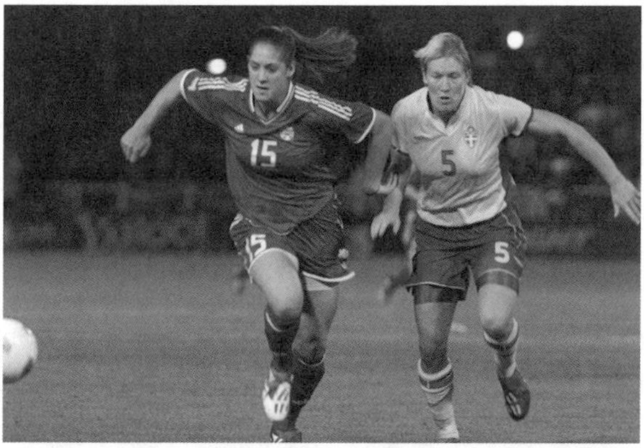

Kara Lang - a dominant young player for Canada

Sportsnet and Gerry Dobson

Ian Bridge's and Pellerud's coaching is highly interactive

Young Canadians (left to right) Tanya Dennis (17), Linda Consolante (19) and Sasha Andrews (20)

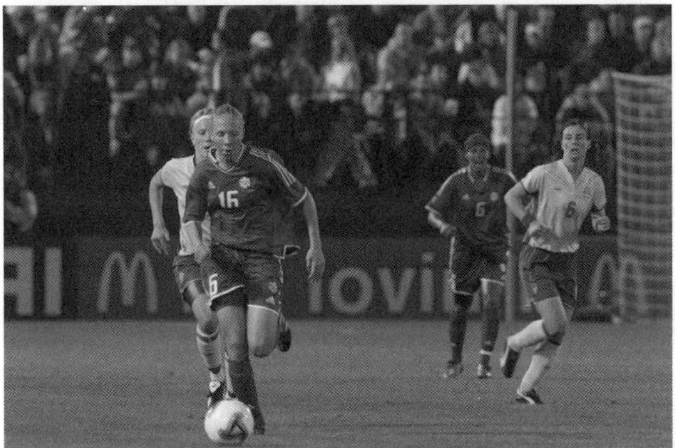

Rising star Brittany Timko - WWC2003 vs Sweden. Timko went on to win the golden boot in the FIFA 2004 U19 Championships

Andrews, Timko, Latham, LeBlanc, Nonen, Morneau and Dennis - The Nebraska Connection

Pellerud's ever watchful eye on technique as Christine Sinclair strikes in practice.

Tony Waiters in North Vancouver with the budding young goalkeepers

In order to optimize the outcomes and, in Canada even more crucially, to effectively utilize the time taken in scouting and talent identification, a coach needs to trust his assistants. His staff and even the regional coaches he is infrequently in touch with have to be on the same page, as to what technical and tactical abilities coaches look for. Coach Pellerud has frequently stated that he wants to see the players in game situations so he can estimate their ability to read the game, how they visualize the play, what's going on on the field and how intelligently they react to the position of the ball and the players on the field. It is understood that hand-in-hand with player development is coaching development, because coaches with a good eye for identifying talent are an asset to any National Team coaching staff. This means that the coaches have to be involved in the evolution of the process at every step of the way.

As he began to assemble his team the structure he had to choose from in Canada included coaches in National Training Centres. With Provincial centers and newly developed National Training Centres the building blocks of centralized scouting and player development were in place.

The philosophy of the National program as described by the CSA is officially stated as: "The National Training Centre Program (NTC) is a development strategy with two focuses for player development:

1) Individual player development through the use of the NTC program
2) Development of youth teams and youth team players."

The long-term goals of the NTC were stated as:

1) "To establish a process by which we produce stability and continuity in the development of international players;
2) To provide an informative structure path along which players can move from an introduction to international soccer at the age of 14 to international maturity between the ages of 18 and 20;

3) To produce international players who are comfortable with and understand what is required of them to perform successfully at the highest level."

The jargon was in place, but now talent had to be assessed.

Some of the questions the National coaches had to deal with included: What does it take as a coach to identify talent and then nurture it? Why does that unusually talented nine-year-old fall away at 14? Are we missing players who can't afford (financially or geographically) to be seen? What does it take to make a National Team and how is that information passed on to the player? How do you as a coach optimize a player's chance of playing at the highest level?

One of the most respected coaches in the women's game is Tony DiCicco, former National Team Coach of the U.S. Women's Team and Commissioner of WUSA. A well-published and Hall-of-Fame contributor to the game in North America, when asked about the most important attribute of a soccer coach, DiCicco replied without hesitation: *"The primary function of a coach, the job he or she has to be good at, is to recognize and develop talent. I have always felt that the ability to recognize and develop player talent is first and foremost the greatest asset a coach could have. To be a good coach--developing talent--is critical, but then putting it together, a piece of a puzzle at a time, is important. One of the exceptional qualities you might look for in the player may be leadership, for example. So, you have to identify not only technical and tactical abilities, but also intangibles, such as character and leadership. Even Pellerud could do that and, in 1995 he assembled what may have been one of the most outstanding women's teams of all time. Certainly, one of the best three teams ever in the women's game. I think along with the U.S. team of '96 and the Chinese team of '99, that Norwegian '95 team was one of the truly great teams in women's football over the past 15 years."* (See Appendix I for the USSF approach to player identification and development.)

Even Pellerud's advice to coaches on talent identification in a recent NSCAC coaching symposium in Ottawa included: "When you see a young team playing and young players playing you will always notice two main things:

1) How the player generally looks. Can she play soccer? Does she move like a soccer player? Does she think like a soccer player? You need a certain level of skills, athleticism, speed, and whatever intangibles that make an athlete. That is the foundation for assessment. It is an automatic assessment. An overall intuitive coaching assessment.

2) More consciously, the exceptional talent/skill of course but also something else they bring to the table. I'm looking for the special competence, the special quality, the amazing quality. Something that stands out that makes this player different than other players. I'm looking for production. Does the player produce for the team? Is he or she particularly fast? Is the player special in passing? Is the pass nice and precise and does it produce penetration, a goal chance? That is more important than the generally nice looking pass. Is the player an especially good leader? His/her impact on the team. Sometimes impact and production is overall more of what I'm looking for, rather than breaking the play down to something technical.

Sometimes a good player, a special player, if you break down all the qualities you just see average skills, nothing special. Take practice, for example, she may not stand out in the practice skills. She's average, maybe even poor. You put her in a game, a scrimmage, however and you will see a player that excels, that produces for the team, that has an impact on the other players, that makes the other players better than they really are. Those more undefined qualities are very important in my approach to assessing a young player. It will make the difference of whether I think that "she's just going to become an average player" or "this could be something special, because she has this special gift or this special talent that is hard develop during the years-it is more a part of her that is intrinsic."

There are other aspects of choosing players that involve timing. Pellerud recounts his first (unfavorable) viewing of Canadian midfielder, Diana Matheson. Unimpressed he made only a slight note of this player. Seeing her again almost coincidentally at a practice session in Toronto, he was more intrigued. Ultimately, he selected her and she has become one of the starters on the Canadian team. Players may duck under the radar if a coach takes a first-impression, black-and-white evaluation. Pellerud believes a player has to be seen more than once and in more than one environment in order to get a true estimation of what her talents are and how she may fit into the team.

Many players may not develop to their full potential until later in their physical and mental development stages. Arguably the best forward in the women's game in the world, presently, is the U.S.'s Abby Wambach. This player came out of university as a good player, developed under the radar in WUSA, maturing in her second year as an excellent player. It was only then that the National Team took notice of her and she has become their most outstanding player over the last year. This player whose National team didn't give her a second glance at the earlier prime stage of player development (19-21) has gone on to become one of the strongest forwards in the World. When the question was posed to Even Pellerud and John Walker in an informal coach's meeting, recently, "what does it take for a player like Wambach to make that sudden transition" they both had the same response: "Maturity. Wambach has decided to get serious. She has essentially 'grown up'. She has focused all her energies into being the best she can be and when a player dedicates herself to the game good things can happen." In Canada it was Christine Sinclair who was one of the most talented strikers Pellerud had ever seen. She impressed him immediately at 20 and already capped over 60 times, she is a big part of the future of the team. He is waiting for her maturity to catch up to grasp the role of leader.

John Walker

John Walker was an assistant with the previous National Team program and has been involved as a guest coach with many of Pellerud's camps. Walker has a strong history in Canadian soccer. He played his early soccer at Queen's University where his father, John, a Scottish football fanatic, was a coach and his love of the strategy involved in soccer led him naturally to a coaching career. Coaching Queen's University following his senior season, he went on to earn a Master's Degree in the Science of Coaching at Miami of Ohio. He is also one of the first graduates of the Canadian Coaching Institute, holds his Level 5 Canadian National Coaching theory certification, and has achieved his highest levels of Canadian/U.S. certification-the Canadian A and USSF "A" Licenses.

As a high-performance coach for Ontario, in a moment of serendipity, John Walker was recruited by the Director of Athletics for the University of Nebraska, at Lincoln, where the Title Nine ruling had led the University to form its first ever women's soccer team in 1994.

Since then, Walker has amassed an outstanding 78% success record, second only to Anson Dorrance in the Women's coaching ranks of the U.S..

John Walker has a unique insight into Canadian soccer, having served as assistant coach of the 1999 World Cup team and assistant on the U-20 women's team. He has trained no fewer than nine Canadian National team players. Presently (2004) on his team are Brittany Timko (outstanding midfield/defender for Canada and in the top five NSCAA scorers as a forward in 2004), Tanya Dennis (a forward used as a defender in the 2003 Women's World Cup) and second-year defender Sasha Andrews. Goalkeeper Karina Leblanc, striker Christine Latham, and defenders Brianna Boyd, Sharolta Nonen, and Isabelle Morneau have all played under John Walker at Nebraska and moved on to the Canadian National Team.

Walker has therefore had a unique perspective on the development of Canadian female soccer players over the past 15 years. He was recently interviewed and had the following to say about the development of the women's game:

- Players are, overall, more complete than they were 10 years ago in every aspect of the game.

- Players are more athletic now. There is a larger talent pool of athletes. It is harder to dominate teams physically and athletically anymore for the simple reason that all good teams are stocked with great athletes.

- The skill level is much higher now. It is higher and moving upward but we are still not there. There are still deficiencies, for example in ball striking technique, long accurate passing, heading, finishing accuracy, crossing (varying the types and accuracy), finishing quality as well as goalkeeping-those are the areas that the female players need to continue to develop in.

- We now look for good players who are good athletes. Five years ago we would be looking for pure athletes and then plan on refining them. Now, there are more pure athletes that are already fairly competent players so the very raw athlete now has so much catching up to do and no longer has the advantage of significant athletic superiority. This makes it tougher for a player who hasn't been in the game technically and skill wise to make it.

- Game understanding - There is still a major problem in the women's game, not enough of our players watch soccer at the highest level and not enough young players in an unstructured or pick-up setting. These two facts contribute to a lack of truly creative players. Most of the players we have had here at the University of Nebraska have developed strictly by going to organized practices and games and rarely played for fun and they rarely watched soccer on television. The little intricate nuances in the game are, therefore, in these players. They enjoy soccer, but the game they know has been taught to them only in structured practices.

- ❑ The changes I have seen in Canadian players coming to the University of Nebraska are evident. The technical abilities are similar since we have already tended to recruit and attract the more athletic player. The advantage that the more recent Canadian players have is an improvement in tactical understanding. Players such as Timko and Dennis have multiple years of training camps and games behind them now with all of the youth National Team and WWC team. They are more seasoned players with a better tactical understanding of the game. In the late 90's players we had here such as Isabelle Morneau, Amy Walsh, Sharolta Nonen and Karina LeBlanc came to University with a minimum amount of National Team experience. Now the players have an understanding and they are well versed in tactical principles by which the National Team plays, as well as the teams they play against. They are efficient with high pressing zonal defending and penetrative attacking. Playing this game against the best sides in the world has allowed a further refining.

- ❑ The progress of the Canadian player is evident in the U.S. College game. It is heartening to see Timko, Thorlakson, Sinclair, Latham, Matheson, Chapman all playing major roles at nationally prominent programs over the past few years. Sinclair was just named Hermann Trophy winner of 2004 as the outstanding NCAA player and she is still only a junior. This didn't happen 10 years ago. Latham was WUSA Rookie of the Year in a league full of American International talent. This wouldn't have been conceivable even as little as five years ago. A lot of the credit for this must go to Even Pellerud and Ian Bridge and the rest of the coaching staff, including all the youth National Team coaches for their philosophy of bringing young players along quickly and allowing them opportunities to "move up" regardless of age. Not all National Team programs think this way and it is working well for Canada.

The Ontario Perspective

Even Pellerud was based for his first five years in Canada at the National Training Centre in Toronto where he interacted with a lot of Ontario Soccer Association coaches, as well as the CSA staff coaches. One of those OSA coaches was Bryan Rosenfeld, a respected former player and Canadian A-licensed coach, who directs the high performance program for the Province of Ontario. Ontario is the largest province in Canada with over 8 million people. He works out of the Soccer Centre in Vaughan (West Toronto), a $12-million facility with multiple grass fields, complete indoor complex and a new outdoor Field-turf facility. It was also the home of the CSA National Team coaching offices.

Rosenfeld came through the National youth program playing briefly for Canada for six years in the Professional Canadian Soccer League. He oversees the National Training Centre, giving support to the provincial program on both the male and female sides. Having recently developed the first goalkeeping certification course with Mark Marshall, Rosenfeld was asked about some of the areas he would like to see improved in the players coming to him. He commented that the players were definitely coming through with better individual skills and he attributed a lot of that to the exposure with more soccer to watch both on the field and on television. The deficiencies he saw, however, were the same noted by Even Pellerud: 1) The inability of players to properly strike a ball over distances; 2) 1v1 attacking (also a prime target in the new German Federation approach); 3) 1v1 defending; 4) heading the ball, particularly in the women's game; 5) receiving the ball. The program is working on improving these aspects at the regional levels and concentrating on coaching development.

On Canada's playing philosophy, Rosenfeld was very adamant about a "made-in-Canada" approach: *"If you look around, the top programs in the world are their own programs. You must create a philosophy that best suits your country. I think we sometimes keep trying to look - there is nothing wrong with gathering information to better what they're doing from Holland,*

Germany, Brazil-but we are our own country that is still, from a soccer point of view, trying to develop and mature. I think the key to success-be it player development for us-is creating a formula for success that is Canadian and best suits our Canadian players, our Canadian athletes, our Canadian lifestyle, and our Canadian culture. This, our soccer culture, is now being created more and more on a yearly basis. That is the only way you can do it. From the women's side the direction that has taken place from the top down has had a huge influence on its success right through to the development teams. There is a large understanding and a consistency through every development team what the technical and tactical priorities for the program are and that is what Even has established and has followed and maintained. So there is a consistency through that whole program. We have good communications with our Provincial and National Training Centres and player identification that has been put in place over the last five years with Even. There is a plan here and the direction has been really helpful towards the women's program and we would like to see that begin to develop throughout the entire CSA program."

Ian Bridge

As stated earlier, Even Pellerud had selected the former Canadian National to continue as his assistant with the National Team program. More importantly, Bridge was put in charge of the U-19 Women's program when FIFA opened its U-19 FIFA World Championship in Canada. Bridge had been an outstanding fullback in the Canadian program for over 10 years in the 1980's. On the only Canadian World Cup team in 1986 in Mexico, Bridge also played for Canada in the 1984 Los Angeles Olympics and the 1979 FIFA World Youth Championships in Japan. A professional player with the Seattle Sounders and the Vancouver WhiteCaps in the North American Soccer League (NASL), Bridge also played in the Swiss National League and the Canadian Soccer League before beginning his full-time coaching career. He was the head coach of the University of Victoria Women's Varsity Team from 1990-2001. Appointed on March 5th, 2001 to head the U-19 team, Bridge was at the helm of one of the most exciting periods in Canadian soccer history.

The first FIFA U-19 World Championship was held in Canada in 2002. Canada's team went on an unbelievable tear winning 14 consecutive games in the lead-up and during the tournament, only to lose to their archrival the U.S. in the final on a golden goal in an evenly played game. A sell-out crowd of close to 50,000 people, one of the largest crowds ever in Canada at a soccer event, watched that game in Edmonton and the television audience was one of the largest ever for a Canadian soccer event. Importantly for Even Pellerud, on that team were Christine Sinclair, who won the MVP and Golden Boot for the tournament, and 15-year-old Kara Lang, who was about to become a big part of the future for the Canadian National Women's Team.

Canada, following a similar approach to Norway, has now expanded to 13 National Teams and the players are getting the necessary international exposure. The importance of international competition and the highest challenges possible are the final building blocks to developing the best players.

The consummate competitor, Bridge avenged the narrow 2002 loss to the U.S. when he led the 2004 U-19 National Team to a win in the CONCACAF qualifying tournament for the 2004 FIFA U-19 World Championship in Thailand. Sealing the irony by winning on a golden goal-a brilliant 50-yard service by Kara Lang to the head of a rising new star, Josee Belanger-Canada moved on past the U.S.A. to the Number One seed and a favorable draw for the World tournament by defeating the U.S. for the first time ever in a FIFA-sanctioned international tournament.

Coach Bridge has shepherded along some of the new Canadian stars who have already made their way onto the senior squad and he sees a bright future in front for Canada: Jodie-Ann Robinson, a 15-year-old from British Columbia; Kara Lang of Ontario, Sophie Schmidt a talented 16-year-old BC-native, as well as the remarkable Sydney LeRoux, a 14-year-old also from British Columbia are strong physical players in the Canadian program. Bridge is particularly high on Schmidt, who possesses great maturity and technical ability for a 15-year-old. Pushed into a starting role in Thailand, the young defender/midfielder played almost flawless football.

Bridge provided the U-19 development team with multiple opportunities to mature their game at the highest levels. As an elite team, international friendlies and tournaments are more readily available to the Canadian squad. This cauldron of international competition is what will guide the Canadian program to its ultimate success. Players who will figure strongly in Canada's future such as Brittany Timko (Nebraska), Christine Sinclair (Portland), Diana Matheson (Princeton), and Katie Thorlakson (Notre Dame) are already dominating in the most competitive avenues currently available next to the International FIFA program-that is the NCAA Division 1 program.

The U.S. College Game

The majority of the Canadian National Women's Team players in the past have played on athletic scholarships to the U.S. universities. With the advent of Title IX over the past 20 years, the women's programs have become solid and coaching has improved. Nevertheless, with the hundreds of colleges participating in the various competitive levels (NCAA Division 1, 2, and 3, and NAIA), it is important to note the stronger teams are in the Division 1 programs and this is where scholarship money is proportionately higher.
In the past 25 years, only six teams have won the Final Four in the NCAA Division 1 and a consistent group of teams make the final 16. In the past five years, that scene has begun to change as programs have spent more money on coaching and the demands on competitive results have increased. For instance in 2004 Princeton made it to the Final Four for the first time and Illinois to the Final Eight.

One of the breakthrough teams in the past several years was Clive Charles and his Portland team. After six appearances, Portland won in 2002. Christine Sinclair, the Canadian National Team member who was in her second year on that team, had an outstanding season and broke Mia Hamm's long-standing tournament record in the post-season. Sinclair and another fellow Canadian striker, Wanda

Rozwadowska, also in the National Team pool were outstanding for Portland in the Final Four, scoring all of the goals. After taking a year off for the World Cup and illness, in 2004 Sinclair continued her outstanding play in Portland. The winner of the 2004 Hermann Trophy (MVP) she again placed in the top five in scoring in the country. She is also a three-time academic All-American.

The Canadian trend has continued with Katie Thorlakson leading the entire NCAA in points (goals and assists) in 2004 playing for Notre Dame. On the Notre Dame team there were no fewer than three Canadian starters, as Notre Dame won the National Championship over UCLA on December 5th, 2004. Thorlakson and Candace Chapman combined on a beautiful goal to score the winner in a 1-0 semi-final win over perennial stronghouse, Santa Clara (coached by Jerry Smith and his wife Brandi Chastain, U.S. National Team star). In addition, Melissa Tancredi (another Canadian National Team pool player and Hermann finalist) anchored the Notre Dame defense as a senior playing strong center back (see picture) and shutting out the powerful Santa Clara squad to gain the UCLA finals on Sunday.

John Walker's University of Nebraska made it to the Final Eight despite the fact that their National Top-10 scorer Brittany Timko was in Thailand for the Canadian U-19. A very difficult rebuilding year, the Nebraska team looked strong with, again, a strong Canadian contingent.

A surprise team in the Final Four in 2004 was Princeton. Princeton had no less than four Canadian starters. A primarily academic school, Princeton built their game around the freshman midfielder and stand-out player, Diana Matheson. Matheson, who deferred her first year, was masterful in the midfield in a losing cause against UCLA. Brea Griffiths, a senior from Burlington, Ontario, anchored the midfield for Princeton. Sisters Janine and Rochelle Willis also played strong starting roles on the team as a defender and midfielder respectively.

The Canadian college ranks are serving as development areas for the Canadian players, but more than that, Canada is gaining an international reputation as an excellent source of skilled players for the U.S. system. The outstanding performance of these young players has led to an increased interest from the U.S. programs in the Canadian youth system. This directly leads to improved player development. With the exception of the National Team level, this is the highest competitive level available for women.

With five months of daily training and 20 official games, college continues to be a big part of the development model for the senior Canadian players. Diana Matheson, recruited by several schools, chose Princeton due to the strong Canadian contingent and the fit with her academic interests (economics) and the coaching staff.

In comparing the college game to the international team experience the 20-year-old felt that, overall, the depth of the players in the international games she has faced were greater in strength and speed, quickness of play being more noticeable. With respect to style of play she felt, defensively, there was more man-marking and overall less of an emphasis on the early penetrating pass and more on possession, but she indicated that individual styles of the teams were becoming more mixed. They were facing more teams with a direct approach and more strict zonal defending. She, herself, was man-marked in the tournament.

Katie Thorlakson was man-marked in the semi-finals and finals due to her outstanding assist-and-goal rate during the year. This was not an uncommon occurrence for her so they have had to solve the problem and she, individually, and her team were able to do that in the tournament. She was Notre Dame's dominant offensive player and MVP for the tournament. Interestingly enough, Thorlakson credits her trip with the National Team to Japan and Even Pellerud's advice for her breakthrough this season. She claims Pellerud's comments on how she was just satisfied to get a shot on net and not being tough enough was what pushed her to increase her creativity around the net.

One of the challenges Pellerud faces as a National Team coach is the release questions both from the college programs where these players are being essentially paid to perform for their schools, and formerly through the WUSA program, particularly in the extensive preparations now being carried out by National teams for the World Cup years the impact can be considerable.

One of the issues that Sylvie Beliveau and the technical group at FIFA is looking at is coordination of the international calendar and these should be improved in the coming years.

A long-time university coach in Canada at the University of Victoria, Bridge acknowledges a great improvement in player development as coaching improves at the university level and some partial scholarships are introduced. The vast majority of Canadian National Team pool players, however, have passed through the U.S. college programs. More importantly for a National Team, Bridge feels preparation time is the key. An ambitious two-month program in Vancouver prior to the Thailand World Championship served to underscore that point as the coaching staff noted vast improvement in their young squad.

While Pellerud is the overall women's program director, Ian Bridge and Shel Brødsgaard and their staff follow the training and tactical philosophy developed by the head coach program. Secure with complete control of the women's program and coaches in his new contract, Pellerud's playing philosophy is being implemented throughout the competitive National Team ranks.

As an indicator of the widespread success of the program, Bridge commented recently that the players now coming in from the Provinces and clubs have been, for the most part, introduced to zonal defending and direct penetrating play. This simplifies the task for the National squad coaches who can now expand training at an earlier stage. He also noted that with the enhanced provincial programs, regional scouting and training centers in place, the National Team is satisfied that talent identification is optimal-few, if any, players are missed now.

In trying to build on Canada's strengths, Pellerud moved his family in mid-2004 to the Vancouver CSA National Training Centre, where the outdoor soccer season exists year round. The headquartering of the new Men's National Team coach, Frank Yallop has also helped the CSA move forward with a pyramid of play concept. In a joint venture the National Training Centre was relocated to Simon Fraser University and an alliance was formed in October 2004 between the CSA, the British Columbia Soccer Association and the Vancouver Whitecaps (Canada's oldest professional club). A shared player development program was formed designed as a model to move player development forward in Canada.

The Program (The Grass Roots and Coaching Development)

The Canadian Soccer Association (CSA) has identified the grass roots of player and coaching development as their primary focus. They have appointed two national capital and community development officers with the daunting task of covering the country. Sean Fleming in the west and former National Team Coach Sylvie Beliveau in the east have been working with clubs and provincial associations as they devote their program to finding a predictable base of training at the recreational and introductory levels of play. The National Training Centres are then devoted to the higher age levels and the development of those players towards professional and National Team pinnacles.

When Even Pellerud took over the women's program in Canada, he came with knowledge of the difficulties in instituting necessary truly National program where all clubs, all coaches, and all players, were on the same page. Although Canada remains a long way from this ideal, at this time (2004) they are in the process of appointing a National Technical Director (expected to be announced in 2005). Pellerud had to deal more of a selection than development process. There was a general concern that even the process off identifying talent, let alone developing it, was poorly understood in the country at that time. Parallel to the increase in the number of players the coaching process has struggled to keep up.

As previously mentioned, Canada is renowned throughout the world with its National Coaching institution and it's National Coaching Certification Program (NCCP). Until recently in Canada, very few opportunities existed for professional coaches. Unlike the U.S., high school coaching positions are generally not manned by certified coaches. The positions are chiefly unpaid even at the university levels. It is only recently that coaches have been professionally appointed and only at a few universities at this point in time. Many of Canada's young coaches have had to leave to coach in the U.S. or Europe.

It is only recently that this has begun to slowly change. In Canada's largest province, Ontario (a population of over 8 million and over 300,000 registered players) a club head coach program has emerged over the past 10 years. This is beginning to happen in other provinces, such as British Columbia. Professional club head coaches are now becoming the norm in large urban areas. In Ontario in 2004 a club head coaches' alliance was formed with over 100 registered club head coaches in Ontario, the vast majority professionally employed.

Regional coaches have been employed in several provinces to identify talent and to also move the coaching development forward.

Summary

In the appendix that follows, some of the CSA and USSF ideals in player development and talent identification are referenced. Coaches are encouraged to use these resources for further depth in the process of player development and identification.

Communication is as important between coaches as it is for players on the field. The chain of communication between a house-league coach, a competitive coach, a club's technical committee, the club head coach, the regional provincial coaches, the provincial team coaches, and the National team coaches is critical if the game is going to be moved forward. This is the lasting communication Even Pellerud brought with him from Norway. The early signs are encouraging in Canada, as senior coaches, such as Ian Bridge, John Walker, and Bryan Rosenfeld, have noted improvement in the tactical sophistication of players. The soccer culture is slowly changing and with the accessibility of premier league teams and international competition both on television and in the media, this serves as an essential part of player development.

Player Development

In his five years in Canada, Even Pellerud has seen:

1) An improvement in facilities;
2) An enhanced talent identification process at the National Training Centres;
3) A satisfactory level of athlete;
4) Implementation of the necessary new National Team age group programs;
5) An enhanced awareness of the women's game in the media and public;
6) An evolving understanding and implementation of zonal defense and direct penetrating attacking play throughout the provincial and now club programs;
7) Successes with the women's and U-19 National Teams

Appendix - The USSF includes the following key factors in its publication on identifying and developing talent in the women's game. For a complete comprehensive review of the USSF approach to development the reader is referred to the USSF website (www.ussoccer.com)

IDENTIFYING AND DEVELOPING TALENT IN THE WOMEN'S GAME

Involvement in youth sports begins in broad base recreational programs that can eventually lead into an elite level. This process takes place over a period of many years and is very complex. As young players work their way through youth soccer levels, they are consistently exposed to an increasing measure of challenges and obstacles. Identifying talent (Club, State, Regional, or National) expresses an interest in the elite performer relative to her current level and daily playing/training environment. The best model to identify and develop talent in America (at any and every level) includes a continuous cycle of evaluation in training and competition.

The continuous cycle of identifying and developing talent includes: Competition-Identification-Selection-Evaluation-Selection-Re-Evaluation (in training and competition) etc...

Competition - watch players play within their daily environment, be it Club or ODP
Identification - identify the most talented players at that level
Selection - invite players to participate at the next level - pools, camps, teams, or tryouts
Evaluation - evaluate players' performances, in training and in competition. Critical to assess their technical, tactical, physical, and psychological dimensions, along with their work-ethic, discipline, and contributions or conflicts toward team chemistry.
Selection - invite player to participate at the next level - pools, camps, or teams
Re-Evaluation - in training and competition/games, evaluate players on and off the field with her level of competitiveness being the ultimate test of her ability to be for your team.

Evaluating, identifying and developing talent in any selection process is a work in progress. 'Talent' and 'performance' is dynamic (it's always evolving). If a player doesn't continue to grow, her teammates will compete more strongly for a position on the team, and opponents are always improving. Players are capable of and do respond to the demands of training and performance, thus elevating their current level to the next level. It is important to remember that evaluating players in a number of different environments contributes to the valid assessment of their potential. Every evaluation and selection process should include the following two (2) environments.

1. Competition
2. Training

Chapter IX
The Physical Factor

Women As Athletes

The attitude towards women's football and, indeed, the physical image of women in athletics, and the acceptance of female participation in sports traditionally dominated by men has changed rapidly in the past few years. Even Pellerud's liberal upbringing was helpful in that he did not significantly alter the training regimen for his teams when he moved from the men's game to women. It was to serve him well as the teams relished this full out approach to training-something previous coaches had stepped around.

Tony DiCicco recounts an interaction at the European Football Trainer Symposium held in London in 1998. "While making a presentation about the upcoming '99 World Cup with video and slides, there was genuine awe that the U.S. Soccer Federation had gone out on a limb planning such a huge event around women's soccer. As the main session was about to break up, a man stood up (Tony recalls the speaker was a from an enlightened European culture, not a backward country) pointed to a poster depicting U.S. player Brandi Chastain fighting a Norwegian player for a ball, and said, 'I look at that and I see ugliness and muscles. This is not what it's supposed to be about.' DiCicco responded, 'If this poster were of men playing you would see fitness, athleticism, and commitment. We need to change people's attitudes to that so they see that when looking at women'." Some of those barriers have been broken and are continuing to be broken to this day, and that is great news for the game. The truly dedicated athlete has always known there was a price to pay for playing at the top of the pyramid.

In Canada, players such as Charmaine Hooper are proud and competitive about the level of fitness they achieve. Quoted in a Fütbol interview in 2002 Hooper quipped: "I'll take on any man in pull-ups, chin-ups and push-ups." She added, "I know when I play a game with men they used to back off a bit, but I don't want that and I think they respect me now-I know it when they play their hardest against me." Perhaps one of the most telling observations on women's dedication to the game can be gleaned from Scott Stossel's piece in The Atlantic in June 2001. Writing about the new WUSA and the Boston Breakers team, the editor of American Prospect wrote:

As American as Women's Soccer?

Everything about the new professional women's soccer league is unorthodox, which is why it may succeed...

It was a snowy morning on the last Sunday in February, too early to be awake, but inside Mike Boyle's Strength and Conditioning center, in Winchester, Massachusetts, twenty-six women were working out, as devout in their exertions as monks at matins. This was not a casual jaunt-on-the-StairMaster sort of workout; Mike Boyle's is not the place for casual jaunts. There are no Pilates classes here, no juice bar, no copies of Cosmo or Glamour-just machines, weights, and a swath of artificial turf laid across the concrete floor. These women were working out: sprints and weights and more sprints, while an imposing trainer in black sweats put them through their paces for two solid hours.

They were the Boston Breakers, one of eight teams in the new Women's United Soccer Association (WUSA), which made its debut in April. The women are already elite athletes; they also represent the future. In the college seminar I teach on sports and culture, nothing infuriates the female students more than the degradation of women that is associated with male sports: bikini-clad ring girls at boxing matches, inanely grinning cheerleaders at basketball and football games, victory-circle girls at auto races. For my students and many of their contemporaries-who have come of age in the era of Title IX, the 1972 law prohibiting sex discrimination in institutions (primarily high schools and colleges) supported by public funds-an increasingly compelling image of femininity is represented by the women at Mike Boyle's: it's not about cheering sports but about aggressively playing them…."

Even Pellerud has always been known as a coach who promotes aggressive play. The Norwegian direct game promoted aggressive and thus physical play and, beyond that, demanded it for success. Pellerud's first step in Norway, as it was in Canada, was to demand the maximum out of his players in all categories of fitness.

Tony DiCicco in recalling games against Even Pellerud made the following comment at an NSCAC seminar in 2002: *"I think it is a mistake for people to consider the game that the '95 Norwegian team played was 'kick and run'. Even's teams were well coached and when that long ball came forward there was a purpose to it. It usually found the target or the space that was immediately attacked in an organized fashion by a group of very physical and disciplined players. Our players would move to the ball and when they looked up there was a group of these 'Vikings' around them and there was going to be a price to be paid. His consistent organization around the ball when it arrived was difficult for us to contend with and that '95 team was big, strong, and fast."*

Pellerud states that his philosophy is to select players to fit his team style. He is clear in what the roles and responsibilities of the players are and, along with that, their physical attributes have to suit the position. (His opinion on player roles and responsibilities are described in Chapter 6-for a summary of technical and physical exercise patterns see Dunn, Ford and Williams in Insight Issue 4, Vol. 6, 2003, pg. 41-45)

As Pellerud's outstanding strong forward Linda Medalen noted in a 2004 interview: *"Even's teams didn't always have the best 18 players in Norway on his team, but they always had the best 18 players for their positions. There were a lot of very talented players who weren't selected for the team, but they didn't fit into the positions or the system that Even saw for the team. Those players had to be physically, mentally, and above all tactically able to play the game Even wanted." Pellerud himself is quick to point out that he will not alter his playing style to accommodate players, but neither is physical size/prowess critical to his style. It's an aggressive player with a great work rate that he's looking for. He uses examples such as Hege Riise (Norwegian center midfielder), Diana Matheson (Canadian National Team center midfielder), Amanda Ciccini (U-19 National center midfielder), Kristina Kiss (Canadian National Team midfielder) as players who are smaller, not overly physical, but who have developed well as players who play their role positions well."*

When Pellerud first came to Canada in 1999, he was happy with the athleticism of the Canadian women, but he clearly understood he was at a disadvantage with the size of the country and the limits travel imposed on the number of times he could bring the players together. *"The Norwegian National Team was much like a club team because we had close communication and cooperation with their coaches and clubs. The club coach would help out in developing the player in the way I wanted. That isn't here in Canada, yet. There our playing philosophy was more consistent throughout the system. I had some control over the players. I could monitor their fitness. We had excellent testing that the coaches and, more importantly, the players could use as a monitor of where they were. Even in an environment like that we depended on the players to monitor and maintain their own fitness level, but we put them in training environments that would push them. We played against boys teams and tested ourselves constantly."*

Medalen, the 1995 World Cup standout also commented on the change in the game in Norway: *"I think one of the biggest problems with Norway's team today (2004) is they are not as fit as we were. Even had an idea of where he wanted the players to be. For me to be as effective as possible Even told me he wanted me to maintain a VO2 max in the 60-65 range, the minimum a forward should have. I worked hard to keep myself at 65 and the whole team did the same for their targets. We would play 120-minute games so when it came to 90 minutes our team was still going strong while other teams were in trouble. I don't think they work as hard as we did on that part of the game now and I think when everyone has such good technical skills that is an advantage you have to maintain for yourself. Even had a clear idea of how physically fit he wanted our team and we knew when we were trained at our best, that gave us a big advantage. We could beat anybody."*

VO2max

VO2 or a player's maximum oxygen uptake can be measured most accurately in a laboratory. A player is run until exhaustion. Fitness is then measured by the volume of oxygen you consume while exercising at maximum capacity. By definition then, VO2 max is the maximum amount of oxygen in milliliters that one can use in one minute per kilogram of body weight. In general terms, those who are more fit have a higher VO2max and can exercise with more intensity than those exhibition lower levels. It is generally accepted that VO2max can be increased if an athlete works out above 65% of the maximum heart rate for at least 20 minutes, four to five times per week. While expensive to measure in a lab in exact increments there are calculators for converting other endurance tests, such as Cooper test or, more realistically, the intermittent yo-yo test, to VO2max estimates. The reader is referred to www.peakcentre.ca and Brian McKenzie's Successful Coaching for more information and references on the indirect testing.

Programming for Fitness

The challenge to Pellerud was to convince the new Canadian team and instill individual training discipline. He had a solid scientific interest in conditioning, strength, and speed training. He had co-authored a significant report and manual on football training in Norway in the early '90s. With his coaches and training staff Pellerud's approach has always been to develop a specific training regimen tailor-made to each player. The players are given the schedules and areas to work on and are followed up at the intermittent training camps and over the phone and by e-mail in the non-camp times.

Most importantly as a coach, Pellerud believes in paying close attention to the individual players and where they fit in with respect to physical factors of play. The individual programs are monitored and changed when necessary based on his observations as a coach. Feedback remains Pellerud's cornerstone. A typical player program is included at the end of the chapter (Pg. 238).

In addition to being a coach setting a standard, he is aware of the importance of leadership from within. Players such as Medalen in Norway and Hooper in Canada were those leaders.

Those players knew the physical factor in the game of soccer was critical to success. Having confidence in individual and team speed, knowing you can beat your opponent to the ball is the first and most significant step in developing the confidence necessary to win at the highest levels of the game.

Finding those players with the gifts of speed, balance, strength, and endurance is one of the first tasks a coach has to undertake in assembling a team. Track speed versus game speed has to be analyzed. Core strength and upper body strength are critical in most positions. Hand/eye coordination. Ability in the air. These factors are bonuses. The ability to pass a long ball (a cross) accurately is a combination of physical and neurologic factors as well as confidence. Finding those players and developing those skills is what Provincial and National training programs are all about in Canada and what the model for development was in Norway.

The best players look after their own fitness. While coaching sessions, particularly small-sided games, can train endurance and build the base levels to train the energy systems, the players have to take responsibility for their own conditioning. Programs are developed by coaching staffs and physiologists, but the bottom line rests with the player. At the National Team level players are expected to come to camp with a normal, high standard of physical conditioning.

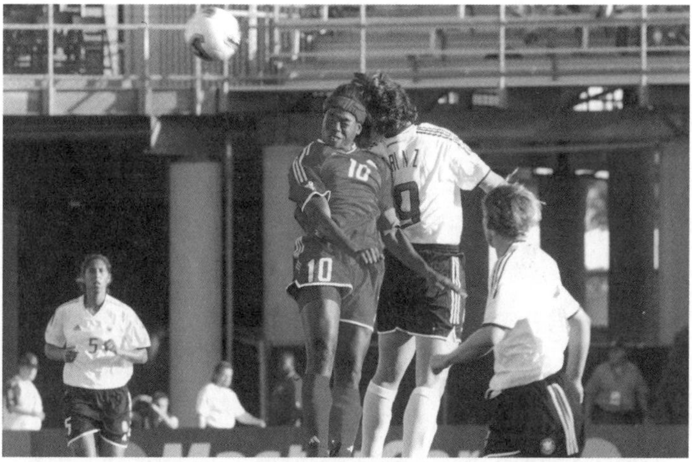

Hooper battling tournament MVP Prinz in opening game

Competition post-game

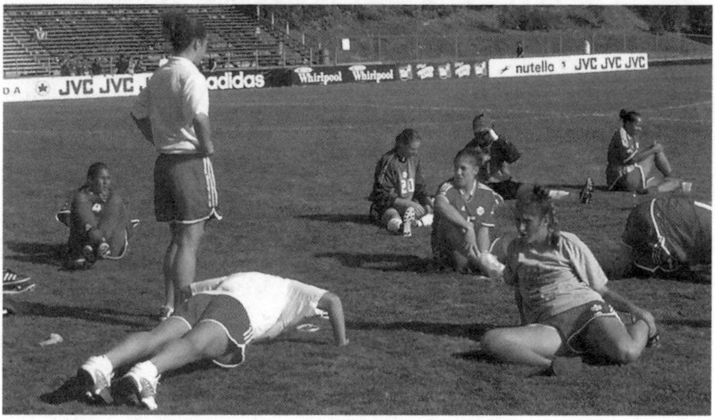

The important cool-down post-game under the eye of the trainer

Speed work is an integral part of practice. Competition is stressed.

Trainer Paolo Bourdignon checking the status of captain Hooper

Taking Their Measure

Even Pellerud's approach to fitness is based on individual analysis. Physical requirements may vary to some degree for each position on the field. Significant variation of distances covered and speed of training has been well documented in science and soccer literature. Stradwick and O'Reilly in the FA Insight (2001 Issue 2, Vol. 4) and William Setal (Issue 2, Vol. 6) have clearly correlated exercise activity patterns as well as technical deficiencies across various training positions.

Don Kirkendall, a sports exercise physiologist involved with FIFA, has worked with the U.S. National Teams for many years. When specifically looking at the game of soccer Kirkendall has indicated that the game has five speeds: walking, jogging, sprinting, cruising, and backwards. Two-thirds of the game is spent walking and jogging. 800-1000m of the six miles covered in a typical 90 minute game, or less than 20% of the game, is spent sprinting. These are multiple sprints of 10-40yds, 40 being the average maximum sprint. One and a half of those miles are spent cruising or making recovery runs to prepare positions and follow the play. A very small amount of the game is spent going backwards-although this can be a critical few steps for a defender.

Pellerud and his staff have taken an approach to training that is position specific and typically develop plans for early conditioning (pre-season), maintenance (in-season), and specific body work, core strength, upper body, and legs. The responsibility for maintaining a fitness level to meet minimal team standards falls squarely on the shoulders of the players, particularly at the National Team level where they are assembled for only short periods of time. A very useful resource for various programs specific to adult female soccer players is outlined in both of Anson Dorrance's excellent books, Training Soccer Champions and Vision of a Champion.

Periodization or appropriate timing and intensity of training in the pre-competition, competition, and recovery phases have to be appropriately planned. Istvan Balyi and Tudor Bompa in

Canada have contributed extensively to this area of training and exercise. Their work is recognized internationally and utilized by the Canadian programs. Istvan Balyi has worked as a high-performance consultant with the Canadian National Men's Soccer Team. He is recognized as a leading world expert in planning periodization, long- and short-term training and performance programming. He has published extensively on training, concentrating recently on pre-training and long-term athlete development including training to train, training to compete, and training to win stages of periodization (further references are included in the appendix).

Tudor Bompa is widely recognized as one of the world's leading experts on training methodology. His books include, Periodization Training for Sports published March 1999, and Periodization Theory and Methodology of Training published June 1999, Serious Strength Training published October 2002 (all three books published by Human Kinetics), Power Training for Sports, Plyometrics for Maximum Power Development published by Midpoint Trade Books, March 1997. Widely recognized for his expertise in the area of the strength and power training, serious coaches refer to his work.

A typical periodization schedule is appendixed from the Soccer Academy prepared by John Bilton. The NCCP (National Coaching Certification Program) run by the Coaching Association of Canada provides extensive courses in coaching including periodization and specific energy system training (see www.coach.ca/e/nccp).

Every good coach should have an idea of a minimum standard of fitness required on his team. While tests of the various energy systems and aspects of speed--acceleration, power, strength-are alternatively available, most of our athletes' fitness levels can be assessed in a short period of time with a few tests. In Norway, Pellerud was involved in the production of a testing "normal" or fitness review with various National trainers in the early 90's. In Norway, as now in Canada, the team fitness was tested on a regular basis. The players find the standards useful as personal benchmarks. (See Figure 3 tables a., b., and c.)

Even Pellerud explains his approach to testing: *"Testing for the sake of testing or the science of it I do not find that important, but more it is important by way of giving the player advice, direction, as to how they should change training and for motivational reasons. Testing has a place in soccer science of course. When I was with the Norwegian Soccer Association I was involved in producing a specific package of testing procedures and I went to all the competitions we had in Norway and put together a program, which is still in use. The basic testing we do at the high level is submax endurance, max VO2 to produce a standard to relate practice and training schedules and regimes. That will be done on a treadmill and with very competent scientific staff doing those tests for us. This is direct VO2 Max.*

"We also do a 40-meter sprint run with sensors to eliminate test error (or cheating!). The third important test we have used a lot is jumping-we use vertical jumps measured electronically. We basically test the time in the air and by that find out the jumping ability of the athlete. This relates to power and speed very directly.

"How often should testing be done? The test equipment and testing tools we use for this can be expensive, but ideally, every team at the highest level, and every athlete at the highest level, should test three to four times a year. It depends on the season and even for us on the budget. Generally, I record the most ideal test schedule as: 1) after the season; 2) before the pre-season training schedule; 3) prior to the season (at least a few months to see if the program works and some can adjust); 4) in the middle of the season, as well, because we know from experience that most soccer players have some problems keeping up the physical qualities during the season because training will get less attention, there will be higher intensity, there are more games, more restitution practices...all these things will drop a soccer player's fitness if she is not very disciplined. You have to be conscious about that as a coach and as a player. It is easy to see fitness slip away in a season and the testing helps us refocus on that.

"Those three or four tests a year are ideal and we are not there yet in the CSA or in Canada on my team. At the moment (2004) we test once a year in the summer to give some ideas about where we are. In the summer of 2003 leading up to the World Cup we had excellent test results, which made the coaching staff feel very comfortable about what the players did at home. We went into the World Cup with good confidence about the physical standards we had. In that way testing is important. A psychological boost for the coaches!" (See standards appendix at the end of the chapter)

The scientific approach to measuring physical parameters in an athlete in order to predict performance is an area of increasing interest to coaches. One of Canada's better-known sports science conditioning centers is PEAK. Exercise physiologist Michael Hart provided an insight into how physiological testing can positively affect coaching and athlete evaluation/performance.

The Importance of Physiological Testing in Soccer

In the competitive world of soccer, games are won by a mere fraction of a second; with a single kick leading to the winning goal. With this in mind, coaches, exercise specialists, and athletes strive to achieve every possible advantage over opponents. Numerous factors, including genetic endowment, training, and health influence athletic performance. Figure 1 illustrates the

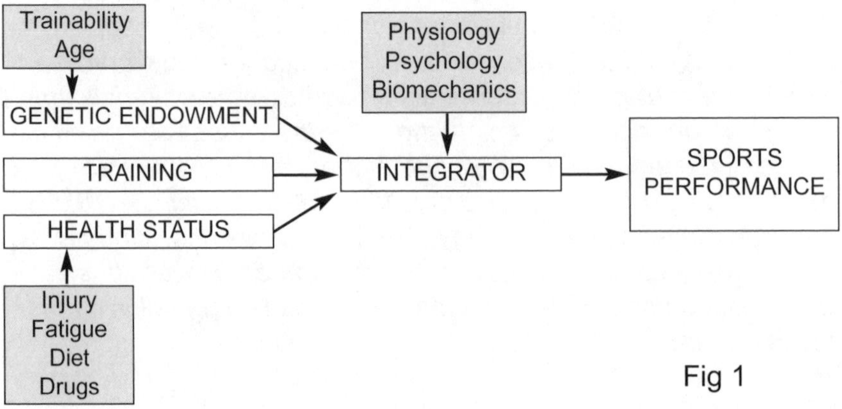

Fig 1

Although little can be done to alter predisposed genetic potential, performance can be optimized through superior training strategies. With training identified as an integral factor in performance enhancement, it is logical to monitor training improvements to ensure positive performance influence. The most effective training methods involve a regulated training structure. This structure incorporates a battery of scientifically developed sport specific performance tests that may be used to (a) provide a physiological "snap-shot" identifying athletic capabilities, (b) identify strengths, weaknesses and general health status and (c) generate a feedback system used to gauge the effectiveness of a training plan.

Laboratory and Field Performance Testing in Women's Soccer

Exercise performance testing may be categorized as either laboratory testing or field-testing. Laboratory tests provide measurements of established variables within a controlled environment, attempting to closely mimic and control conditions within a given sport. These tests are very accurate and reliable, providing consistent, repeatable results under a given set of testing conditions. In contrast, field tests reflect measurements obtained during a simulated competitive situation. In this respect, field tests are generally more specific to sport competition.

Because of the specificity of these testing conditions (environment, equipment, distances, work to rest ratios, etc), the results obtained from these tests are an invaluable tool in tracking sport specific fitness improvements over time. Both laboratory and field tests, if conducted properly, are valid and reliable forms of testing and should be considered complimentary to one another. Results from neither form of testing should stand-alone as an ultimate measure of performance.

There are many laboratory and field tests regularly performed in exercise science and it is important that the most appropriate tests be chosen for a given sport. The following discussion provides a brief synopsis of tests that may be appropriately used with soccer athletes (refer to Table 1 for a summary of these tests).

TEST	TYPE	WHAT IT MEASURES	PRACTICAL UTILIZATION
VO2 Analysis	Lab Test	- Aerobic system capacity - Ability of the aerobic system to perform at given exercise intensities	- Identification of maximal ability to utilize oxygen
Blood Lactate Analysis	Lab Test	- Endurance capability at sub-maximal exercise levels	- Identification of training thresholds and corresponding training intensities - Improve recovery efficiency
Repeated Sprints with Lactate Recovery Analysis	Field Test	- Ability to sustain repeated high intensity sprints - Fatigue Index (speed drop) - Acceleration - Recovery ability following repeated high intensity sprints	- Develop individualized sprint training strategies based upon individual needs
Resisted Repetitions (1RM, 4RM, 8RM)	Lab Test	- Muscular strength, power, endurance	- Enhance individual strengths and improve weaknesses that may relate to improved play or reduced injury rates
Vertical Jump Assessment	Lab Test	- Instantaneous lower body power and resistance to fatigue	- Enhance individual strengths and improve weaknesses
Flexibility Assessment	Lab Test	- The range of motion about a given joint or series of joints	- Identify muscle imbalances - Identify athletes predisposed to injury
Body Composition Analysis	Lab Test	- Percentage body fat - Total muscle mass	- Optimize movement efficiency and overall performance - Ensure optimal training health

Table 1: Performance tests, what they measure and how they can be used

While measurement of oxygen uptake (VO2) may be beneficial, perhaps a greater indicator of performance resides in the measurement of blood lactate levels. Blood lactate analysis detects the ability of an athlete to sustain critical submaximal exercise intensities. This form of assessment is important in determining optimal training intensities to enhance base fitness, recovery efficiency, and endurance capacity.

The ability to recover efficiently following repeated bouts of high intensity exercise is crucial to the success of any athlete involved in soccer. Using a repeated sprint test with lactate recovery measurement, it is possible to determine an athlete's rate of recovery as well as the ability to sustain individual maximal sprint speed.

Development of lower body as well as trunk strength and power are also invaluable tools to possess in soccer as this sport involves very powerful movements. The development of specific strength and power are important keys to performance enhancement. It is important to note that there are numerous variations of strength and power testing enabling the sport scientist, coach, and athlete to determine the optimal area for improvement focus. Flexibility assessment is essential as limited range of motion (ROM) or muscle imbalance about a specific joint (such as the hip joint) may negatively affect performance and predispose athletes to injury.

Body composition must be monitored to ensure optimal performance and health. Numerous methods are utilized to estimate body composition. Referred to as the "gold standard", hydrostatic (underwater) weighing is a precise, yet costly method of determining body composition. Less costly methods such as skinfold assessment and bioelectrical impedence analysis (BIA) are more commonly used. Skinfold assessment provides greater accuracy and reliability than BIA. It should be noted that dual-energy x-ray absorptiometry (DEXA), a new form of x-ray technology is emerging as the superior method for body composition assessment, however, DEXA equipment is very costly and generally only operates in regulated medical institutions.

Performance Testing Guidelines

Figure 2 illustrates a guideline for integrating exercise testing into an exercise training plan. This format involves conducting a "needs analysis" to determine specific performance requirements. Initial tests determine baseline measures of athletic performance. Training plan design should reflect results attained during the initial testing sessions, as well as specific requirements of the sport as determined via the needs analysis. Further, it is important that a form of test-retest cycling be implemented within the program design. Frequent testing (every 2-3 months) is used to gauge the effectiveness of a training plan.

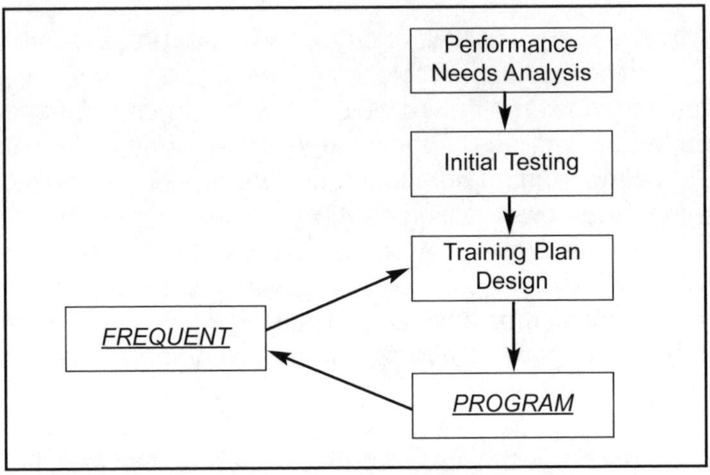

Figure 2. Test-retest cycle for performance diagnosis and subsequent training plan evaluation. Modified from Newton et al. (2002).

Summary

Many factors influence athletic performance. Training is a controllable factor that may be monitored regularly. Physiological tests provide a "snap shot" of current performance levels as well as a sound feedback system through repeated testing during the course of training. This enables regular augmentation in training (if necessary) to ensure that optimal performance results are achieved.

Michael Hart M. Kin., PFLC, CSCS
Exercise Physiologist
PEAK Centre for Human Performance
613.737.PEAK (7325)
www.peakcentre.ca

The PEAK Centre for Human Performance has emerged as one of North America's leading High Performance Fitness Testing and Training Facilities. Being one of only eight Nationally Accredited Centres located in Canada, the PEAK Centre has provided sport science support to many of North America's top National and Professional athletes.

References

Newton, R. U. and Dugan, E. (2002). Application of strength diagnosis. **National Strength & Conditioning Association**. 24 (5): 50-59.

MacDougall, J. D. and Wenger, H. A. (1991). The purpose of physiological testing. In: **Physiological testing of the high performance athlete (2nd ed.)**. (eds. MacDougall, J.D., Wenger, H.A. and Green, H.J.). pp. 1-6. Human Kinetics: Champaign, Ill.

Getting There

While a typical between-camp program is shown in Appendix I at the end of this chapter, the players all follow a personal program, as well as a club program for training. Sharolta Nonen, outstanding defender in the WUSA for the Atlanta Beat, and Charmaine Hooper, forward in Atlanta (and more recently defender for Canada), were two of the outstanding Internationals on the Atlanta Team. The conditioning coach and trainer for coach Tom Stone was Jeremy Boone at Atlanta. Boone, an outstanding speed and strength coach who also trains the NFL Carolina Panthers, remarked on the two Canadian players.

Charmaine Hooper:

- "Charmaine's advantage as a player is that she knows her own body so well. She is aware of what her body can and cannot do and how far she can push herself."
- "At the end of just about every practice, when every other player is walking off the field exhausted, I look over and see Charmaine doing extra pushups or running hills. Her work ethic is unbelievable."

Sharolta Nonen:

- "Sharolta's advantage is that she is one of the fastest players on the team. In terms of athletic ability, she has more raw athletic potential than just about any other player I have worked with."

The following Figure 4 shows a typical Atlanta Beat one-week training program from early pre-season.

ATLANTA BEAT
April 23-28, 2002

Major Emphasis
Recovery
Competition
Speed Endurance

Minor Emphasis
Strength
Speed Acceleration

Mon	Tues	Wed	Thu	Fri	Sat	Sun
- WU #1 - Conditioning	- WU #1 - Straight ahead speed - Strength training	- WU #2 - Lateral speed and agility	- Strength training - Recovery	- WU #2	GAME DAY	- Active recovery - Reserve game

Warm-up #1

Jog 3-5 minutes	
Partner Leg Swings- 10 each leg	
Dynamic Stretch- standing position	
Calf	
IT Band	
Hamstring	
Hip Flexor	
Hurdle Walks- forward & backward	2 x 30yds
Partner Balance	
Skip	2 x 30 yds
Heel Kick- right leg only/left leg only	2 x 30yds
Crossover Skip	2 x 30yds
Carioca	2 x 30yds
Backward Run	2 x 30 yds
Team Agility Ring Game	

Warm-up #2

Jog 3-5 minutes- incorporate forward/backward/lateral movement
Dynamic Stretch- standing position
- Calf
- IT Band
- Hamstring
- Hip Flexor

Medball Balance Game

B Skips	2 x 30 yds
Crossover Skip	2 x 30 yds
Lateral Shuffle w/ Change of direction	2 x 30 yds
Carioca w/ Change of direction	2 x 30 yds
Plant & Cut- forward & backward	2 x 30 yds
360s forward/backward	2 x 30 yds
Zig Zag Bounds- 4 into a sprint	2 x 30 yds

Speed Tag- two rounds

Conditioning

Field Players

SPRINT INTERVALS
10-yards & back in 3 seconds x 5 reps; 6-second rests;
20-yards & back in 6 seconds x 4 reps; 9-second rests;
30-yards & back in 10 seconds x 3 reps; 12-second rests;
40-yards & back in 12 seconds x 2 reps; 16-second rest;
50-yards & back in 15 seconds x 1 rep

Goalies

Hill Sprints (2 reps) followed by 15 sec. all out run
Perform 5 sets @ 2 min. rest b/t each set
Incorporate ball juggling during rest periods

Straight Ahead Speed

Hoop Starts (into 10 yd sprint with ball)

Soccer Start
Balance Start

Speed Ladder Footwork (into 5 yd sprint)

2 In (1 set ea foot leading)
Shuffle (in-in-out)
In-in-out-out

Lateral Speed & Agility

6 Point Star Drill (5m radius)
Complete 2 reps ea way

Cool down

Jog 5-8 minutes

Hurdle Walks 2 x 20 yds
Partner Leg Swings
Forward/back x 10 each leg
Side/side x 10 each leg
Static Stretch -hold ea. Position for 20 sec.
Order (calf-hamstring-quad-hip flexor-groin-low back)
individual athletes choice as to which particular stretch

Strength Training

Dumbbell Complex

High Pull x 6 reps
DB Curl & Press x 6 each arm
Upright Row x 6 reps
Squat & Overhead Press x 6 reps

*Circuits 1 & 2 use two arm movements
*Circuits 3 & 4 use alternating single arm movements

<u>Pushup Progression</u> - complete 3 trips of 8 reps ea. In a circuit format

Rotational
Stagger
Crossover
Butt-up
Regular

Step Up

3 x 10 each leg
Body weight only

Core

As a group

Jeremy Boone maintains an active sports fitness performance company in North Carolina and can be reached at www.athletesbydesign.com.

Charmaine Hooper demonstrates how personal dedication to the physical factor in the game can bring success. Her approach has always been to push herself.

Charmaine Hooper on Fitness

Charmaine Hooper credits a lot of her ability to play the game at speed and with strength to her "playing up". She recalls, it was difficult in the early years: *"My first year I did it I was terrible. When I was 13 I played U-16 and when I was 14 I played U-18. I actually look back on that and wish I could have been challenged even more. There is one regret I have about my career: if I could have played against boys sooner, that would have been a better development for me. I started playing with guys when I started university. They were mostly from our men's team. I improved a lot after I finished school. With the girls I wasn't being pushed enough. With the guys I was being stretched every time I went out to practice. The difficult thing is when you leave playing with a guys team and go back to playing with girls. Your level of playing drops as well. It's frustrating not to be able to maintain that level. Our biggest obstacle right now as National Team players is to be able to play at a high level consistently. It is a mental thing."*

Tom Stone, Hooper's coach at the Atlanta Beat, pointed out: *"Her strength is her game. When I coached against her, I used to spend a week drawing up a plan to stop her. I figured the best way to stop Charmaine Hooper was to draft her."*

Hooper brings a very strong mentally committed presence onto the field, and a rare combination of speed, power, and aggression to the game. Coach Stone comments: *"All great goal scorers have the ability to separate from a defender physically, but what makes Charmaine unique is that she can separate with her upper body strength or she can separate with an explosive first step."* Stone also sees Hooper as a positive role model, adding: *"Here's someone who is 5'7", 160 lbs. A young female soccer player can look at her and see that Charmaine is a quality athlete who is still feminine, who is still lady-like on the field and off."*

Charmaine Hooper's physical strength and speed come from a work ethic within. Jeremy Boone, the trainer of the Atlanta Beat recalls: *"When I did the first round of testing on the athletes, I was amazed to see that our oldest player, Charmaine Hooper (32 at the time), was our strongest and most fit athlete."* This fitness was recognized by her fellow players and many in the sports world. Picked as one of the most fit women in sport by Sports Illustrated, Charmaine was chosen for a feature piece on how different female athletes trained and balanced health, fitness, and their workouts.

Hooper married her long-time college sweetheart from NC State, Chuck Codd, in 2002. When asked about her longevity in the game and her ability to stay fit, Hooper responded: *"I have always taken my health seriously and I'm very keen on stretching, hydrating, and recovering after workouts to help my body be healthier and fitter. The mental part, being motivated to get better and knowing I could improve and be constantly challenged is more motivation. It has made me a better player."*

Her advice to young players is to push themselves and to play with male teams whenever possible. If you can, try out for the highest levels possible. Find the most competitive pro-leagues (England, Norway, Sweden) and play in those leagues.

Intensity and Dedication

Every program in the world can be put in front of the players, but if they don't take personal ownership of it, maximum results will never be achieved. Coach Pellerud is not shy in pricking his players' conciences so they maintain both quality and volume of their training away from the team. The importance of intensity in training, whether for endurance, strength, or speed, has recently been outlined in a review by Norwegians Jian Hoff and Jan Helgerud (Faculty of Medicine, Norwegian University of Science and Technology, Trondheim, Norway. 34: (3) Page 165-180). Even Pellerud utilizes the small-sided 4v4 approach to maintaining a work rate to rest ratio of 1:1 in training camps-averaging to operate at 80-90% of maximum heart rate. Hoff and Helgerud review the scientific basis for this approach in two recent articles: 1) Endurance training improves football performance. Hoff and Helgerud. Insight, Issue 4, Vol. 6, 2003, Page 38-40; 2)

National Team players are in a unique situation. Coming together for a few days at a time for camp with the National Team will not produce the level of endurance (aerobic base) development of strength, power (acceleration/speed), investment necessary to produce/reach the elite athlete level. Club and university training have to be valid and reliable to gain the peaks necessary. Pellerud as National Team coach personally keeps a close eye on players' training regimes. They are responsible directly to him.

Appendix I

Example of a Team Training Program - Sent out by coaching staff prior to International tournament for the Canadian WWC team

Period: February - March — Objective: To peak for Algarve Cup

Principles:		
	Volume:	12-15 hours/week
	Quality:	High
	Intensity:	High

Content and Execution

Soccer play
4 times/week (The more/the better)
HIGH INTENSITY

Soccer skills
5 times/week — Often, 30min, 5-7 times/week
About skills: Practice skills that apply to the game as we did at camp

- receiving balls
- heading
- accurate long driven pass
- 1v1's

HIGH QUALITY

Endurance
2 times/week — 16/14's - 15 reps
Rest 2 min - repeat 3 series
INTENSITY - But do not produce lactate. If so, reduce speed, do NOT extend pause (Additional longer runs, 45-90 min is still good for body and mentality and recovery, for instance once a week - low intensity)

Sprints — Yes
2 times/week — Well rested prior to every single sprint
QUALITY

Jumping (plyometrics) — Yes
2 times/week — Same principles as sprints
QUALITY

INDIVIDUAL ADJUSTMENTS ACCORDING TO PLAYERS/COACH MEETINGS THAT TOOK PLACE, WITH PLAYERS IN FLORIDA CAMP

Table 10 - Average Values on Field Tests of Fitness for American Youth Players in North Carolina, 1997-1999

Age Group	Speed* (m/s)	V.J. (cm)	20 yd Pro (s)	Illinois (s)	300m shuttle (s)	Int Rec (m)
GIRLS						
U12	5.65	40.25	5.85		76.26	528
U13	5.40	40.65	5.88	18.71	77.66	529
U14	5.68	42.82	5.45	19.11	75.64	586
U15	5.63	44.88	5.49	17.79	73.88	755
U16	5.60	45.53	5.34	18.62	75.81	625
U18	5.79	47.56	5.35	18.77	73.76	585
BOYS						
U12	5.26	45.47		18.62	80.22	723
U13	5.79	46.23		17.93	74.92	717
U14	6.10	51.57		17.62	71.78	1043
U15	5.68	56.69		17.34	67.21	1148
U16	5.54	55.25		17.68	70.78	938

V.J. = Vertical Jump
Int Rec - Yo-Yo Intermittent Recovery Test
*Speed data mostly from 20-yard sprint from a standing start

Table 11 - Average Values on Field Tests of Fitness for US Women National Team Players, 1996-2000

	20m Speed (m/s)	30m Speed (m/s)	V.J. Pro (cm)	20 yd (s)	Illinois (s)	Shuttle (s)	Int Rec (m)	Sprint Fatigue (%)
Elite Univ.		6.21	51.24		16.83	67.37	1216	9.8
U21	7.17	6.08	52.84		16.68	64.27	1374	7.99
Full	7.33	6.33	56.36	4.75	16.20	61.55	1310	6.37

TABLE 14. VERTICAL JUMP (NO STEP)

High School varsity average	17 inches
College average	20 inches
Elite athlete average	23 inches
U.S. Women's soccer team	24 inches
Top score on the team	29 inches

TABLE 15. THREE HOP

High School varsity average	17 feet
College average	20 feet
Elite athlete average	23 feet
U.S. Women's soccer team	22½ feet
Top score on the team	25 feet

TABLE 16. 20-YARD DASH

High School varsity average	3.2 seconds
College average	3.1 seconds
Elite athlete average	3.0 seconds
U.S. Women's soccer team	2.9 seconds
Top score on the team	2.7 seconds

TABLE 17. 300 YARDS SHUTTLE TIME (AVERAGE OF TWO TESTS)

High School varsity average	66-67.9 second
College average	62-63.9 seconds
Elite athlete average	58-59.9 seconds
U.S. Women's soccer team	58.9 seconds
Top score on the team	56.2 seconds

TABLE 18. SIT-UPS ONE MINUTE

High School varsity average	35-39
College average	45-49
Elite athlete average	55 plus
U.S. Women's soccer team	61½
Top score on the team	75

TABLE 19. PUSH-UPS ONE MINUTE

High School varsity average	18-20
College average	24-26
Elite athlete average	30 plus
U.S. Women's soccer team	51½
Top score on the team	72

Tables 10, 11, 14-19 taken from **Soccer Performance Series - A Guide to Soccer Field Testing** Pg 22-23, 28-29

Chapter X

Leadership, Mentorship, and the Mental Side of the Game

Leadership from within a team is what coaches crave. This hard-to-define quality can be recognized by good coaches from across the field. Heidi Store, the Norwegian captain in 1991, perhaps epitomized the description of a leader in action. Tony DiCicco, at the time a USA assistant coach while standing across from Even Pellerud and his team in China noted: "One of the true leaders on the Norwegian team was Heidi Store. I witnessed her in 1991. I was at the opening game of the World Cup and Norway was beaten 4-0 by China. It was an interesting game because Norway was all over them and then all of a sudden, China started breaking them down defensively and Norway missed a penalty shot and then missed an easy save and the final score was 4-0. Norway was very powerful coming into this tournament so I was just watching, wanting to see how the Norwegian team was going to respond to this. I noticed Heidi Store going up to every player. I didn't know what she was saying, but I think she was saying, 'We'll be back. We just need to stay together. Keep working together. We will be back in this tournament'. She went to every player. Of course they got stronger in the tournament, they got to the final and they almost won the whole thing. They probably outplayed our U.S. Team and we won it against the run of play." Leaders present themselves in different forms. Even Pellerud, upon arriving in Canada and surveying his team, discovered one of his leaders quickly. In one of his earliest team talks, he asked for combativeness. He indicated that he was looking for someone to get in there and put themselves in harm's way, risking a "blue eye". The next day at the end of practice, Andrea Neil showed up in front of him with significantly blackened eyes chiefly from her aerial combativeness. He knew he had one of his leaders.

Andrea Neil, one of the co-captains going into the 2003 Women's World Cup, in a wide-ranging interview about leadership and her role on the team as a leader and mentor, gave a great insight into what makes the Canadian team tick:

Andrea Neil - The Blue Eye - On the Team and Her Coach

Andrea Neil, one of Pellerud's co-captains, represents what leadership is all about for the Canadian team. Capped over 100 times, Neil came to soccer late. She was a gifted athlete in British Columbia playing at the National team level in badminton when she took up soccer in her mid-teens. She tried out simultaneously for the Provincial and National Soccer Team at the age of 17 and has been on the Canadian National Team since its inauguration in 1990. The National Program itself came into existence in the mid-'80's but the first official team designated for World Cup trials was 1990 and Neil played midfield on that team.

Typically, Neil's early days started out with playing on boys' teams. She was the only girl in a boys' baseball league. Being naturally left-footed, Neil has played all positions in the National Team over the years, including marking back, sweeper, mid-field, centre mid-field, and left mid-field. She has played up front and has even been a back-up goalkeeper. She considers herself more natural in the centre-mid position.

Being very conversant with different coaching and playing approaches over the years, Neil found Even Pellerud's approach to the team and coaching very logical. Pellerud's early description of the team to his players was that of a good fit: *"You can have a ball winner, a very skilled player, or a very skilled ball controller. You don't necessarily have to have the whole package, but it is how everyone fits together to dovetail together that's important."*

Even looked at Andrea Neil as a piece of the puzzle and she brought her skills in the air and her leadership as her main points of value, and she and Even agreed on this.

Andrea Neil looked at leadership in a similar way to her coach, Even Pellerud-essentially "going to your strengths".

Pellerud knew Neil had what he wanted in a leader when he challenged his players to compete with more intensity in practice-"get some bruises". At the end of practice the midfielder had not one but two "blue" eyes. Neil had made a very favorable impression on her coach.

As a co-captain with Charmaine Hooper, Andrea Neil shares the role of leader, and quite candidly recently stated: *"As one of the captains on the team, for me an armband is never important. As captains we've made that clear to him. I think, for me he understands what I feel is important. I'm a fairly stable person. I have the experience of both life and on the field a little more than most and I think Even values that about me. My competitive desire is also something he appreciates. With Charmaine it's more she's the face of the team and, for obvious reasons she has leadership abilities just on her own. She puts up numbers. Her skills and desire and ability to produce are amazing. She is a quality person that way and her leadership is up front. For me, my leadership is more behind the scenes. I would never be satisfied just to be a cheerleader and I think the coach looks at me, even as Neil Turnbull looked to me before, to speak the mind of the team. To get the general feel of what the players are thinking."*

Without a full-time sports psychologist or mental trainer, team leaders are gravitated to and Neil noted that there were a lot of young players on the team. The balance is now tipped towards youth under Even so there is a lot of life experience that is useful in helping players avoid problems and understanding the pressures that are going to come with the team.

Neil notes that the players will come to her, but she has no hesitation about going to players and talking to them. *"That's more my style. I mean there's the intense Andrea on the field that is sometimes intimidating and hard to approach. And, I've had some of the young players tell me, 'you're intimidating sometimes' but then we talk about it afterwards and make sure we're all on the same page and they know the other side of me that's approachable. When on the field we have to be all business and that's something we have to teach the younger players, as well. Players tend to gravitate to certain personalities and there will be other leaders on the team. Sharolta Nonen is one who is a little younger and some players may feel more comfortable chatting with her."*

As far as the prospect of involving a sports psychologist in the team Neil states: *"We tried a sports psychologist previously and it was a bit of a problem. A very reputable man who used a lot of theories and models of sports psychology, but nothing that was really applicable. Most players didn't find it very practical and I think we need someone who fits with the team. I don't think the coach would want to change too much in the environment now. We're keeping it pretty tight and making sure those around us are the right people, but at some point, we would probably find a sports psychologist that would help the team if he or she was the right fit personality wise.*

"Even himself has provided us with some focus. A lot of the young players come from different environments and there were issues on concentration, getting into the game as quickly as possible. There is a time for being rambunctious in the locker room and a time to start thinking about the game. I think, particularly in the last year (before the 2003 World Cup), the culture has developed and a lot of that comes from his preparation. Pellerud prepares a team very well off the field so we as individual players know our roles and responsibilities before we leave the hotel for the locker room and the field. This helps immensely to get people into the mind set. When you're traveling on the bus, when you get to the locker room, you can concentrate on what he's given you to focus on, what he's given you to be your job in the game, on the two or three things that you have to do.

"How that's different from before is that the culture really wasn't established. The winning attitude wasn't there and I think the winning attitude has to be learned. Some teams find a way to lose and they need to develop an attitude of winning. The team may be a better team on the day, but they don't often win. I think that we've had to learn that as a team and that goes along with how we prepare ourselves. As people gain experience, core members become older and their experience allows the establishment of routines.

"Personally, I like to go into myself. I like to focus on things. I don't like to be focused on outside distractions and loud locker rooms because for me it is only about the game at that point and I'm building my intensity. Off the field I'm pretty passive, but on the field I think you have to reach within yourself and find that aggressive side. For me that's not very natural so I have to have a routine. I have to gear myself up for it. I have to go somewhere and find it."

To understand Andrea Neil's determination it is important to point out that this venerable National Team veteran came to soccer through a motorcycle accident. *"I was a badminton player and soccer player at the same time. The Junior National Team for badminton and then Senior National Team for soccer. Both coaches were pushing me to quit the other and play and I couldn't make that decision. So I went away and traveled for a year and tried to get my mind straight and I got in a motorcycle accident that resulted in a large injury for me. I had a very bad laceration in my knee and ended up with an infection that became gangrenous. I had a major surgery that took some quad out and some of my tissues and I was very fortunate to recover. I had two more surgeries and rehab and it seemed more natural to lean towards soccer. I loved the comraderie of the team sport. So it was that instead of the long dreary hours by yourself in a gym doing footwork for badminton that appealed to me. So I started to hone some of my communications skills and some of the intangibles on the field and it has grown to be a part of me. So I was interested in heading in that direction.*

"I have had other injuries to work through. I have had multiple stress fractures, a broken toe, broken wrist three times, broken thumb, a nasty geographical bone bruise that ended up as an impaction fracture of my femur. I had ACL reconstruction in 1998. So unfortunately I have had a lot of time out. Interestingly they knew I had hip problems when I was young. I was born with dislocated hips and my surgeon back then said I would never play competitive sports, let alone soccer. So I still struggle a little."

As is true in so many great athletes, adversity contributes to the very character that is critical to team success. Neil came from a close-knit family background with one brother and her father, surviving her mother's death in 1996. During the World Cup in 2003 Andrea was able to share that great time with her dad and family. Her father, and greatest supporter, was terminally ill and passed away shortly after the competition. Neil's play on the field was consistent and as aggressive as always during the entire Women's World Cup, in no way reflecting the personal stress she was under.

Andrea Neil continued with her thoughts on the role of testing and practical training for elite athletes: *"On the physical testing side, I think it is important for the players and the team because you can't hide from physical testing. I think on the soccer field, as a player you can hide sometimes and even in practice. But, in a physical test, like an exam, you can't cheat. It shows up in black and white. I, personally, don't compare myself with anyone else. I compete with myself and I like to know how I'm doing. I try to keep myself as balanced as possible. It is important with my hip problems, but I like feeling strong. I like knowing I can compete at the higher end of the test results. So for that it is personally important.*

"With respect to practices, the preparation for this World Cup was a lot more pointed towards how we were going to play rather than lots of technical touches and small grids, as we did in the past, Even did a lot of things structured. It is purposeful about how we need to go out and play. We work on shadow play and formations constantly in practice and we will consciously

practice the tactics of the style of penetrating play and zone defense. I think the players weren't as confident and understanding of what the coach wanted from us as a team and individually as they are with Even. Even Pellerud makes it very clear what he expects of the players and how he expects us to play. What I liked about Pellerud as a coach when he came in is that you, as a player, knew what he was trying to accomplish. He built the team slowly from the ground up. He kept adding layers and you never really thought you had it completely because every time you did he would just add something else. There's always something more that you don't fully understand. But he gave it to us so slowly that I think we're starting to get it as a team.

"His first approach was zonal defending and that was hard. He really worked on that and, for the players, we had to understand it. In the last year, he has been adding up the layers of the attacking play and focus and getting more and more success and I think we can see we will become more sophisticated in our attack and be able to use more approaches to bring the ball forward as time goes on.

"What I see, as a player, though is that once we've got the full background of defending, you can truly understand what the attack is all about and then use the weapons we know that we have. I know that a lot of soccer fans and coaches want to see more of that American or South American style-the "beautiful" soccer. We know some fans complain when they see us play. But, we went out and tried to play the beautiful game and we got stomped. But we see the beauty in this game, too. When we see a 40m ball that connects up and links with players and then we surround the ball in an organized fashion, I think that's an amazing and beautiful thing too.

"So, for the players, we know what we're trying to accomplish and it's the linkages, sending the ball with a purpose that's important.

"I think we started to get it after the Gold Cup when we did so well against the U.S. And, even more recently, I think we're trying to use each other and have an overall tactical approach to

the game, much more now than we did before. We're more confident now attacking as a team. The counterattack is still one of our biggest weapons, but we know that we're learning more weapons and we're getting an understanding of how to use those."

Neil went on to talk about player development and how a lot of it had to do with players knowing when to say 'no', when to concentrate on their sport and their position: *"As a player who's been there I can read often in their lines and the way they hold their body and the looks on their faces. I can read when some of these younger players are under stress and a lot of them will tell the coach what they think the coach wants to hear and not really say what's on their mind, and that can be damaging and hold them back in some ways. I think that has a lot to do with being young and not having confidence.*

"The other thing that is very important in developing a player is the ability to keep yourself fit. You can lose it so quickly so you have to be individually disciplined to keep at it year round. These days, physical people come in and they know physical testing is going to be done and what's required of them and the players who care come in more prepared and you have to compete with that. You have to maintain it all year round.

"With respect to where players can develop maximally, we do have the W-league and, until recently, WUSA, but I'm worried that some players head off to American scholarship programs and there are some bad programs down there. For the most part, the Division 1 schools are great and there is the top 20 teams where the level of play is excellent. We still can't compare to that level in our Canadian universities, but hopefully we'll get there. Part of it is lack of money. The scholarships and the professionalism that you have to weigh. There is probably more value in an academic degree from UBC than the University of Nebraska."

Finally, Andrea Neil stated in 2004: *"Five years from now, I don't see myself playing beyond this World Cup, but I would still love to be involved in the game. I would love to be involved with coaching. As tough as it is to make a full-time living at coaching, that is changing with head coaching jobs and paid University jobs. I'd like to think I will have something to contribute."*

Mentorship/Leadership

The role of both motivator and mother hen is critical on a team that's going to go to any higher level. Mentorship when younger players are being brought into the mix is critical in bringing a team together. Do you, as a coach, create leaders or are leaders born? Anson Dorrance posed this question in his leadership lecture at the NSCAA Convention 2004 (see his website for lecture http://www.ncgsc.com/04leadconv.htm). The answer may be that leadership develops in players that have the right stuff. Experience without arrogance is one of the qualities that promotes respect in team leaders. One of the game's true classic leaders by example plays for Canada. Charmaine Hooper is invaluable on the Canadian team. While not always the most diplomatic, Hooper challenges her teammates on the field and in practice and her leadership on the pitch cannot be challenged. Early in a National Team training camp with a lot of new young players, Charmaine was playing in a scrimmage. When a rookie intercepted a ball forwarded to Hooper, the veteran flattened the new player-a yellow card offense in any game. Without apology she turned away. When Hooper was questioned about the incident in an interview later, she replied: *"It's my job to let these kids know what to expect-what it's going to be like in international games. They've got to be tough enough to take it or give it or we're not going anywhere as a team."*

As one of the co-captains of the team and one of the most respected players in women's professional soccer for the past 15 years, Charmaine brings the credentials. What impresses Pellerud about Hooper's personality on the team is her willingness to do anything that is asked of her. Her successful conversion to a defender (ultimately first team all-star in the 2003 Women's World Cup) defines self-sacrifice with focus. What Even finds more important about Charmaine is her recognition of the importance of team experience to be passed on to younger players.

Pellerud has noted that Hooper spends virtually all of her spare time with other younger players passing on her international experience, hurdles she's had to overcome, advice on the type of commitment and sacrifice that's going to be necessary to make the team successful and achieve the goals they've set for themselves. This indispensable quality and her leadership by commitment and total involvement on the field of play is something that Pellerud feels the team should benefit from for as long as possible.

Michelle Akers had the same effect on the U.S. team. Never was a leader's commitment more evident than the 1999 Women's World Cup final when Akers kept the Chinese team at bay, putting herself in harm's way and, indeed, suffering the consequences.

The coach is expected to be a leader. Indeed, he has the badge or the power of the law to make him the defacto leader of the team. But it is the chemistry of the combination of that coaching leadership and what comes from within the team that seems to define greatness in teams. The Norwegian '95 team had it, the U.S. has it, and the Canadian team has it and is in the process of developing it.

The Mental Coach

It was only a few short years ago that coaches and sports organizations scoffed at the concept of leadership from without. Any reference to the mental side of the game was to come from the players themselves-their innate toughness. The science of sports psychology has been around for decades, but, ironically, it has been in practice at the levels it should be most effective-that is, the coaching staff-for a very short period of time. Pellerud was a pioneer in this area.

In 1995 he was able to convince the Norge Fotball Forbund that the team would benefit from the inclusion of a sports psychologist on his coaching staff. Not taking it lightly he was not willing to take just any sports psychologist, rather, he wanted a "fit" for the team. He was looking for someone with knowledge and background in soccer and a way of personally imparting the important aspects of sports psychology or mental training to the game his team played.

"When I coached Norway for seven and a half years I introduced a mental program to the players early on. I was looking for a person with a lot of competence in that background and found Anne-Marte Pensgaard in Norwegian University of Sports and Physical Education (NUSPE). She had the soccer background and I found out through an interview with her, in my opinion the right approach that would fit with the team. She had the commitment level, which I think is really the key here, because I don't believe in outside doctors coming in once in a while to heal the players or entertain the players or accommodate the players or staff. If you bring in a team doctor or sports psychologist, this person should be a part of the staff that the players see around them again and again. Not as a novelty or experimental coach, but as a person with competence that can complement the rest of the staff and being a part of the staff, even to kicking balls and chasing balls and the next minute she's talking to a player, talking to a group of players and giving them information, letting the players be challenged, allowing the players to think. That is what Anne-Marte Pensgaard did for us and has continued to do for10 years+ with the NFF.

"Since coming to the CSA I have been thinking a lot about doing the same thing here. I'm still searching for that right person. I am searching for the funding to do it, as well. At the moment that is tough, but going into our next cycle of preparation there is no doubt that I will intensify my search for a person with that type of competence. I didn't really make that a priority for the first two or three years in the program because we had to produce certain developmental standards on the field before introducing the mental trainer as a more sophisticated part of the staff.

"We had a lot to work on from a technical standpoint and to bring in a mental coach too early would have been too much information for them at the same time. We had some mental breakdowns last year during the World Cup and Olympic qualifi-

cation, as well, and in my opinion it is time now because the technical standards are in place. We need to take the next step, which is the "dot over the i". I think all the standards from a technical standpoint, a physical standpoint, and from a skills standpoint have reached the level where we need some new input and that will probably be a mental input. I'm a believer in that. It has worked well in Norway and in the U.S.A. program where they began soon after us in 1996 with a team psychologist.

"No doubt about it, I believe in it. I think that could make us a better team. I think that could help us take the step from number four in the world to number two or one in the world and I think the evidence is out there. Canada has great, quality leaders in the field of sports psychology, such as Terry Orlick (University of Ottawa) and it is my job as a coach to convince my association that those expenses are valuable for our team performance and our team performance development."

A well-enlightened coach recognizes the enhanced ability of a professional in sports psychology to impart important tools of mental pre-game preparation, focus, mental imagery, self-talk, and goal setting skills to the players. It's widely accepted that a player's optimal performance and that of the team can be enhanced 5-10% with proper training in the mental side of the game. What coach wouldn't want a player and team that was 5% better. Coach Pellerud selected Anne-Marte Pensgaard as an obvious fit for the Norwegian team. She currently works at the Olympic Center in Norway and remains the National Women's Team's Sports Psychologist 10 years later.

Pensgaard recalls her recruitment as a young professional in 1995: *"They didn't have a particular problem they needed to solve. On the contrary, they were playing quite well. Even wanted to add a new dimension to the training regimen, develop them further. He was particularly interested in my educational approach, which was not clinical and problem-focused. I was delighted with what seemed to be someone who was thinking the way I was and I said 'yes'.*

"My background was a Master's in Sports Psychology and I had started on my Ph.D. I had some soccer and downhill skiing

experience and had been involved in many seminars for different sports associations where I presented on my philosophy of mental training. I was responsible at the time for the mental training preparation of the Norwegian Olympic Committee's elite female athlete project. This group also funded my work with the soccer team.

"It was perfect that there was no particular problem to solve, but we were part of a development program for the players. That's a very good time to implement mental training, when things are going well.

"I worked with Even from '95 through the Olympics in '96. With the new head coach, Per Mathias Hoegmo, I left and came back in 1998 and have stayed with them since. Presently, I'm moving a little towards the men's Olympic team, but my basic philosophy stays the same and that is an educational approach-always thinking long-term, no quick fixes!

"Generally, my time with the team is at most of the training camps between 50-70 days a year depending whether we are working towards a championship tournament or not. I work with some players individually between camps. I approach them from an educational perspective grounded in humanistic psychology. I believe in personal growth and positive psychology. I believe intrinsic motivation is a core value and critical in order for a player and team to succeed.

"One of my greatest influences has been Terry Orlick of Canada and Gloria Balague of Spain/USA, who I know and admire. I have received much valuable advice from these pioneers in Sports Psychology.

"My sport science background is also something I rely heavily on and it helps me to understand the culture of soccer and sport and I feel that's very important to the success of a team sports psychologist. I always work on a close relationship with the coach. He/She always approves whatever plan I do with a team and we talk a lot about how to work with the team as a whole and as individual players.

"The players need to know that they are very fit, stronger and fitter than any other player. It is a good base to work on and then the self-confidence will start to emerge and then the self talk will improve and then it is easier to see themselves break through barriers. But, they have to have a strong physical base. That is an important key. When that is in place it becomes very individual. The self-confidence is very important and I feel the women can gain that through knowing they are fit.

"To facilitate that, I like to be present at as many practices and training camps as possible. I want to observe the players and coaches when they practice. That tells me a lot about attitudes. I try to help out wherever I can, collecting balls. I want to be part of the team so the players get to know me comfortably and it makes it easier to discuss things.

"How a sports psychologist fits into a team still depends on the coach's philosophy and also, of course, on the resources allocated to the team. There has to be a good match or fit between the coach and sports psychologist.

"I think every elite team has to have a sports psychologist today, either traveling with the team or working with players between camps. It is an advantage to have that extra edge."

Dr. Pensgaard reflects further on her time on the Norwegian team in 2000 by giving some background for those interested in delving further into the mental training side of things. She also reviews her concept of mental training through physical training in an original paper here.

Reflections from working as a psychological adviser for the Norwegian female soccer team - Olympic Champions Sydney 2000

Anne Marte Pensgaard
Norwegian Olympic Sport Center/Norwegian University of Sport Sciences

The importance of refined mental abilities in order to achieve outstanding results within sport is hardly questioned. Anecdotes from world-class athletes underline the vital role strong mental capacity plays in these achievements (e.g. Orlick, 1990, Pensgaard & Hollingen, 1996). Although there is consensus that strong mental skills are important, there is less agreement upon how mental training should be conducted and organized. My involvement with the Norwegian Female Soccer team commenced in January 1995 and initially lasted until the Olympic Games in Atlanta 1996. In the fall of 1998 I was approached by the new head-coach and asked to work with the team again, and was given a two year assignment. In March 2001 I started a four-year assignment to work with yet another head-coach and the team toward the World Championship in 2003 and the Olympic Games in Athens 2004.

The philosophy behind my Mental Preparation Program is based partly on the humanistic approach advocated by Orlick (1990), and partly on the motivational paradigm developed by Nicholls (1984, 1989) and by Deci & Ryan (1985). One important aspect is that the initiative is expected to come from the athlete herself. Each session is like a discussion between the athlete and myself where the theme of each session is driven by the need of the athlete. The MPP has an educational approach. The players are provided with a textbook, workbook and a CD (Pensgaard & Hollingen, 1996), and one goal is to develop an intrinsic interest to develop mental strength. Everything is of course discussed and approved by the coach before it is introduced to the players. To me, it is essential that the coach is an active part in this process too.

After the World Cup in 1999, where the team finished fourth, an evaluation concerning the mental preparations of the team was conducted. One important finding occurred, namely that there was a major discrepancy between the players' goals prior to the World Cup. While not even reaching the final hugely disappointed some of the players, others were pleased with having qualified for the Olympic Games in Sydney! Therefore, one of the first things that was done the following season was to agree upon and clarify the goal, namely going for gold in Sydney 2000. In hindsight, this proved to be one of the most important moves in order to direct the effort and energy of the players and support staff during the months leading up to the Olympics. Deciding the goal in itself is just one little step, the major move is to take the consequences of the goal set, and work towards the goal every day, little by little, focusing on the process goals.

During the pre-camp and the Olympic Games itself, one of my objectives was to be available 24 hours a day throughout the whole period. It was a great advantage that I had been travelling with the team on a majority of their training camps the last two seasons, so the players were used to having me around. I made sure that I talked with every player on a regular basis, and during the evenings I made sure that I always spent some time at the "social room" where we had gathered videos, cards, and games like Trivial Pursuit. I also had regular discussions with the coach, which was important in order to be able to make the right moves at the right time. The administrative leader also had regular meetings with the "player group" - an appointed group of five players - and that also prevented minor issues from developing into major issues because they were detected at an early stage.

One major challenge for a sport psychology adviser is wanting to do too much in order to justify your mere presence at the Olympic Games. Since I had been working with the team for a long period I felt confident that both the players and the coaching staff felt that they could contact me whenever they wanted, and that proved to be the case. I urged the support staff and especially the coaches to express confidence and belief whatever happened, and that was needed when the results went against us in the first match. Everything considered, I believe this was one of our greatest factors of success, the innate belief that we could do it, no matter what.

Another aspect of my Mental Training philosophy that has developed over the last decade is that it is important to integrate a vast majority of the mental training into the physical training regime. Each sport has its characteristics and demands, and the mental training should be conducted accordingly. I believe we can talk about mental skills on a general and a sport-specific level. The general level can be developed through performing other activities (e.g., rock climbing to develop courage and trust), while the sport-specific level must be practiced while performing the sport in question (e.g., simulate situations such as penalty shots that may occur in a World Cup final). I believe we still have a long way to go before we have managed to integrate the mental training into the physical training in such a way that the athlete is aware that she has, for example, been practicing concentration as well as endurance, but I am convinced that this is the way to go in the future!

References

Deci, E. L. & Ryan, R.M. (1985). *Intrinsic motivation and self-determination in human behavior.* New York: Plenum Press.

Nicholls, J.G. (1989). *The competitive ethos and democratic education.* Cambridge, MA: Harvard University Press.

Nicholls, J.G. (1984). *Conceptions of ability and achievement motivation.* In R. Ames & C. Ames (Eds.), *Research on motivation in education: Vol.1. Student motivation.* New York: Academic Press.

Orlick, T. (1990). *In pursuit of excellence. 2nd edition.* Champaign, Ill: Human Kinetics.

Pensgaard, A.M. & Hollingen, E. (1996), *Idrettens mentale treningslære [The mental training method of sports].* Universitetsforlaget, Oslo.

Coincidentally in 1995, Tony DiCicco petitioned the U.S. Soccer Federation to bring a sports psychologist on board for his U.S. National Women's Team. Colleen Hacker had been doing some work with the team and DiCicco saw her value. The USSF refused the budget and took it a step further by failing to recognize the importance of the aspects of sports psychology on a National team. "Tell your players to play harder" was one of the suggested solutions to the fine-tuning DiCicco was trying to put in place for the American team. He did not give up. He eventually convinced the U.S. Soccer Federation to hire Colleen Hacker as an assistant coach, and then as sports psychologist to the U.S. National Team. Ironically, he may not have been able to do that if they hadn't lost to Norway in 1995. Hacker has been recognized as a key factor in the success of the National Team, as she was on board for the '96 Olympic win and the '99 Women's World Cup. She continues to work with the U.S. Women's National Team and has published extensively.

In 2002, Hacker and DiCicco produced an excellent book on coaching and the associated psychological skills training in Catch Them Being Good (Penguin Books, 2002). This best-selling soccer book has become recommended reading for coaches.

Colleen Hacker shares her experiences and her approach to doing her job as one of the pre-eminent sports psychologists in the game of soccer.

Colleen Hacker with Joy Fawcett and Julie Foudy

Psychological Skills Training for the United States National Soccer Team

Colleen M. Hacker, Ph. D.
Professor, Assistant Dean
Pacific Lutheran University
Mental Skills Coach, Sport Psychology Consultant
U.S. Women's National Soccer Team

Carla Overbeck. Kristine Lilly. Joy Fawcett. Mia Hamm. Brandi Chastain. Those are the names of the five players who jogged the long 40 yards from where they gathered with their teammates in front of 91,000 screaming fans at Rose Bowl Stadium on July 10, 1999. It was their turn to strike a penalty kick to help determine the team soon to be crowned World Champion. The final game ended after 90 minutes of regulation play followed by 30 minutes of overtime in a scoreless draw. All five of these veteran players scored on their penalty kick opportunities to win the World Cup. In the 2004 Olympic Games in Athens, Greece, a newer name, Abby Wambach, scored the game-winning goal (in overtime) for the United States to win the Gold Medal. Much of the team's success reached the sporting consciousness of the global community and appreciation for their accomplishments remains strong among soccer pundits and fans worldwide. What few people know, however, is the magnitude and the details of the adversity, challenges and changes (both individual and collective) that this team has faced over the years. Perhaps the most illustrative, even symbolic, glimpse into that drama can be found in the National Team's own history.

In 1991, the United States National Soccer Team won the first-ever Women's World Cup in China. They had triumphed in the most prestigious world event in their sport. Many professional sports "claim" to crown a "world champion" even though teams represent only a handful of nations. In soccer, the World Cup involves teams from every continent and every corner of the globe. The 1999 Women's event drew over 650,000 fans to the stadiums, and on television over 40 million viewers in the United States watched the Final game along with more than a billion people worldwide. When the 1991 team won the World Cup, they returned home largely to an empty airport and to a home country that had little knowledge and even less interest in what they had just accomplished. America had not yet experienced a watershed event in a women's sports event - at least not since the Billie Jean King - Bobby Riggs tennis match in the 1970's.

Favored to win the next World Cup in 1995, the games in Sweden were played in front of sparse crowds and an American press that virtually ignored the team's quest to win its second world title. Although talented, prepared and competitive in every match, the United States lost to Norway in the semi-finals and had to settle for third place. It was into that environment that I was invited to join the team.

Although my first training camp and international event with the team (in 1995) was prior to the second World Championship, because US Soccer had never utilized the services of a Mental Skills Coach or Sport Psychology Consultant, there was neither awareness of nor support for sending me with the team to Sweden. After the third place finish, however, the coaching staff decided to make several changes in the program including player personnel, staff and team tactics. I was one of those changes.

I have served steadily on the coaching staff of the US Women's Soccer Team since early 1996, beginning our quest for a Gold Medal in the Summer Olympic Games. Since that time, the team has won a gold medal in the 1996 Olympic Games, a gold medal in the 1998 Goodwill Games, the 1999 World Cup, a silver medal in the 2000 Olympic Games, a third place finish in the 2003 World Cup and most recently, a Gold Medal in the 2004 Olympic Games in Athens.

This amazingly consistent performance in the world's most prestigious events is made even more remarkable when one considers that the United States is the only country in the world to finish in the top three of every World Cup and Olympic Game competition.

Many people have asked me over the years how I got involved with the team and then usually follow that question with "is it a dream come true?" Both answers may surprise the reader. My background at the time was strictly as a professor and collegiate soccer coach at Pacific Lutheran University. At that point, I was teaching full time and coaching collegiate sports for over 17 years. We competed in the NAIA (now NCAA Division III) and were fortunate enough to earn a berth in the National Collegiate Championship five consecutive years, ultimately winning three national soccer titles. My professional "dreams" were to teach graduate and undergraduate classes, coach collegiate soccer and to conduct performance enhancement training for athletes of all ages and abilities. I had already begun consulting with pre-elite and elite athletes in a variety of sports by that time and hoped one day to continue to provide psychological skills training for some of the world's top male and female athletes in a variety of sports.

In 1994, I was selected to join the National Soccer Coaches Association of America (NSCAA) Academy coaching staff. It was a group of coaches, primarily from large Division I Universities, that provided coaching education to soccer coaches from youth to professional levels. When I joined that group, the former Women's National Team Head coach (Anson Dorrance), the then-head coach (Tony DiCicco) and one of his Assistant Coaches, and the current National Team Head Coach (April Heinrichs) were all serving as members of that same Academy Staff. It was quite an honor to serve alongside these and other illustrious coaches of the men's and women's game and it was also an incredible professional opportunity. From those interactions, my philosophy, approach and perspective to psychological skills training caught the attention of the national team's coaches. My "try-out" period with the team apparently went well and I was asked to join the coaching staff prior to the 1996 Olympic Games. At that point, it was clear that I could not continue to coach our collegiate team, teach full time and serve as the mental skills coach for the United States National Team. Something had to give and I resigned my University soccer coaching position.

The National team moved into a full-time residency program in Florida that same year (the first of three residency programs in which I would eventually participate) and my immersion into the challenges, demands, joys and pressure of serving as the Mental Skills Coach for the United States Women's National Soccer Team began in earnest. At every conceivable break in the University calendar, I was on a plane joining the Team either for a training camp or an international match. I carved out a week here, 10 days there and long weekends at numerous opportunities. When the semester ended, I often moved to the residency location with the team in order to prepare for a major world event such as the Olympic Games or a World Cup.

Fate, flexibility and athletic event planning have been extraordinarily kind to me over the years. The Goodwill Games in 1998 were held over the summer months so I was able to live and train with the team full time. The 1999 World Cup was held from May through July so I was again in residency with the team throughout a major championship. The 2000 Olympic Games were held in September and October in Australia but fortunately I was scheduled for a teaching sabbatical that same year and I was able to take a leave of absence to work in the 2003 World Cup.

Obviously, this challenging schedule required that the Head Coach and University officials be understanding and flexible with the demands placed on my time. My priorities have to be narrow, clearly delineated and firm faculty responsibilities at PLU and the United States Women's National Soccer Team.

During the time that I served on the National Team Staff, there were two different head coaches, more than a half dozen assistant coaches, at least four different goalkeeping coaches and significant player turnover every year. What many people do not realize is that of the 20 members of the 1999 World Cup team, five were not invited to the next national team training camp for Sydney, a mere six months later. From a staff of 12 or so for the World Cup (including coaches, trainers, medical Doctors, equipment personnel, etc.) only two members returned to the team for the Olympic

Games. A similar turnover of staff and player personnel also occurred between the Sydney Olympic Games and the 2003 World Cup. Athletes in our player pool experience similarly high pressure and turnover rates. No spots are guaranteed and no players ultimately feel secure. The age range of athletes, while different for every major event, vacillates consistently from ages 16 to the mid-30s. For most events, we bring in a range of players from high school to professionals, veterans of three World Championships and two Olympic Games and younger players hoping to make the National Team for the first time.

One advantage of being the Mental Skills Coach with the Women's National Team is that I have also served in a similar capacity with several Youth National Teams. Over the years, I consulted with the U-16, the U-19 and the U-21 National Soccer Teams. While only a small percentage of the players who are members of the Youth National Teams go on to play for the senior National Team, more often than not, I have encountered these players at earlier ages. This familiarity makes the transition and efficacy of our working relationship much easier. Recently, US Soccer in conjunction with the USOC, has developed its own Performance Enhancement Team (PET) of sport scientists. These individuals from sport psychology, sport nutrition, strength training, media technology and exercise physiology have helped coaches create a master plan of vertical integration to bring the best of what sport science has to offer to all of the national soccer teams. I am fortunate and challenged by the charge to head the sport psychology branch of the PET Team.

Our national teams operate under the premise that the training effects accrued from psychological skills training mirror those of physical skill training. Specifically, we believe that both are developed, refined and improved with consistent, qualified and systematic practice throughout one's competitive career. Because of my academic background, the sport psychology services I provide are fundamentally educational in nature. No counseling occurs from a clinical perspective and should those types of services be required, individuals are referred to a licensed, clinical psychologist. Primarily my role centers on the teaching of psychological skills for performance enhancement (or maintenance). Psychological skills training includes: relaxation techniques, imagery, concentration skills, distraction control, pre performance routines, self-talk patterns, performance cueing, goal setting and team building. Team building activities serve a critical role in our team's evolution and aids the assimilation of strong personalities into a unified and collective whole. We "work for" rather than "hope for" team chemistry. We make it a matter of individual responsibility and players take pride in demonstrating actions that facilitate a 'team-first' perspective. Athletes also receive assistance in dealing with competitive pressures, team selections, playing status, sleep patterns, travel demands, family and life challenges as well as team dynamics. All of my work is conducted in concert with the coaching staff although the specific details of my individual work with athletes remains strictly confidential. When I conduct full team meetings, topics usually follow the needs identified and requested by the Head Coach. It has truly been a team effort. My goal is to complement the philosophical and programmatic vision of the coaching staff. Their support has proved invaluable.

My approach has been eclectic from the start. It represents a combination of knowledge and experience gained over the years from my own competitive background as an athlete (playing at a national and Olympic Trials level in several sports), my tenure as an intercollegiate coach and my formal education and experience in sport psychology. This integrated approach is practical, user-friendly and individually tailored. At the heart of our program is the athlete herself. Players are first encouraged to effectively and systematically self-monitor and to honestly self-report psychological strengths and mental toughness goals for a particular training block. Athletes function as active agents in the design, implementation and evaluation of their own performance enhancement techniques. No one knows better than they do what issues they face, what challenges they are confronted with and what obstacles they must overcome. Their world is one of high pressure, high demand and high stakes virtually every day of the year. The typical focus is on three types of (although certainly not discrete) intervention strategies: somatic relaxation and energizing strategies, cognitive appraisals and restructuring skills and finally, behavioral modification techniques. While both educational and remedial interventions are employed, the educational component clearly is the most utilized. Our goal is to not only facilitate optimal performance for both individual athletes and for the team, but also to foster enjoyment and the intrinsically satisfying aspects of performance.

We employ a variety of teaching and learning tools and strategies all aimed at actively engaging athletes. We have developed written workbooks, "homework" assignments, and work sheets. We use imagery videos, movie clips, audio CDs, verbal cueing, hands-on practice in training and international competition, team and individual video footage, team building activities and both small group and full team meetings. The ultimate goal is to consistently employ techniques that work best for individual athletes rather than requiring and implementing some predetermined intervention strategy for the entire team. Listening closely to athletes, offering alternative perspectives to solve problems, maintaining confidentiality and providing successful, athlete-friendly solutions to actual challenges are essential to program success. The process is long, intensive and individualized. It requires a mutual commitment from the athletes, coaching staff and support personnel.

I am frequently asked to describe what a typical day is like as the mental skills coach for an Olympic or World Championship team, and I've often said to the team that I believe: "one national team day equals four traditional 'earth' days". That analogy illustrates just how much activity occurs each day including: team meals, training sessions, fitness workouts, medical rehabilitation and preparation, team meetings, youth clinics, public appearances and media demands. Because knowledge of each athlete's personal style, preferences, needs and idiosyncrasies are vital to the design and effective implementation of the psychological skills training program, I attend every training session, all meals, all team meetings, group meetings and coaching staff meetings. Our coaches' meetings include the head coach, the assistant coach (or coaches), the goal keeping coach and the mental skills coach. I offer mental skills services primarily though individual consultations but also conduct full team and small group meetings in every training block. Because these athletes are committed to psychological skills training year round and since almost every athlete is competing nearly 11 months of the year including the Women's Professional league (WUSA) or their collegiate programs (in addition to the national team), I spend approximately 15-20 hours per week working via email, phone or through written communication with the athletes and coaching staff.

Gaining trust and credibility at this level of performance and professional scrutiny is essential. It must be developed over time and then, only after solutions, competence and guidance have resulted in performance improvements. I approach mental skills training from a practical, application-oriented perspective. I do not "fix the head cases" or offer "quick fixes". If we can make even minute improvements in performance, most Olympic, Professional and World Champion athletes are motivated to participate. Certainly, the most rewarding aspects of my position have been to witness the extraordinary success of athletes and teams in their quest to narrow the gap between current and potential highest-level performance. Seeing that feat accomplished on a consistent basis and in the biggest competitions is indescribable. Beyond that, the opportunity to work with some of the world's most talented, brightest and dedicated human beings is the greatest gift of the entire experience. The challenges, the joys and the rewards are unending. Our future competitive challenges remain essentially unchanged, namely, assemble the best possible team to represent the United States of America in future world soccer events.

Back row (L to R): Brandi Chastain, Mia Hamm, Colleen Hacker, Julie Foudy, Joy Fawcett. Front row: Kristine Lilly.

Summary

Progressive coaches such as Even Pellerud and Tony DiCicco have moved the game of soccer forward in ways other than on-field technique and tactics. The introduction of consummate professionals such as Pensgaard and Hacker to the highest levels of women's sports and achieving success with this innovation has helped move the game along yet further.

It is noteworthy that the England FA under Andy Cole has recently introduced an on-line sports psychology course for soccer coaches. Even without the financial/human resources of National Teams, soccer coaches may still introduce some of the fundamental advantages that sports psychology practice has to offer to the modern sports teams.

Chapter XI

Player Wellness/Sports Medicine

Even Pellerud's Canadian World Cup Team entered the preparation phase of the Women's World Cup 2003 in excellent condition. As the coach would recall later, "the 12 months leading up to camp for WWC2003 were the smoothest in my career as a coach." An ominous precursor of things to come indeed!

"We experienced an extreme example of the impact of injuries on the game before and during the World Cup in 2003. I had no injuries in three years coaching Canada and then suddenly the summer leading up to World Cup we experienced two ACL injuries-Amber Allen and Candace Chapman. Christine Sinclair was recovering from mononucleosis when she finally joined the team in late August. Then we had a stress fracture in Randee Hermus and a foot fracture with Carmelina Moscato. We had two concussions, Brianna Boyd in the summertime playing for her WUSA club team, and then during the World Cup her replacement Tanya Dennis. During the World Cup there were also major lower extremity injuries to Silvana Burtini and Isabelle Morneau. Minor leg injuries also cost games for Andrea Neil and Kristina Kiss. This was an extremely challenging World Cup campaign. The players worked hard to compensate for the injuries and we came through it as well as we could. But it takes a lot of energy out of the team, a lot of energy out of the staff and a lot of focus away from us as a team. One thing that is really helpful in that situation is that you have a competent medical staff you trust. We have that and, I must say, I am very impressed with the medical staff we have had involved in my four years in Canada. They are very competent and pleasant people to work with and they have been extremely good in taking responsibility and letting us, as coaches and players, concentrate on the task at hand--competing.

"I approach the staff with the attitude that they are the experts. That would be my advice to all coaches-find experts you can trust and communicate with. If they tell me that a player cannot play then I'm not going to let that player play. That would be disastrous for the mutual trust within the staff and I can't recall ever opposing the staff's recommendation even though it is most often offered only as their opinion. Sometimes the medical staff is unsure, of course. There are gray areas for how much pain a player can take and where things are dangerous health-wise that can become worse than the injury. Then there is a little bit of discussion about whether it is just pain or if there is risk of major injury if the player is placed on the field.

"The mutual trust between the coaching staff and the medical staff is extremely important. It has to be there. If not, we are in trouble and the players will find a way to play us against each other. Some players will try this, and I'm talking about highly motivated players here, very ambitious players...there is no doubt they are concerned about medical staff going to the coach and talking about injuries. These players want to play every game and there is no doubt that there is a potential conflict situation between honesty and denying reality on their part. There are also instances where a player may go so far as to hide things from the medical staff; smaller, minor injuries creating an ethical dilemma for a physician, doctor, or physiotherapist and that can be hard to live with for that person. So good honest communication between coach, players, and training and medical staff is very important.

"I have been very fortunate with my medical staff here in Canada with the CSA. They are very competent people with high ethical standards. They have a robust work ethic. They work long hours night and day. They are excellent in communicating to both the players and the staff. They spend a lot of time with the players giving information on an individual basis, on a group basis, both formal and informal. I remain impressed by the quality and competence that the medical staff has shown and that is important for a coach to be free to concentrate on the other areas.

"There may be dilemmas where, for example, a player sustains a minor or possibly major injury leading up to kick-off time. Worst-case scenario is, of course, when a player gets injured during warm-up leading up to a game and that actually happened last World Cup in the fall 2003 in the lead-up to the quarterfinal against China. A player went down in warm-up and it was a very delicate situation for the player and staff and the coaches. A player goes down and the medical staff has to assess in a very stressful situation. The player is stressed, the medical staff is stressed. The coaching staff is stressed waiting for an assessment and, at the same time trying to stay focused on the players who are healthy and ready to play in that five or ten minutes before kick-off. There are a lot of people in the stands. It is in this challenging situation where ethical standards are tested, as well as the relationship between the medical staff and technical staff.

"In assessing injuries a doctor has standards to relate to, ethical standards and all the routines to follow. This is more important these days when we talk about injuries to the head (concussions). The actual decision based on a doctor's recommendation in a situation like that will also depend on how sure the doctor is in an assessment. The evidence medically seems to be changing more to the cautious side with concussions. The more sure and clear the evidence that a player is injured reduces the pressure on the coach. A doubtful or cautious assessment where there are question marks definitely give the coach more freedom to go with the family physician or other opinions. It is an ethical dilemma. A wrong decision in that situation could lead to lack of trust in the future and could become a serious problem with team chemistry if there is not a good relationship between the medical staff and the coaches.

"Remember, as the coach in that injury scenario leading up to a game, you also have to talk to the sub and prepare her to play in this position. You have to consider whether to change spots for players-should one player move from right to stopper and who goes there now? You have to take this myriad of tactical circumstance into account while at the same time listening to the assessment, talking to the player, talking to other coaches,

talking to the subs, and that extremely stressful situation is one of the worse scenarios a coach can have. It disrupts everything when I see a starter go down in warm-up or limp into the dressing room.

"It is important to note the approach your medical staff has in general. Some of them will be conservative and follow the routines and the standards that are laid out from higher levels and tradition. Some are used to working with sports and athletes and more aggressive, knowing that athletes can take much more pain than normal people.

"As a generalization, I would say that most physicians have a tendency to be very much on the same wavelength and follow standards, while physiotherapists and athletic trainers have a tendency to give a more individual assessment based on their background, experience, and education. There are a lot of alternative routes to go today for therapists and I guess that is the background for different approaches to injuries. Some are using needles, and some are using massage, while others go to stranger alternative therapies.

"I like an aggressive approach much better than a conservative one--giving the players a lot of work to do from an alternative standpoint, putting them back on the field as quickly as possible and giving them a hard time so they are challenged to recover more quickly. Soccer is a game of movement and if the doctor clears things I like to have the therapists keep activity (alternative) levels up."

Dr. Cathy Campbell, National Team Physician, shares some of her thoughts on the medical care of a women's team here. Dr. Don Johnson, orthopaedic surgeon, and Rudi Gittens, orthopaedic surgeon and CSA Medical Director, and Don Kirkendall Ph.D. contribute their thoughts on approaches to sports injuries, hydration, and nutrition respectively.

Cathy Campbell has been the team physician for the Women's World Cup Team since 2000. A national level track and field athlete from 1968 until 1998 (as a Master's athlete), Dr.

Campbell is a graduate in Physical Education with her Master's in Exercise Psychology from Dalhousie University. She worked as a sports administrator for the Coaches Association of Canada from 1977 to 1980, at which time she entered medical school and graduated as a family practitioner, finishing her residency in sports medicine at the University of British Columbia. She then worked in the U.S. as a clinical fellow in sports medicine in Connecticut followed by a 12-year practice in family sports medicine in Houston, Texas, before returning to Canada and joining the National Team.

Medical Problems/Musculoskeletal Injuries in Elite Women Soccer Players
By Cathy Campbell MSc, MD, DipSportMed,
Team Physician, Canadian Women's Soccer Team

There are an estimated 200 million women involved in women's soccer worldwide. Historically, it is not a surprise that there is scant literature on women in soccer when one considers that the European Football Union imposed a ban on women's soccer in 1921 that lasted 50 years! It was not until 1971 that the ban was repealed and opportunities opened up for women to play soccer. There were no university women's soccer teams in 1971. Field Hockey was the only field team outdoor sport available for women. In North America, today, there are over 500 women's soccer programs in colleges and universities in the U.S. and over 100 in Canada. Field hockey, rugby, and lacrosse are also rapidly developing as outdoor field sports for women. The first FIFA World Cup for Women's soccer was not held until 1991 in China!

Women soccer players are similar to male soccer players in several respects. One important note: unlike, for instance, ice hockey, soccer is played the same way for women as for men. The rules regulating field dimensions offending are identical. The intensity of training, the number of kilometers run, and many physical aspects of the game are the same. There are some areas, however, where the frequency of physical and medical problems might be greater in women elite soccer players (for a variety of reasons, which will be explained later). It is important for coaches and staff to be aware of these differences to assist in their recognition and prevention.

Such Medical issues include:

1. Anemia
2. Nutrition
3. Travel
4. The Female Athlete Triad

SUGGESTION #1: ARRANGE A HEALTH MAINTENANCE/PRE-PARTICIPATION EXAM FOR EACH ATHLETE WITH HER SPORT ORIENTED FAMILY PHYSICIAN EVERY YEAR

The traveling and playing schedules for the typical national level female athlete often do not permit regular medical check ups and, subsequently, the player's general health maintenance is neglected. The physiotherapist or team trainer may provide excellent musculoskeletal care but the athlete should get a general physical and lab check up annually.

I decided to do a complete physical exam and obtain lab work on every member of the team (including staff) at one of our camps that was held in Canada in 2002. As the team physician only sees athletes for a brief time, and as a complete physical exam means a minimum of ½hour+ per person scheduled in between two practices per day, meals, meetings and travel time, this is not typically the responsibility of the team physician. But, upon questioning the athletes I realized that none of the athletes or staff had been medically assessed for a long time.

In light of this revelation, I arranged for a phlebotomist from one of the local labs to come to the hotel to save us time, at minimal expense. When I received the lab results by fax the hotel the next day I prepared an individual package for each player and staff member in the form of their physical exam, lab results, and point form recommendations. This provided a useful baseline assessment for each athlete in the program.

SUGGESTION #2: ANEMIA IS A SIGNIFICANT PROBLEM IN FEMALE ATHLETES-A SERUM FERRITIN LEVEL HELPS TO IDENTIFY THOSE WITH LOW IRON STORES

Anemia

Female athletes are more likely to experience anemia then their male counterparts because the women menstruate each month and often have diets deficient in iron. There are two kinds of iron: heme and non-heme. Heme iron is derived from animal and fish sources whereas non-heme is obtained from vegetable sources.

The lab results from the 2002 camp mentioned above revealed three players with significant anemias. I routinely obtain a serum ferritin level (which reflects the iron stores in the body) drawn on female athletes because of the higher occurrence of iron deficiency anemia. One athlete, who was also to play on Canada's U-19 women's soccer team as part of the Silver medal effort in the U-19 Women's World Cup in Edmonton in August 2002, had been complaining of fatigue, keeping up with others, and difficulty in recovery in between practices. When tested, her hemoglobin was 80mg/dl (normal levels are over 120mg/dl,) and a serum ferritin level of 0ng/ml (normal is over 20ng/ml). Since the Under 19 World Cup was still three months away, she had time to restore her levels with iron supplementation and performed incredibly well in Edmonton. Two other athletes on that team were also found to be anemic.

The website www.anemiainstitute.org provides additional information on the anemic condition and reviews various sources of iron.

Nutrition

SUGGESTION #3: FAMILIARIZE YOURSELF AND YOUR TEAM WITH THE CANADA FOOD GUIDE--
http://www.hc-sc.gc.ca/hpfbdgpsa/onpp-bppn/food_guide_e.html

Following the revised Canadian Food Guidelines is certainly a good sound start to a proper diet. It is important to include a variety of food portions from each of the food groups to maintain general health. Because women's diets are typically deficient in iron and calcium in particular, I always make a point of addressing these topics briefly throughout the camps. Women in this age group need approximately 1200-1500mg of calcium per day and it is important to provide some general information so that the athlete can do simple arithmetic to see if she is consuming sufficient calcium. For instance an 8oz glass of skim milk contains about 300mg of calcium and a small container of yogurt (low fat) can contain up to 460mg of calcium in one container. Rather than concentrate on calculating the exact percentages of the various minerals and carbohydrates it is easier to establish a diet that is composed of the correct amount of the various food groups.

I will not discuss the pros and cons of "supplements" but it is safe to say that all nutrition required should be obtainable through a proper balanced diet. Many supplement products are laced with banned substances (1 in 6 supplements used by athletes in the 2000 Sydney Olympics contained banned substances that were not listed in the ingredients). The position of the Canadian Center for Ethics and Sport (CCES) is that supplements should not be used for the above reasons.

Athletes like to try the latest product or protein bar and focus on this instead of attending to their basic needs. There is no advantage to spending money and energy finding the latest 'best' protein or other bar or product when you are not including sufficient iron, calcium, and minerals in your diet. More research needs to be done in the area of supplements and elite athletes--the athletes need to work hand in hand with the sport scientists who need to provide guidance in nutrition for excellence (see Kirkendall).

SUGGESTION #4: BRING FRUIT, GRANOLA BAR OR SNACK TO THE PLAYING FIELD WITH YOU

Research has shown that the best time to restore glycogen stores is during the 30 minutes following practice. Be sure to tuck a snack into your bag to eat following practice (unlike Kirkendall's work).

Nutrition Recommendations for Canadians

- The Canadian diet should provide energy consistent with the maintenance of body weight within the recommended range.
- The Canadian diet should include essential nutrients in amounts specified in the Recommended Nutrient Intakes.
- The Canadian diet should include no more than 30% of energy as fat (33g/1000kcal or 39g/5000kJ) and no more than 10% as saturated fat (11g/1000 kcal or 13g/5000kJ).

- The Canadian diet should provide 55% of energy as carbohydrates (138g/1000kcal or 165g/5000kJ) from a variety of sources.
- The sodium content of the Canadian diet should be reduced.
- The Canadian diet should include no more than 5% of total energy as alcohol, or two drinks daily, whichever is less.
- The Canadian diet should contain no more caffeine than the equivalent of four cups of regular coffee per day.
- Community water supplies containing less than 1mg/ltr should be fluoridated to that level.

Travel

Many teams are now traveling on a frequent basis to compete nationally or internationally. There are many issues that should be considered routinely when planning the trip. If it is not a National Squad, the planning often falls on the parents, coaches and manager to arrange the details. From a medical planning perspective there are many things to consider. A few items that will be briefly covered here include some tips on:

1. Jet lag
2. Health risks
3. Immunizations
4. Nutrition and water
5. Medications

The International Olympic Committee in its second Consensus Conference on nutrition (Journal of Sports Sciences Vol. 22, no. 1 Jan, 2004) prepared the following statement for the athletes at the Athens 2004 Olympics Games.

> The amount, composition and timing of food intake can profoundly affect sports performance. Good nutritional practice will help athletes train hard, recover quickly and adapt more effectively, with less risk of illness and injury. Athletes should adopt specific nutritional strategies before and during competition to help maximise their performance. Athletes will benefit from the guidance of a qualified sports nutrition professional, who can provide advice on their individual energy and nutrient needs and also help them to develop sport-specific nutritional strategies for training, competition and recovery.

A diet that provides adequate energy from the consumption of a wide range of commonly available foods can meet the carbohydrate, protein, fat, and micronutrient requirements of training and competition. The right diet will help athletes achieve an optimum body size and body composition to achieve greater success in their sport.

When athletes restrict their food intake, they risk nutrient deficiency that will impair both their health and their performance. Careful selection of nutrient-dense foods is especially important when energy intake is restricted to reduce body and/or fat mass. Fat is an important nutrient and the diet should contain adequate amounts of fats.
Athletes should aim to achieve carbohydrate intakes that meet the fuel requirements of their training programmes and also adequately replace their carbohydrate stores during recovery between training sessions and competition. This can be achieved when athletes eat carbohydrate-rich snacks and meals that also provide a good source of protein and other nutrients. A varied diet that meets energy needs will generally provided protein in excess of requirements. Muscle mass is maintained or increased at these protein intakes, and the timing of eating carbohydrate and protein may affect the training adaptation.

A high carbohydrate intake in the days before competition will help enhance performance, particularly when exercise lasts longer than about 60 minutes. Dehydration impairs performance in most events, and athletes should be well hydrated before exercise. Sufficient fluid should be consumed during exercise to limit dehydration to less than about 2% of body mass. During prolonged exercise the fluid should provide carbohydrate.

Sodium should be included when sweat losses are high, especially if exercise lasts more than about two hours. Athletes should not drink so much that they gain weight during exercise. During recovery from exercise, rehydration should include replacement of both water and salts lost in sweat.

Athletes are cautioned against the indiscriminate use of dietary supplements. Supplements that provide essential nutrients may be of help where food intake or food choices are restricted, but this approach to achieving adequate nutrient intake is normally only a short-term option. The use of supplements does not compensate for poor food choices and an inadequate diet. Athletes contemplating the use of supplements and sports foods should consider their efficacy, their cost, the risk to health and performance, and the potential for positive doping test.

Excessive training and competition are associated with some negative consequences. Robust immunity and reduced risk of infection can be achieved by consuming a varied diet adequate in energy and micronutrients, ensuring adequate sleep and limiting other life stress. Attention to dietary intake of calcium and iron is important in athletes at risk of deficiency, but use of large amounts of some micronutrients may be harmful. Female athletes with menstrual disorders should be promptly referred to a qualified specialist physician for diagnosis and treatment.
Food can contribute not only to the enjoyment of life, but also to success in sport.

Lausanne, 18 June 2003

Jet Lag

Jet lag is caused by a disruption of the body's circadian rhythm (or the body's built in clock), which dictates its various physiological activities. As the team crosses four or more time zones, a significant shift occurs in the day and night cycle. This shift causes physical and mental disruptions. This means that the athlete's mind is telling her to perform when the body is telling her to sleep.

SUGGESTIONS TO COMBAT JETLAG

- Pre-adapt sleep/wakefulness patterns and practice times to those of the destination and allow three days at the destination to adjust to the competition environment.
- If this is not possible, allow one day's rest for every time zone crossed over four time zones
- Increase fluid intake and food containing laxative material, such as bran, because constipation may be caused by flight dehydration
- Mild isometric exercises on the plane may relieve stiffness and alleviate fatigue
- When possible, schedule arrival time for evening and schedule a very light practice upon arrival which can enhance sleep
- Research the environment before you arrive so that you can prepare the team for possible problems and ways to adapt

Health Risks

Research the area to which you are traveling during the planning stages so that you can make members of the team aware of problems or things to avoid. Many websites provide excellent information about diseases or illnesses common in the area. Recent events (eg: the cancellation of the China venues for the Women's 2003 World Cup) have pointed out the potential health hazards of traveling to foreign locations.

The Canadian team traveled to China in January 2003 in the midst of a resurgence of SARS and a new epidemic of Avian or "Chicken" flu. In addition to conferring with appropriate government officials about the advisability of traveling there, I prepared handouts on both illnesses for all members of the team and held a briefing session upon arrival at our hotel. One of the clear messages to the team was NOT to go to any of the live animal or chicken markets.

SUGGESTION #5: A VERY USEFUL RESOURCE IN CANADA IS THE WEBSITE: www.TravelHealth.gc.ca

This website provides valuable information on a variety of topics related to travel including regular updates on sites for traveling to any country and useful tips on things to avoid. It is useful to prepare a package of information downloaded from various sites on the web, and copied and stapled together to use as a resource package for the team members. It can also give historical, geographical and historical information on the destination.

SUGGESTION #6: PREPARE A QUIZ WITH A REGIONAL FLAVOUR A FEW DAYS AFTER ARRIVAL FOR AN EVENING ACTIVITY, FORMING TEAMS OF 3-4 TO POOL THEIR ANSWERS AND GIVE FUN (INEXPENSIVE) LOCAL GIFTS OR AWARDS FOR PRIZES.

All ages seem to enjoy this and it forces some of the players that are quite focused on the sport to perhaps take a moment and learn about a new country or environment.

Immunizations

It is important to remember that immunizations need to be checked long before the trip and should be considered in the planning process. Current status is monitored on an ongoing basis for national traveling teams. For example, Hepatitis B immunizations need to be started six months prior to traveling to countries where this is endemic. Again, the Canadian website www.TravelHealth.gc.ca is very helpful in describing the recommendations for each country. The official website for the American Center for Disease Control, www.cdc.com, is also very helpful.

Nutrition and Water

It is a great idea to put a menu together prior to traveling to another country listing food preferences and menus. Most hotels have e-mail, making it easy to find the best contact person, usually the catering manager or chef, and develop a personal relationship. Upon arrival, search them out and review the menus ahead of time so that misunderstandings or changes can be clarified. A souvenir or pin from Canada goes a long way in enhancing good will.

Remember that many countries have unsanitary drinking water and so bottled water must be obtained quickly. Hotels will often provide this at a steep price so plan bus stops at the local markets enroute to purchase water if the local organizing committee does not provide it. It is important to remember to remind the players and staff to use the bottled water for making hot drinks in their room, or even brushing their teeth!

Medications

If no medical personnel is accompanying the team there are many over the counter (OTC) medicines that should accompany the team. The types of medications a team can carry depend upon the region and the local health risks, but it is probably reasonable to include the following in your travel bag:

For colds/allergies--Advil cold and sinus, Advil, Tylenol, Vicks rub, throat lozenges, Robitussin DM cough syrup, Claritin. It is critical to remain current with Sport Canada/International banned substances when involved in sanctioned competitions.

For gastro-intestinal problems--Pepto-Bismol, Gravol, Imodium, Preparation H (which is also effective in stopping minor skin bleeds during the game).

For skin--30SPF (sun protection factor) sunscreens, blister

treatments, sunburn lotions.

This is an abbreviated list but there are many sources of information on stocking the medical bag. This can readily be available through a variety of websites including the Canadian Academy of Sport Medicine Website:
www.casm-acsm.org

The Female Athlete Triad

The Female Athlete Triad is a syndrome consisting of disordered eating, osteoporosis and amenorrhea. This syndrome was first observed in sports where physical appearance was important in scoring, such as ballet and gymnastics, but was quietly present in other sports. The athlete tends to become obsessed with their appearance. Believing she has too much body fat or is too heavy she changes her eating habits in an attempt to achieve a personally idealized body appearance. Unfortunately, while attempting to decrease body fat, the athlete fails to eat the proper nutrients or consume sufficient calories. This results in a change in the hormonal structure of the body. It feels that it is in danger and makes changes to conserve energy.

Although certainly some female athletes may develop anorexia nervosa and/or bulimia (well recognized eating disorders), the Female Athlete Triad Syndrome is usually not as extreme as these diseases but certainly can be. The insufficient diet will lead to physiological and hormonal changes, resulting in amenorrhea (stoppage of menses) and osteoporosis or osteopenia (thin bones) which, in turn, can result in many health problems including an increase in stress fractures and other related problems.

It is important to recognize an athlete who seems to be experiencing sudden changes in weight or eating patterns or frequent or multiple stress fractures.

THE COACH, STAFF AND PLAYERS MUST BE AWARE OF SUDDEN CHANGES IN WEIGHT, CHANGES IN EATING BEHAVIORS AND FREQUENT STRESS FRACTURES (Female Athlete Triad)

Competition/Training Injuries

Within the musculoskeletal area, there are a variety of injuries, which occur frequently in female soccer players:

1. Ankle sprains
2. ACL tears
3. Stress Fractures
4. Concussions

Ankle Sprains

Ankle sprains constitute one of the most frequent injuries in soccer. There are three grades of ankle sprains. A Grade 1 sprain is the most common and involves minor injury to one of the ligaments on the outside of the foot. There is no disruption of the ligament, minimal swelling and no loss of playing time. A Grade 2 is more serious with disruption of one of the ligaments causing swelling, bruising and often requiring various amounts of time from play. A Grade 3 is obviously more severe and involves more serious injury and greater time lost from play.

In a study I authored involving the Canadian National Women's soccer team in 15 training camps over a three-year period, there were twelve Grade 2 ankle sprains. This is not an insignificant number and necessitated reminding all of the need for prevention exercises as part of the training session. As with most injuries, RICE (modified rest, ice, compression and elevation) is necessary as early post injury treatments. The important part of the post injury process begins soon after this with rehabilitation/proprioceptive exercises that are discussed elsewhere is this book. Although exercises designed specifically to strengthen the ankles have been found to help prevent these sprains, they will still occur. Time is spent at many of the national camps reminding the athletes to include these exercises in their training programs. Often they are performed after a sprain has occurred, but it is also necessary for all athletes to perform them as part of every practice since the likelihood of sustaining an ankle sprain is high.

SUGGESTION #7:INCORPORATE ANKLE STRENGTHENING EXERCISES INTO EVERY PRACTICE

Anterior Cruciate Ligament (ACL) tears

This injury is the fear of every soccer player since it typically requires up to a year to get back to playing form. The look in the eye of the athlete on the field, the severity of the injury, and their inability to continue playing after the injury is the typical beginning of the cascade of medical treatments required for this problem. ACL tears appear to be occurring more often in women athletes for a variety of reasons. Research is ongoing, but there are some preventative programs that should be incorporated into the training programs of all athletes.

The Santa Monica Orthopaedic and Sports Medicine Group has developed a prevention program that has been shown to reduce ACL injuries in preliminary studies. For a copy of this program and further information visit their excellent website at: www.aclprevent.com/pepprogram.htm

SUGGESTION #8: INCLUDE EXERCISES, STRETCHES AND PLYOMETRICS IN TRAINING TO HELP PREVENT ACL INJURIES (SEE ABOVE WEBSITE)

Stress Fractures

The causes of stress fractures are as numerous as the bones that they affect. Stress fractures, simply put, are partial fractures of the bone usually involving the cortex. These can occur from practicing or competing on hard surfaces, incrementally increasing the intensity/frequency and duration of practices too rapidly, and ill-fitting or designed footwear. Disordered eating, previously discussed, may also be a cause.

The pain of a stress fracture is significant and first draws the athlete to seek attention when it does not subside. There may be some swelling, but the initial plain x-ray is usually negative since the bones are not typically displaced. The diagnosis is usually clinical, but other imaging studies can certainly help to confirm the diagnosis. If a plain x-ray is negative and an immediate diagnosis is required, a bone scan or CT is often ordered to confirm. Plain x-rays turn positive in a few weeks and the diagnosis is made not by the sign of a fracture but by the sign of the healing callus that is observed over the stress fracture site.

This is a difficult injury to treat and can take many months to heal. The Canadian World Cup Team lost one of its starting defenders with a fibular (small thin bone that runs down the outside of the calf to the ankle) stress fracture three weeks before the start of the 2003 Women's World Cup. She did not return to the team until several months later. She stopped weight bearing training for that period of time and used pool running, biking and weights to assist in the maintenance of her fitness.

SUGGESTION #9: MAINTAIN FITNESS THROUGH ANY INJURIES...THE BIKE AND THE POOL ARE TWO OPTIONS

Concussions

Concussions are the scariest and one of the most serious injuries that the medical staff may encounter. The reason for this concern is twofold. First, if the initial injury is not managed properly in the first instance there is the potential for future damage to the brain and related consequences. Second, if an athlete returns to play too early she is at risk for "second impact syndrome", which occurs when an athlete, who returns to play before she has fully recovered from the effects of the concussion, suffers another minor head trauma. This minor head trauma can result in acute brain swelling, unconsciousness and even death.

It can be difficult to diagnose, stage and recommend guidelines for return to play following a concussion. Over the past 20 years the importance of a relative classification and treatment protocol has become increasingly appreciated. There have been many systems of diagnostic determinators designed over the years that require a physician to recall elaborate criteria and classifications, which is difficult to do when attending an athlete in the middle of play on the field.

In November 2001, the first International Symposium on Concussion in Sport was held in Vienna (Aubry et al.). A group of leading experts in the field of neurology and concussions gathered and were given the mandate to draft a document describing the agreement position by those attending the meeting. This group assessed all the grading systems that have been used but no single system was endorsed. The grading systems have been developed using subjective criteria and are NOT based on any scientific data.

REMEMBER - YOU DON'T HAVE TO BE KNOCKED OUT TO BE DIAGNOSED WITH A CONCUSSION

Signs and Symptoms of Acute Concussion:

If any one of the following symptoms or problems is present, a head injury should be suspected and appropriate management instituted.

1) Cognitive features
   a. unaware of period, opposition, score of game
   b. confusion, amnesia, loss of consciousness, unaware of time, date and place
2) Typical symptoms
   a. headache, dizziness, nausea, unsteadiness/loss of balance
   b. feeling "dinged" or stunned or "dazed"
   c. "having my bell rung"
   d. seeing stars or flashing lights
   e. ringing in the ears or double vision

Other symptoms such as sleepiness, sleep disturbance, and a subjective feeling of slowness and fatigue in the setting of an impact may indicate that a concussion has occurred or has not resolved.

3) Physical signs
   a. loss of consciousness/impaired conscious state
   b. poor coordination or balance
   c. concussive convulsion/impact seizure
   d. gait unsteadiness/loss of balance
   e. slow to answer questions or follow directions
   f. easily distracted, poor concentration
   g. displaying unusual or inappropriate emotions, such as laughing or crying
   h. nausea/vomiting, vacant stare/glassy eyed
   i. slurred speech, personality changes
   j. inappropriate playing behaviour (for example, running in the wrong direction and decreased playing ability)

What to do?

When a player shows ANY symptoms or signs of a concussion:
- the player should not be allowed to return to play in the current game or practice,
- the player should not be left alone and regular monitoring for

deterioration is essential
- the player should be medically evaluated after the injury and
- return to play must follow a medically supervised stepwise process.

A player should **NEVER** return to play while symptomatic!!

One of Canada's top starting defenders had a significant concussion in July 2003, while playing with WUSA in the US, played another game within a week, sustaining another concussion and has not played with the Canadian National Team since, including the World Cup 2003, because of recurrence of symptoms. This shows the seriousness of this injury and the importance of carefully monitored return to play.

Conclusion

This chapter has touched on a number of topics relevant to medical issues affecting the female soccer player from medical problems to musculoskeletal injuries as well as travel tips. Many current reference websites and publications are available for athletes and coaches interested in pursuing further knowledge in these areas.

References

Aubry, M, R Cantu, J Dvorak, T Graf-Baumann, K Johnston (chair), J Kelly, M Lovell, P McCrory, W Meeuwisse, P Schamasch (the Concussion in Sport (CIS) Group). Summary and agreement statement of the first International Conference on Concussion in Sport, Vienna 2001. Br J Sports Med, 2002; 36:6-10.

Ireland ML. The female ACL: why is it more prone to injury? OrthopClin North Am. 2002; Oct; 33(4): 637-51.

Practice Parameter: the management of concussion in sports (summary statements). Report of the Quality Standards Subcommittee. Neurology 1997; 48:581-585

Guskiewicz KM,Marshall SW, Broglio SP, Cantu RC, Kirkendall DT, No evidence of impaired neurocognitive performance in collegiate soccer players. American J of Sports Med 2002; March-April; 30(2): 157-62.

Junge A, Rosch D, Peterson L, Graf-Baumann T, Dvorak J. Prevention of soccer injuries: a prospective intervention study in youth amateur players. Am J Sports Med, 2002, Sep-Oct; 30 (5): 652-9.

Beynnon BD, Renstrom PA, Alosa DM, Baumhauer JF, Vacek PM. Ankle ligament injury risk factors: a prospective study of college athletes. J Orthop Res, 2001; Mar; 19 (2): 213-20.

Fluid Intake and Sports Performance

It is important to note that the body can only regulate water balance in a functional way through the sensation of thirst because, in actual fact, thirst is quenched before an adequate amount of fluid has been drunk. Studies indicate that players who exercise in hot surroundings and are allowed to drink as much as they wanted only drank 70% of their required fluid to restore losses.

An often-quoted study has three groups of soldiers marching (6 hours) in temperatures of about 25°C. The first group was not allowed to drink. The second group was allowed to drink as much as they wanted and the third group was instructed to drink at regular intervals. When performance was evaluated the group without water performed worse. The third group who ended up drinking the most performed better than the other two groups. The implication is to maintain fluid balance-more fluid has to be drunk than that to satisfy thirst.

With respect to drinks before, during, and after a match, Bangsbo wrote that players who do not drink before a match reported a feeling of discomfort. He encourages players to drink during the day prior to a match even when not thirsty and limiting during the last hour before the match (not more than 300mL every 15 minutes). During the match, small amounts of regular fluid intake is important. Recommended sugar levels of not greater than 5-10% (often 3%) are suggested. It is also important to remember that after a match, restoration of body fluids is critical and most studies find that it takes 10 hours for body fluid to be restored when players do not drink at regular intervals. Bangsbo's findings can be summarized as follows (used with permission, page 329):

1. Drink plenty of fluid the day before a match and on the day of the match-more than just to quench thirst.
2. Drink frequently just before and during a match as well as at half-time, but only small amounts at a time - not more than 300ml of fluid every 15 minutes

3. Drinks consumed just before and during a match should have a sugar concentration lower than 3% and a temperature between 5 and 10°C. The addition of salt or other sub - stances is not necessary.
4. Drink a lot after a match - even several hours afterwards.
5. Use the color of the urine as an indication of the need for fluid - the more yellow the urine, the greater the need for fluid intake.
6. Experiment with drinking habits during training so that any difficulties in absorbing fluid during exercise can be overcome.

In Canada, most games and tournaments are played in summer months where temperatures can exceed 35°C and playing times over 150 minutes a day. Dr. Rudy Gittens, Medical Director for the CSA, has provided this brief overview of the importance of fluid intake in soccer athletes.

Soccer, Fluids, and Performance

Water! Without it, life would be unsustainable on this planet. Without it, physical and mental activity would grind to a decisive halt. Without it, there would be no soccer played. The exploration of the planets has, as one of its most important goals, the search for water.

Hydration

Human body weight is 60-70% water. This water is distributed in the circulatory system, in the cells of the body's tissues and in the spaces between these cells.

Fluids in the body perform the following vital functions:

- ❑ Maintain normal temperatures;
- ❑ Distribute nutrients and other essential materials to all parts of the body;
- ❑ Transport cells and chemicals in the fight against disease and harmful agents
- ❑ Eliminate waste products from the body.

The body at rest produces an amount of heat. The muscles of an exercising athlete can generate a substantial amount of heat, as much as 20 times more than at rest. Inability to efficiently dissipate an excessive heat load can significantly intefere with athletic performance, as well as physical and mental well being. Loss of body fluids results in a decrease in overall blood volume and, as a result, efficiency of the heart will be reduced as it is not filled with each contraction. It must beat more frequently to make up for the decreased volume. With dehydration or loss of total body water, the body temperature will increase more during normal exercise, as there is less blood volume transporting the excess heat to the skin (sweating).

A typical 70kg player may lose a liter of sweat (up to 1.4% of body weight) in a game and physical performance will also be affected negatively.

Proper hydration is therefore essential for performance. It is important to note that thirst, while an indicator of the need for water will be satisfied before adequate intake/replenishment has occurred. It is advised that players drink frequently the day before a match. Before competition/training, adequate amounts of water, fluids or sports drinks should be ingested. In soccer, it is advisable that two hours before the activity begins, the player should consume 150ml of fluid every 15 to 20 minutes. This should provide adequate hydration and allow time for elimination of any excess. In addition, intake during a match of small amount of fluid at regular intervals is recommended.

Dehydration is the result of loss of fluids and/or an insufficient intake of fluids.

The following factors are of importance in causing or contributing to dehydration:

- ❑ Duration and intensity of the activity;
- ❑ The ambient temperature;
- ❑ The level of hydration;
- ❑ The timing and amount of replacement fluids taken;
- ❑ The physical condition of the player;
- ❑ The position played.

Dehydration is classified as:

Mild	=	loss of 2% body weight
Moderate	=	loss of 3% body weight
Severe	=	loss of 5% or more of body weight

The following are some of the symptoms and signs of dehydration:

- ❑ Thirst
- ❑ Dry mouth and lips
- ❑ Headache
- ❑ Weakness
- ❑ Lightheadedness
- ❑ Nausea
- ❑ Cramps
- ❑ Dry skin
- ❑ Irritability
- ❑ Difficulty focusing
- ❑ Difficulty breathing
- ❑ Rapid pulse
- ❑ Coma

Untreated, the severely dehydrated player could die. Deaths at football training camps are not infrequently reported. The physiological effect on all body organs is significant.

Thirst is a late indicator of dehydration and as stated previously is satisfied before adequate intake is achieved.

Rehydration

Rehydration should be instituted at the start of the activity and should end some hours (~24 hours) after activity.

One way to scientifically determine weight loss is to weigh immediately before and after the activity. For every kg lost, drink 1 liter of fluid. Since water is the main ingredient that is lacking, then it should be replaced by drinking frequent small amounts over a 24-hour period.

Sports drinks may also be used. They contain carbohydrates, potassium and sodium. It is advisable to take drinks of sugar levels not greater than 5-10%.

Hyponatremia

Hyponatremia happens with low sodium levels in the blood. This may be due to a fluid overload or significant loss of salt in sweat. Cramping can be a side effect and replacement (through sports drinks or other NaCl sources) is recommended.

Conclusion

Coaches and players must be aware of the risk of poor hydration and take into consideration the climate and playing conditions they are exposed to. Coaches and players must:

1. Recognize fluid losses during activity;
2. Pre-activity/practice good hydration;
3. During activity replace lost fluids by drinking frequently;
4. Post-activity rehydration.

Nutrition & Performance

While maintaining good general nutrition is critical to optimal performance in athletes, we as coaches have to understand how nutrition applies directly to the performance of our athletes. The levels of muscle glycogen and how the body uses it during football matches has been studied extensively in Scandinavia. In Bangsbo's Fitness Training in Soccer: A Scientific Approach an evaluation of eight professional Danish players illustrated the importance of muscle glycogen levels in relation to performance.

Analysis of the carbohydrate (glycogen) in the quadracep muscles indicated that those with depleted glycogen stores covered less distance than other players during the second half of a match. They concluded that the ultimate football performance would have been enhanced if the players had prepared by increasing higher muscle glycogen stores before the match. Glycogen stores are provided almost exclusively by carbohydrate intake and most professional and elite level athletes "load up" with their intake of carbohydrates in the days prior to important matches.

For optimal training as well as individual match results, optimal carbohydrate intake is suggested in all elite athletes. The enclosed schematic from page 308 of Bangsbo's book details the total energy levels derived from carbohydrates, as well as other fat and protein nutrition in their nutritional balance, supporting the benefits of increased carbohydrate intake to achieve the best possible physical performance.

A similar study assessing food intake was performed with Danish top-class players. The players completed food intake questionnaires over a 10-day period. Based on this information and an individual interview, the consumed amount of carbohydrate (CHO), fat (F), and protein (P) was calculated (see Scheme NU1).

Scheme NU1

	Energy Distribution in %			Total energy
	CHO	F	P	MJ
Football players (male)				
Danish	46	38	16	15.7
Malmo FF	47	39	14	20.7
National average (18-34)				
Males	43	43	14	12.5
Females	46	39	15	9.2
Recommended				
Males	50-60	20-30	10-20	11.9
Females	50-60	20-30	10-20	8.6
Recommended in football				
Males	60-70	10-20	10-20	15-25
Females	60-70	10-20	10-20	10-20

The study revealed that the carbohydrate content in the diet of Danish top-class players does not differ significantly from the national average for individuals in the same age group and that the intake of carbohydrate for the players was lower than recommended. Thus, as with the Malmö FF team, the diet of the elite Danish players was inadequate for optimal physical performance.

While national team coaches have medical and nutritional staff, coaches have an opportunity to optimize performance when educating their players on best nutritional practices. Don Kirkendall, a Ph.D. exercise physiologist, has published extensively in sports literature and with FIFA. Presently at the University of North Carolina, Don shares some of his recent work on nutritional balance and athlete performance.

Eating to Play

by Dr. Don Kirkendall

This has been one of the most intensely researched topics in the sports performance literature and there have been many advances from the "Saturday morning steaks" that dads might remember from their high school football days. Research can be grouped into four categories regarding the timing of eating: training days prior to competition, day of competition, during competition and after competition. In brief, carbohydrates are the best choice, so choose foods that give the most carbohydrates per serving.

Days Prior to Competition

This was the first real focus of study that led to the "glycogen loading" concept. Without going into a lot of scientific history, the typical routine now is to gradually reduce training volume and intensity while increasing the fraction of the total diet that is carbohydrates. This will help the muscles load up extra glycogen (the main fuel for muscles) for the game. Unfortunately, this is not a common practice in soccer. Most research shows that the muscle glycogen levels of soccer players are no better than the spectators in the stands - not good. Studies on soccer players have shown that those with the most pre-game muscle glycogen run the farthest at the fastest speeds during a game.

Day of Competition

There is probably no area more full of misleading information than eating the day of competition - the proverbial pre-game meal. Most pre-game meals are eaten in the 3-4 hours prior to competition. But realize that the food eaten will have little to do with the energy expended in the game. That comes from what was eaten in the 2-3 days prior to the game.

Most players eat what they like so they won't still feel full come game time. Remember that the more calories (i.e. fat and protein) in a meal, the slower the food leaves the stomach.

Carbohydrates are always the best choice (fruits, cereals, juices, pancakes/waffles, etc.) over sausage, eggs, steak, or many choices on the breakfast menu at a fast food restaurant.

Food in general, and carbohydrates in particular, should be avoided in the last hour before play. Carbohydrates stimulate an insulin response, which lowers blood sugar and also stimulates the production of serotonin, a chemical in the brain that reduces arousal (makes you listless and sleepy). Both are obviously counterproductive to competition. If something must be eaten, choose low glycemic index foods as they cause less of an insulin response.

Immediately prior to competition (in the minutes before kickoff), carbohydrates can be taken in. The excitement of the game will counteract the insulin response and the fresh carbohydrates give the muscles an extra source of fuel. The type of carbohydrates is important. Foods should be of a moderate or high glycemic index (see table). Carbohydrate supplement drinks work great. "Clear" candies (jellybeans, "Gummy" candy, Skittles etc. you the idea) are another choice.

Eating During Competition

During the game, carbohydrate supplement drinks given before the game and at half-time have been shown to increase running volume and intensity in the second half in soccer players. This is important to consider because goals become more frequent later in the game as players get tired.

If you have more energy than your opponents do, you are more likely to have an advantage over the opposition and hopefully, score more later in the game. As you can see from the table below, the ubiquitous orange slices at half-time are pretty low on the priority as a carbohydrate source.

Eating After the Game

The game uses muscle glycogen (carbohydrates) so it must be replaced. Research has shown that muscle is the most receptive for carbohydrate replacement in the first two hours after exhaustive exercise. Therefore, it is important to eat some moderate to high glycemic index foods in the first two hours after a game.

From the table, you see there are quite a variety of options for food, most of which require a little planning and typically do not come in a bag or a tray from a fast food restaurant. With games at 12 noon and 4 pm, it is necessary to get some carbohydrates back into the muscles quickly.

Remember, fast foods are high in fat and protein and can remain in the stomach at the start of the next game (depending on when it was eaten and how much was eaten), and don't return much in the way of carbohydrates to the muscles, and therefore should be avoided.

A nutritionist gave me a good suggestion: make up bags of Chex Mix with some pretzel sticks added (forget the oil and baking requirement0 and let the players eat this after the game. Clear candy is also good, as are raisins, cakes, pies, and bagels.

But don't get the idea that all the carbohydrates can be replenished in a couple of hours. Under the best of conditions, it can take 20 hours to fully replenish muscle glycogen from muscles that have been completely depleted. Eating for sports performance requires a bit of planning and clock watching but can lead to improvements in performance. When done properly, the players will notice they have more energy late in games, as well as when they have multiple games with minimal recovery between games.

Glycemic Index Table	
High Glycemic Foods	Syrups (eg. Maple, corn, cane); honey; bagel, white bread, jams, jellies; potato, most cereals; raisins, banana, watermelon, pineapple; carrots, cooked; white rice; maltodextring; jelly beans, skittles pretzels, most candy bars.
Moderate Glycemic Foods	Whole grain bread; spaghetti; corn; oatmeal; oranges; grapes
Low Glycemic Foods	Yogurt; Peanuts; beans; peas; apple, peach, pear; milk and milk products

For more information, try:
http://www.olympic-use.org/inside/ - USOC website for nutrition information including some sample menus
http://www.mendosa.com/gi.htm - a complete discussion of the glycemic index
http://www.mendosa.com/gilists.htm - for a long list of foods with their glycemic index
(These last two sites are written for diabetics, but contain much useful information.)

This sports science article comes from the Sports Medicine Section at the Duke University Medical Center and UNC Hospitals. The authors are members of the US Soccer Sports Medicine Committee including from UNC Dr. William E. Garrett, Jr (US National Teams Physician and Committee Chairman), and John Lohnes. From Duke are Dr. Don Kirkendall (exercise physiologist) and Patty Marchak (athletic trainer for 1996 US Women's Olympic Team).

http://tempestsoccer.org/smarts/eat2play.html

In this section, renowned surgeon and sports medicine director Don Johnson of Ottawa, Canada gives some insight into current and upcoming thinking with common sports injuries.

New Concepts in Sports Medicine

by Don Johnson MD FRCS (C)
Director Sports Medicine Clinic, Carleton University
Assistant Professor Orthopaedic Surgery, University of Ottawa

Introduction

In the past, an athletic injury often spelled the end of the athlete's career. Now, with improved diagnostic and therapeutic techniques, most athletes can return to their previous sporting activities and levels of performance even after a major injury.

There have been significant advancements in drug therapies and biotechnology that speed recovery and/or are used to repair athletes' 'moving parts'. These new therapies, in combination with a common sense approach to rehab and chronic injury management, help athletes at all levels heal faster and stay healthy.

The following sections describe the diagnosis and treatment of some of the more common sports injuries. The biomechanics of both acute and chronic injuries are explained in simple terms and, in the case of chronic injuries, some approaches to the management of ongoing problems are discussed.

Achilles tendon tear

In the literature, there is controversy among health professionals about repairing the torn Achilles tendon. However, for an athlete with a torn Achilles, there is no real controversy. The athlete wants the method that will produce the best function and shortest healing time, and that is the operative repair. The use of minimal incisions, and accelerated rehab, with no immobilization, reduces muscle wasting and allows faster return to sport.

There are numerous randomized studies in the literature comparing the operative versus the cast immobilization treatment for Achilles tendon tears in the non-athletic population. These all show that the end result of both treatments is fairly equal, but it is generally felt that, for the running athlete who wants to return to sports as quickly as possible, an operative intervention is preferred.

Anterior cruciate ligament tear

In the past, this was often the injury that sidelined the athlete for more than a year, and, in many cases, permanently. But, through research and clinical studies, we have learned to change this injury from career-ending to a 45-minute outpatient operation with a 90% good result rate and return to sports in three months or less.

We found that the diagnosis can be made both clinically and by MRI (magnetic resonance imaging). This early diagnosis is important to prepare the knee for surgical reconstruction. In most cases, the athlete should not continue the season with a torn ACL. There are some situations, such as a football lineman, who can play with a brace, and the ACL repair can be delayed until the end of the season. However, should there be any damage to the meniscus, it should be repaired soon after the initial injury and the ACL repair deferred. It must be noted that if the athlete continues to play with a torn meniscus, the damaged meniscus becomes irreparable. The surgical repair of the torn ACL involves replacing it with a tendon from the same knee. The patellar tendon, the hamstring tendons and the quadriceps tendons are all popular choices. An allograft (tendons donated after death) are useful for complicated or difficult situations. Ways of attaching the grafts to the bony tunnels have improved significantly in the past few years. With the grafts more firmly attached the athletes can begin early aggressive exercises and vigorous rehab that prevent joint stiffness, and loss of muscle function.

If the athletes meet all the milestones of recovery--including a full range of motion, strength equal to the opposite knee, no swelling, and a stable knee--they can start to participate in their sports by three to four months post-op. It may take much longer to regain their full proprioception (sensory awareness of a part of the body), which can be said to have returned when the athlete feels confidence running and pivoting on the repaired knee.

Incorrectly placed tunnels are the most common cause of the failure of ACL reconstruction and this happens more frequently where the surgeon does not have extensive experience repairing ACLs. However, the use of computer guided surgery or fluoroscopic computer guided surgery has made it easier for the occasional ACL surgeon to place the tunnels in the correct anatomical position. This technology is currently available as a commercial program call Orthopilot.

The prognosis after surgical reconstruction depends as much on the status of the meniscus and articular surface at the time of reconstruction as it does on the tunnel placement. In one study done by Shelbourne, if the patient had normal articular surface and normal meniscus at the time of the surgical reconstruction, almost 90% of these patients will have a normal x-ray at 10 years. This follow-up study emphasizes that the athlete can return to sport without worry of developing arthritis if the knee is reconstructed and both cartilage and meniscus are normal. It also highlights the fact that the vast majority of athletes should not return to sports with a torn ACL, as this could result in further and irreparable damage to the joint surfaces and menisci.

What will the future bring? Latter day surgeons will view the technique of harvesting tendons from around the injured knee as barbaric. The ACL will be replaced with a biodegradable collagen stent that is taken from the shelf in the OR. The graft will be implanted arthroscopically and the fixation in the tunnel augmented with growth factors to speed healing. The return to sports will be measure in weeks rather than months, as is currently the case.

Suggested reading:

ACL Made Simple, Don Johnson, Springer-Verlag New York NY, 2003

Meniscus tear

A tear of the meniscus of the knee joint is one of the most common athletic injuries and it is usually caused by flexion and rotation injuries. If this injury is detected early with clinical examination and MRI, it can be repaired. The common methods of repair involve suturing the torn fragment back to the remaining rim. In some cases, the meniscus is repaired with bioabsorbable arrows or darts. The removal of any substantial portion of the meniscus will result in long-term degenerative changes in the knee.

The healing and rehab after a meniscus repair may take several weeks longer than excision of the meniscus, but the delay of return to sports will be offset by better knee function in the future.

Articular Cartilage Injury

Injury to the articular cartilage can be due to a single episode or repeated microtrauma, such as running and jumping. However, damage to the articular cartilage does not heal, and leads to late development of osteoarthritis. Cartilage transplantation, as pioneered by Petersen from Sweden, has been done as an open operation with an 80%, 10-year success rate.

These days the procedure can be done by applying the patch arthroscopically, which is preferable to the open operation. The matrix patch (MACI or Hylaugraft) has been implanted with cells that are harvested from the patient and grown in a lab. The cells then produce a new covering for the cartilage defect which is very similar to the original surface. This process of replacement and healing may take as long as one year.

Stress fractures

A stress fracture occurs when muscles become fatigued and are unable to absorb added shock. Eventually, the fatigued muscle transfers the overload of stress to the bone causing a tiny crack called a stress fracture. Stress fractures often are the result of increasing the amount or intensity of an activity too rapidly. They can also be caused by the impact of an unfamiliar surface, improper equipment, and increased physical stress.

In addition to a review of the athlete's training habits, a physical exam and plain x-rays, the diagnosis of stress fractures requires a bone scan.

The most important treatment is rest from the activity that caused the stress fracture originally. It takes six to eight weeks for most stress fractures to heal. During this period, athletes must modify their training programs to non-impact sports, such as cycling or cross-country skiing. Treatment includes icing and stretching before and after modified activity. In cases of delayed healing of stress fractures, as confirmed by follow-up x-rays and/or bone scans, bone stimulators are used. Even with this stimulation of the healing process the complete healing of the fracture may take as long as one year.

Chronic tendonitis

Achilles tendonitis in the runner and rotator cuff tendonitis in the swimmer are the bane of the sports medicine physician. These injuries prevent the athlete from training at the maximum level. During the active treatment phase, training modification is essential to allow the healing of the tissue. For the runner, that means converting training sessions to the pool, using the kick board for longer periods.

The early treatment should be RICE: rest, ice, compression, and elevation. The therapist will assess the athlete and determine the appropriate modality of treatment, such as ultrasound, interferential therapy, or laser. Stretching and strengthening are essential aspects of any treatment program. For chronic tendonitis, progressive strengthening with eccentric exercises has helped many chronic Achilles problems. The resistant bone tendon junction pain can also be successfully treated with Sonocur, or extracorporeal shock wave therapy. After three to five, 10-minute treatment sessions, 75% of the lesions heal, and allow return to sports.

Treatment of the osteoarthritic knee in the older athlete

Athletes who have been involved in sports for many years frequently develop osteoarthritis of the hip and knee. The conservative treatment of the worn knee in the older athlete has evolved and improved over the years. The mainstays of treatment are:

1. Patient education and activity modification. It is important that the athlete continue to be active because it helps the musculoskeletal system as well as mental outlook. The main activity can be changed from weight bearing to non-weight bearing, such as switching from running and walking to swimming and bike riding.

2. Glucosamine. There are several randomized controlled trials comparing the use of a placebo to oral glucosamine and chondroitin. The patients using glucosamine show improvement and there are no significant side effects.

3. Non-steroidal Anti-inflammatory Drugs (NSAIDs). The use of anti-inflammatory drugs should be restricted to acute flare-ups of symptoms. The use of these potent drugs is very effective if there is pain and swelling of the joint. They are not as effective if there is no active inflammatory reaction.

4. Viscosupplementation. This involves injecting a preparation of hyaluronic acid, a naturally occurring substance found in the synovial (joint) fluid, into the knee joint. It acts as a lubri cant to enable bones to move smoothly over each other and as a shock absorber for joint loads. The literature supports the use of viscosupplementation for acute painful episodes of knee inflammation. The usual series of three intra-articular injections will last six or more months. There is an occasional reaction from the injection, but this is rare.

5. Bracing. The use of a brace takes the pressure off the arthritic joint that is in either varus or valgus malalignment, relieving pain and wear and tear. When combined with some modification of activity, the aging athlete can continue to participate in sports much longer. It works particularly well for sports such as golf that involve twisting of the knee.

8. Non-weight bearing exercises. The use of non-weight bearing exercises to strengthen the quadriceps and hamstrings often give significant pain relief. In addition to the use of machines or weights, exercise on the stationary bike should be part of every conservative treatment program. The bike should be used with toe clips, and the patient instructed to use low tension and a high cadence. This prevents stressing the patellofemoral joint, but allows motion and strengthening of the quads and hamstring muscles.

Summary

In order to prevent long-term disability, the athlete should be assessed early by a sports medicine physician to diagnose and adequately treat the injuries, some of which may become chronic and career ending.

Conclusion

The modern coach has to stay conversant with the mountains of health/wellness/sports medicine information that is constantly changing.

As Coach Pellerud clearly outlined, the modern team and it's training and medical staff are intricately tied together with a common goal of maintaining a well athlete. The professionals associated with the elite National team athletes have given us an insight into some of the common concerns. Hopefully, these insights will serve coaches to be a little more aware of the player as a whole person.

Chapter XII

Breaking it Down: Match Analysis

Reading the Game

A great coach, very much in the tradition of the best players, has the ability to see the entire game and its parts at the same time. To be an effective coach one must remain a student of the game and ideally that thirst for knowledge has to be passed on to the players. A coach's dream team would be a room full of players who were intent on studying the game and solving the problems posed on the field.

Soccer is a complex game with 22 players on the field and multiple adjustments to be made offensively and defensively by players both individually and as units. It is important to have resources available to identify problems during a game as well as to conduct an effective post-mortem. Effective solutions are only as efficient as the information they are based on.

While North American games such as NFL football, baseball, and NHL hockey have solidified the concept of teams of coaches, soccer has come only slowly to this point. It is not unusual to employ eight to ten coaches on college football teams with an overall head coach, defensive and offensive coordinators, line coaches, special teams coach, quarterback coach, receiving coach, and spotters in the overhead stands. This is not to mention the teams of scouts and statisticians employed these days even by amateur teams. While the last 20 years have seen an increase in the number of coaches and managers involved in preparing teams in the international game of football, it has also been a time of technological innovation. Video and computer analysis and statistics packages now abound. Lost is the modern team that does not employ technology.

Technological Innovations

Tony Waiters, former National Team Coach for Canada in the 1986 Men's World Cup in Mexico and the President of the National Soccer Coaches Association of Canada, recently commented on the prozone system in an editorial in NewSoccer: *"The thing that really got my attention though was the system they are using at Middlesborough called prozone (www.prozone.com). Twelve digital video cameras are positioned around the stadium by remote. A flick of the switch and off they go. At the end of the game the files are sent to Leeds...edited and returned 24 hours later. Every player, every move they make is recorded and not only can they see what they are doing with the ball, but, just as importantly, what they are doing when they are without the ball."*

Waiters goes on to note that only the wealthiest professional clubs can afford this technology these days, but certainly it's the wave of the future.

The use of GPS (Global Positioning Satellite) and video editing systems are becoming commonplace in the game.

Feedback

An individual coach is severely limited in his ability to gather and process information during a game. Øyvind Larsen, former Norway National Team assistant, has published a discussion on the factors limiting a coach's effectiveness as an analyst (See Football in Norway). Some of the problems encountered by a head coach when coaching and analyzing a game include:

1) Coaching position (at field level and central for the poorest overview in the park)
2) Coaches' emotional state (Swedish studies have shown blood pressure changes during a game at pathologic levels)
3) Complexity of the game (too many things to see-example: can't watch the front line and back line at the same time)
4) Multitasking -- decisions being made on game plan, substitution, time elements, half-time injuries, and so on, while attempting to analyze the game.

Even Pellerud's approach, one which underscores the importance of statistical analysis, has never wavered. Carrying on from his tradition in Norway he engaged his assistant coaches in the process early on. Presently, Shel Brødsgaard and Ian Bridge serve to break down the video of each game, noting and recording their teams' and opponents' strengths and weaknesses for practice and game planning. Pellerud uses this information for motivational purposes and as factual and demonstrative feedback for his players. Tony DiCicco, in his book Catch Them Being Good, refers to feedback as the ***breakfast of champions***. Pellerud's fellow Norwegian coach, Egil Olsen, offers these comments: *"The most important thing I have learned as coach of the national team is that people like feedback. I have never met anyone who did not like it. This makes it an obsession for me: players must receive feedback about what they do. This has been the basis for both player analysis and match analysis. Players must be able to see what they have done in black and white and should talk about it as well as watch it on video-written, verbal, and visual feedback."*

There is more to analyzing a match than simple statistics and goals for and against. In explaining his personal approach to game analysis Pellerud recently reflected: *"Starting with a coach's worst nightmare, losing a game, it is my character to be very rational. I go to a game completely calm and come back from the game with an intention of analyzing the game. I want to analyze what we did both right and wrong. I want to analyze my decisions as a coach before the game: line-ups, formations. I want to assess my work on the bench, such as changes of formations and personnel moves. Also my half-time talk. That is part of assessing myself after a game. It is especially important if you feel your team underachieved, to look back and see what you did right and wrong and learn from that.*

"Whether we lose or win, I strongly believe in looking beyond the result. Giving the players concrete objective feedback based on performance, not on results. Results in soccer frequently are random. Scoring in soccer can be random. To reduce the random effect I remind the players that creating goal-scoring opportunities is not entirely random although the end result may be. We measure scoring chances. The better you

are over time at creating more goal scoring opportunities than your opponent-the more games you will win. This is the role of the "big numbers". The fact that a lot of soccer is random is bad news for a lot of people, but we know after all the studies of soccer that sometimes you win games you deserve to lose and sometime you lose games you deserve to win. If the ball hits the post, it may go in or it may go out. If you base your feedback to the players on results only, that will give you a very emotional and irrational approach to the game. That is not an approach I employ or believe in.

"I think it is important to give the players feedback. They need objective, constructive criticism, both positive and negative, when we win games as well as when we lose games. There are games that you may win and that is great, but you know as a coach when you analyze it that it may not have been a good game-a game you are happy with. You go back to the tape and see that there were problems. We have to change this and we have to change that. Where can we and how can we be better? Then we go back to the players and give them credit for winning the game, but at the same time let them know objectively what we need to do better next time in order to win again.

"The same thing happens when we lose games. The most important point of the outcome is that you go back and tell them what you see that is right and what is wrong and what to do to fix it.

"There are three ways to analyze a game: 1) general technical analysis of a game; 2) goal chances analysis, and; 3) individual player analysis--which is very deep and thoughtful and objective. All these analyses are a part of my retrospective work with the game and the players. It takes a lot of time, but it is very useful feedback to players. We also use VCRs and computers to edit material from games to show the players different scenarios, usually to analyze offensive patterns, defensive patterns, counter-attacks, defensive shape, and dead ball situations. Shel Brødsgaard and Ian Bridge have become very proficient at putting the game tapes together and we get a lot of good information there."

Using the Information

Pellerud points out that it is critical to keep a consistent data set and Figure 1 is a format he commonly utilizes as a collection form.

Fig. 1 - Game Plan Analysis

GAME: _ _ _ _ _ _ _ _ _ V_ _ _ _ _ _ _ _ _ TEAM ANALYZED: _ _ _ _ _ _ _ _ _

TYPE OF GAME: _ _ _ _ _ _ _ _ _ _ _ _ DATE:_ _ _ _ _ _ _ _ _ _

PLAYING COND: _ _ _ _ _ _ _ _ _ _ _ _ LOCATION:_ _ _ _ _ _ _ _ _ _

A. TEAM PHILOSOPHY/STYLE OF PLAY

1. Defensive tendencies: Marking/Zone/Mixed

Marking ———————————————— Zone

2. Offensive tendencies: Possession/Penetration

Possession ———————————————— Penetration

B. SYSTEM OF PLAY

<u>On defense</u> (use drawings)

1. Formation (changes or variations during game? Line up)
2. Pressure height - high/medium/low
3. Pressure quality - 1D / 2D
4. Quality of defensive organization/shape
5. Weak parts of defensive

<u>In attack</u>

1. Formation
2. Attacking pattern(s)
3. Particular players involved in up building or penetration
4. Set Plays (drawings)
5. Strengths

C. TEAM PROFILES

Name - Position - Qualities

D. GOAL SCORING CHANCES

Minutes - Type of attack - Number of passes before finish - Touches before finish - Players involved

Summarize numbers of GSC, both teams

E. KEY POINTS TO BEAT THIS TEAM

As he did while in Norway, Pellerud also uses a modified format of the DOMP analysis. Figures 2, 3, & 4 are examples of some Norwegian games and also Canadian/U.S. games. How the players perform with and around the ball is recorded from tape. The goal scoring opportunities are also recorded and analyzed.

Pellerud, as all coaches should, will use the analyses of his team and also that of his opponent (see WC 2003 Chapter) to develop game plans.

The Game Plan

A typical example of a pre-game talk during a two-game friendly in Japan in June 2004 demonstrates how Pellerud uses the analysis of his team and opponents to develop game plans.

Game Plan - Japan

Game 2 - August 2nd, 2004

Pellerud and the coaching staff prepared the following game plan for the second game in two international friendlies against Japan. Game one was a 1-0 loss and there was limited pressure on the Japanese in the central midfield. Game two, ultimately a 2-1 victory for Canada, was played with a starting formation of 4-2-3-1. The game analysis indicated that Canada had to improve its numbers in the midfield and pay attention to the speed flank play of the Japanese squad. The pre-game talk included the following information (the team was involved in sorting out the priorities and the input was listed on flip charts in front of the group):

JOB PRIORITIES
TEAM/PARTS

List the Main:
a) Defensive jobs/duties - 2-4
b) Offensive jobs/duties - 2-4

GOALKEEPER + BACK 4

Defensive

- Communication
- Pressure/cover
- Controlling the space between mid/defensive
- BFCs (Clearances)
- Balancing the line (the full back pressures and the other three shift over)

Offensive

- Connections to mids and strikers
- Full backs pushing up and getting involved
- Quick counterattacks

The coaches added: quick passing and short corners

MIDFIELD 2

Defensive

- First and second defender pressure
- Cut off the passing lanes
- Tackle
- Communication

Offensive

- Penetrating balls into space 1 and space 2 (between and behind defensive line
- Keep possession - balls into target
- Knock downs to teammates

MIDFIELD 3

Defensive

- Shape - the right side of the ball
- Pressure - cutting off passing angles

Offensive

- Getting forward
- i) Wanting the ball
  ii) Keeping the ball

STRIKER

Defensive

- Cutting off passing angles
- Go hard when it is on (pressure)
- Double back when possible

Offensive

- Be a big target and demand the ball/hold the ball/flick when on
- Make penetrating runs
- Shoot/score
- Take on 1v1

The implementation of the game plan worked well. Canada controlled the game and won, splitting the overseas series with their much improved Asian Conference rival.

Preparation

Pellerud is quick to point out that material for analysis on the other team, although important, is not as important as the attention you pay to your own team. Using his principles of play and adjusting the formation to highlight the strengths of his team and get the match-ups against the weaknesses of the other team is one step. More critical to success is the coach's ability to make sure the team is fully prepared and ready to play at their peak level. Here the coach outlines a typical game-day preparation in an international tournament. Although he has auxiliary staff for the details, he, as head coach, plans the schedule.

Game Day Plan: Even Pellerud

The day for the big game. The day for an international game. We will be very much influenced by routines, repetition, all the standards that have been introduced over a long time so the players will do the same thing from game to game.

The day itself will be very much influenced by the time for kick-off. The later the kick-off, the more challenging the day. But whatever the kick-off time is, I am always preparing backwards from kick-off time and to set up the meals. That will be the first thing I do.

Let's say kick-off is 7 PM. I will count three and a half hours backwards for the match meal. Then I will go back to lunch time and then go back to breakfast time to allow for the right amount of time to digest. It's an important part of game preparations that we keep those schedules and itineraries from game to game.

We also plan in the game preparations, the game talk, which may be half an hour before or immediately following the match meal. It depends on the facilities we are in, extra meeting rooms and so on. Many players prefer the game meeting after match meals so they can get pumped up before they go back to their rooms to do the last part of their preparations.

Normally, with a late kick-off (7 or 8PM), which is very usual at the international level, we will need some activities to kill time that day. Game day preparation is challenging for the players because most of the players at this level have a natural high level of activity in them and they are eager to play, so to get through the time for them in a reasonable way without stressing them requires some creativity. To take the pressure off on these long days we might want to keep attention on things other than soccer. Normally, then we have breakfast in the morning according to schedule and very often we have a quiet relaxed team walk where everybody gets outside and chats informally (never a problem with our women). Some players stretch their legs, which functions as a physical stress-down as well as a mental stress-down for them. Sometimes, especially in longer camps, there may be a little bit less stress for games and we may even need to wind the players up. We may also go for a short bus ride or perhaps a walk or a guided tour to occupy the mind that morning after breakfast and before lunch. Anything to kill time with a little activity.

We will also sometimes take an hour and a half at a matinee movie or sometimes shop for an hour (no more!) when kick-off is late.

The meals themselves on that day are planned-low protein. We normally have a very strict routine for meals. We have a content of nutrition that is based on the medical staff's recommendation and acknowledged competence in that area. I depend on the staff to assure the modern approach-good healthy food for the athletes-easy to digest and still produce energy. We always have carbohydrate loading in the days before a tournament.

Most of the time, with some variation, the players will know the line up and perhaps maybe also the formation the day before. We, on occasion, give them the starting line up at lunchtime at the latest, then they have some hours to digest and think about it. Normally, most of the game preparations from a tactical standpoint are done on the soccer field in the practices on the days leading up to the game so they know how to play and they know something about their opponent.

The final part of the game preparation is done at the team meeting just before or right after match meal. Other than the meetings and the meals and a possible team activity, the players will spend most of that free time on game day in their rooms. Many will rest or sleep. Some will have treatment or muscle massage and some will do school work. There are different kinds of activities, but they stay calm, they stay quiet, they stay basically in their rooms or the treatment room and they avoid activity that is physically challenging, of course. We head to the field and changing rooms two hours before the game.

The Warm-Up

Forty-five minutes before the game the team begins it's warm-up. Pellerud's approach is consistent and he has a format. The players do five minutes of loosening up, relaxed as individuals and small groups. The team then does a team run across the pitch with various lower and upper body movements: skips, hops, stretches. There is then some ball work: circle drills with touches, headers, thighs, volleys. The Head Coach and Assistant Coaches will speak with players individually about roles and match ups. The keepers then work with the goalkeeper coach working at a good intensity. The starters go into a 5v5 game with the coach, moving in a small grid end-to-end with the coach restarting the play. Substitutes work on long balls and passing, generally in groups of three. Pellerud finishes the warm-up with the starters with five sets of sprints. There is a break for a five-minute team talk in the dressing room and the team comes out ready to play.

Statistics and Analysis

Even Pellerud has a solid foundation in statistical match analysis, which he honed during his time at the Norwegian University of Sport and Physical Education. As noted in Chapter 3, Pellerud's National Team colleague Egil Olsen did his Master's thesis on match and performance analysis in 1973. Olsen's work was presented at the first Science in Football meeting in Liverpool in 1987. At that meeting Olsen was introduced to the work of Charles Reep. He was interested to see that Reep had produced statistical evidence over a period of 40 years that supported his own independent work. Reep, in 1951 at Swindon Town, recorded over 10,000 consecutive goals, goal scoring chances, as well as all attempts on goal, and team formations. Known as the father of "notational analysis", Reep was contacted by Olsen and they began correspondence in the early '90's. Pellerud recalls a visit where he personally hosted the 90+-year-old Reep in Norway. He recounts a passionate Reep at a Norwegian National Team match leaping out of his seat in frustration when a player opted for a short pass when a direct long ball was a better option: "Why are they doing that? It won't work." Reep was completely convinced he had statistically proven the only effective way to play football. (For more information on Charles Reep and his impact on the game of football, see Øyvind Larsen's article in the Frank Cass Journal Soccer in Society Volume II Number 3 Autumn 2001, pg 58-78.) (Reep passed away in 2002.)

While the ability to see the game clearly is part of the art of coaching, it is entwined with the science of the game. A good portion of modern senior coaching certification involves match analysis and comparative views of the game. UEFA recently created a professional license position as the highest European license. Proposed as a pre-requisite for coaching at the professional level, to be implemented over the next five years, this UEFA pro license curriculum involves over 50% of its content in match analysis.

Pellerud and his assistant coaches, Shel Brødsgaard and Ian Bridge, have recently collected a set of statistics through video review and FIFA Technical Committee data on the 2002 Men's WC and 2003 Women's WC (See Appendix, Page). The importance of set plays and the necessity of quick movement of the ball from player to player over distance were borne out in the statistics and utilized by the coaching staff as further validation for the players with respect to the design of the training sessions and game plans. This data summarizes the micro-statistics that Pellerud finds useful for coaching purposes.

Coaching is Seeing

Always immersed in the game, Pellerud sat in the stands at a recent W-league final. A fan/enthusiast sitting a few seats away had been passing comments to his friends throughout the game. Pellerud commented to his seatmate, "That fellow knows what he's talking about. He understands the game of soccer. I would have him on my coaching staff. He sees the things you should see in a game and he understands what the players are doing and what they should be doing. That is rare with most people who watch and comment on games." The ability to see what's happening on the field and articulate it is a very important part of what makes a coach whole. It's also just about the last thing a coach develops expertise in and like anything else worth doing well, has to be practiced.

One of the areas Pellerud and his staff are passionate about is the necessity for the equipment and staff to gather the information that will make the program better. At a recent international tournament, no fewer than 12 Swedish coaches and scouts were involved gathering statistics, doing performance analyses, and generally supporting the team's efficiency. This serious teamwork approach to the game is a modern requirement he would like the CSA to improve on.

Thinking analytically about the game, being a perpetual student of the game, and having both the opportunity and the means of exchanging views with your peers is felt by Pellerud to be critical for any coach to ultimately be successful in the game of soccer.

He cannot imagine a group of coaches discussing soccer without a game board in hand.

STATISTICAL ANALYSIS
FOR THE 2002 FIFA MEN'S WORLD CUP IN JAPAN/KOREA
AND 2003 FIFA WOMEN' WORLD CUP IN USA

REPORT PREPARED BY: Coach Even Pellerud

STATISTICS AND RESEARCH/VIDEO ANALYSIS:
Brødsgaard, Bridge, Pellerud

May 6, 2004

2003 FIFA WOMEN'S WORLD CUP

89.2% OF GOALS COME FROM 3 PASSES OR LESS

43.9% OF GOALS FROM DEAD BALL SITUATIONS

86.9% OF GOALS SCORED FROM INSIDE PENALTY-BOX

86.8% OF GOALS WITH 2 TOUCHES OR LESS TO FINISH

2002 FIFA MEN'S WORLD CUP

80% OF GOALS COME FROM 3 PASSES OR LESS

35.6% OF GOALS FROM DEAD-BALL SITUATIONS

83% OF GOALS SCORED FROM INSIDE PENALTY-BOX

88.1% OF GOALS WITH 2 TOUCHES OR LESS TO FINISH

Comments provided above are from Table One (see next page)

TABLE ONE

	Category	Sub-Category	MWC #	MWC %	WWC #	WWC %
Tournament	Total Gms		92		56	
	Total Goals		162		107	
	Goals/Gm		1.76		1.91	
Goal Type	Dead Balls		58	35.8	47	43.9
		Corner Kick	20	12.3	14	29
		Free Kick	18	11.1	22	46
		Throw-in	4	2.4	3	6.3
		PK	14	8.6	8	17
		GK	1	0.6	0	0
	Breakdowns/ Counterattack					
	Long lasting attacks					
Finishing Details	Inside Penalty Box		134	83	93	86.9
	Outside Penalty Box		28	17	14	13
Goals after crosses	Total Goals		64	39.5	44	59
		Inswinger	12	18.8	8	18
		Outswinger	52	81.3	36	81.8
Passes before finish	Zero		42	25.9	30	28
	One		35	21.6	32	29.9
	Two		22	13.5	21	19.6
	Three		30	18.5	13	12
	Four		8		6	
	Five		8		3	
	Six		4		2	
	Seven		2			
	Eight		2			
	Nine		2			
	Ten		1			
	Other	Eleven	4			
		Fifteen	1			
		Seventeen	1			

	Category	Sub-Category	MWC #	MWC %	WWC #	WWC %
Touches to Finish	One		125	77	79	73.8
	Two		18	11.1	14	13
	Three		8		10	
	Four		4		1	
	Five		1		1	
	Six		1		1	

Practical Considerations deducted from data

- High priority in training of fast attacks, especially after break downs

- Finishing practices/techniques should focus on:
  1) One-touch finishing inside the penalty box
  2) Side-foot shots
  3) Near post headers and volleys
  4) Outswinging cross balls

- Free Kick specialists are vital to a team's goal scoring potential

- Dead ball strategies and execution must be given high priority (both offensive and defensive)

- Defenders must avoid losing the ball - breakdowns - in their defensive third

- Defending in the box must be a defensive focus

- Defensive and goalkeeper clearances are of great importance

- Goalkeepers must be able to deal with all types of crosses

- Defenders -- especially fullbacks - must make stopping crosses a high priority

Chapter XIII

Women's World Cup 2003: Canada Breaks Through

Even Pellerud's commitment to the Canadian women's soccer program was cemented in mid-2003 when he re-signed with the CSA for another five-year term. His new contract with the program was based on a goal to win the Women's World Cup 2007 and a real sense of loyalty to his players. In a 2003 interview with the board of the CSA, Pellerud stated, "There is no better place in the world to be in Women's Soccer right now than Canada." He was hooked on Canada. The incredible success of the first FIFA U-19 World Championship, which was held in Canada in 2002 fueled Pellerud's conviction that Canada had the talent to move up on the world stage. The first task in front of him was a dress rehearsal of sorts for 2007. Canada had to improve its showing in the World Cup. The quarterfinals were the goal Pellerud set for the team.

In the three previous Women's World Cups, Canada had failed to qualify for the inaugural FIFA event in 1991 in China and then failed to win a game in Sweden in 1995 or the U.S. in 1999. Because CSA CEO Kevan Pipe's stated goal in '99 was to advance out of their group into the quarterfinal, it was Canada's poor showing in that Women's World Cup that led to the shake up in the program. The pressure was now squarely back on the head coach. Neil Turnbull left the program shortly after the dismal 1999 showing. In another ominous indicator for head coaches of National Teams, the CSA had recently parted ways with National Team men's coach and Technical Director, Holger Osieck, after he failed to fulfill the promising start of the Canadian men's team in five years.

Canada had made great strides forward in the women's game in the mid-'90's and the disconnect in the program between the players and the coaching/management had come to a head following the 1999 World Cup debacle. Amateur sport in Canada suffers the ignominy of being a major political hotpoint. Funding has yo-yo-ed and see-sawed over the years depending on which national political party was in power and it was not uncommon to hear national sports federations or even individual athletes publicly harangue the government in attempts to embarrass the politicians into improving funding of programs.

After frequent less-than-desirable showings at International games and Olympic qualifications, National angst would rise in Canada. It was not uncommon for athletes or federations and even the public to speak out against the government with respect to performance. Promises were frequently made in the aftermath of both the good results and the bad, but few were kept. Only ice hockey in Canada seems to prosper at the International level and that may have more to do with the professional business that ice hockey is in North America. These external influences Pellerud did his best to ignore. Coming from a country (Norway) where government and community commitment to amateur and, indeed, professional sport was a non-question, Pellerud made tremendous inroads into calming the waters. Direct, as always, in his approach to bureaucrats it was clear what he required to achieve his goals and the association was extremely supportive of his suggestions of investment. The road was not smooth but he was persistent.

The first order was to prepare the team properly. Pellerud proposed the most ambitious pre-tournament preparations any national team had undertaken to date. With a total of over 60 days in-camp and pre-tournament team preparation Pellerud was able to use his international contacts and arrange some excellent, competitive matches with the U.S., England, Mexico, Brazil, Australia, and Ghana. More importantly, he was able to showcase the team in some of the major Canadian venues-Montreal, Ottawa, Vancouver, Edmonton, Toronto, and Kingston. A lot of the preparations were also last-minute due to the tumultuous scheduling nightmare when the 2003 Women's World Cup (originally scheduled in China) was cancelled due to the SARS (Severe Acute Respiratory Syndrome) outbreak which surfaced in China in 2001.

The CSA themselves were set back when the great momentum towards a solid place in the FIFA world, originating at the U-19 FIFA World Championships, was critically interrupted by the epidemic. The possibility of staging the 2007 Women's World Cup in Canada was a real possibility after FIFA officials had their eyes opened with the huge crowds that came out for the U-19 games (over 50,000 at Commonwealth Stadium for each semi-final and final games) in 2002. The economic and political benefits of attracting such a huge event to Canada gave the CSA a renewed purpose. What was critical was the establishment of reasonable soccer venues for the competition and it was felt that the five-year interval would allow Canada to get at least the West Coast and Toronto-sites prepared (the Federal Government had promised a new stadium in Toronto if a significant world event were awarded by FIFA).

When the SARS epidemic began to spread, the effect hit Canada hard, as Toronto became one of the world epicenters for the virus. The decision was made to cancel the World Cup in China because of the uncertainty of travel and health safety of the athletes and visitors. A short list of possible new host countries including Canada, Sweden, and the U.S.A. was looked at with the U.S. ultimately being awarded the games. A short-lived proposition to share the games between the U.S. and Canada was looked at quickly and dropped due to logistical problems, sponsorship issues, and Canada's hopes for the 2007 Women's World Cup.

Once the venue of the U.S.A. was chosen (based largely on the reasonable infrastructure that still existed four years after the previous very successful 1999 event) Canada was able to continue their pre-tournament preparations with renewed purpose now in a familiar friendly North American environment (China got the tournament back for 2007, dashing Canada's hopes). Pellerud's main goal was to put the finishing touches on the team-a group of individuals that he began with four years earlier and, to that end, it was important to have them together in a camp format for the summer leading up to the September kick-off. They had qualified successfully at the Gold Cup the year before and now the business of PREPARATION was at hand.

The coach shares with us, here, his observations on the lead up and World Cup 2003 competition.

The summer was planned as a significant preparation for the Canadian Women's Team. The CSA and Pellerud wisely optimized the exposure for the women's team by playing in five of Canada's largest cities. The start was excellent as Canada ran off wins over England and Brazil in four July matches. Team confidence was building. The real job was in front of the coaching staff and the team now. Even Pellerud shares his daily thoughts on the team's progress and results during the 2003 World Cup.

Diary of Women's World Cup Preparation Camp

The following insights were provided by Even Pellerud, recorded in August and September of 2003 as the team prepared and competed in FIFA's WWC 2003.

Monday, August 18th
Following 5 days of camp in Vancouver
All players were available including four from WUSA
(Latham, Hooper, Nonen, and LeBlanc)

Brianna Boyd from the Carolina Courage was not playing in the play-offs for WUSA. She has been in camp, but is suffering from a concussion and had to go home for a rest. She is coming back later.

We were missing five players who were participating in the Pan-Am Games in the Dominican Republic. They are some of our younger players including Kristina Kiss and Taryn Swiatek. Because of the power problems in North America we are a little confused at the moment when the players are coming into camp. (There was a huge three-day blackout in the Northeastern U.S. and Southeastern Canada in mid-August 2003.)

We had a break in the camp, today, as well as a day off yesterday, Sunday the 17th. Today, Monday morning, we are heading to camp in Kelowna (British Columbia). The purpose of the five-day camp is to get the players familiar with each other and directly some soccer fitness. We have worked on individual technical skills, some physical adjustments over the summer at our Montreal, Ottawa, and Vancouver camps.

Now, we are heading into a camp where the objective is team building. Seven days with practices, but also with a lot of team building activities such as barbecues, fishing, concerts, and different activities in that environment.

From Kelowna on the 25th, we are heading to Edmonton for game preparation, playing Mexico in two games. The first in

Edmonton August 31st then heading to Vancouver to play Mexico in game number 2 on September 4th.

From September 5th to 11th we will have a break and send players home for some recovery. We will come together again on September 11th in Kingston for the last preparation game, which is against Australia September 14th.

We will stay together for the 15th, but we will have that day for restitution and some fun and then we will head down to Columbus on the 16th of September for the last couple of days of preparation before the big kick-off against Germany, September 20th.

Player Status

As previously mentioned, Brianna Boyd is suffering from a concussion. We are expecting her back in a couple of days, but she has had this concussion for four weeks now and she tried to come back here, but had to take some more days off and that is worrisome. She is a normal starter and a very important member of the team either as a fullback or a centreback. So we will see how we cope with that.

Isabelle Morneau is back after her shoulder surgery and is fighting hard to get a spot in the roster. It is a long shot for her, but she is a typical veteran giving everything she has. We will see how that goes in the next 14 days.

The final selection will be done September 5th.

Carmelina Moscato, midfielder, is still suffering from a foot fracture that she was unlucky enough to experience two weeks ago and she is out since she probably won't have enough time to recover from that. That's an injury that we can't control at the moment.

It's the same thing with Amber Allen (forward) who suffered an ACL injury in the game against Brazil in Montreal in July. She is crossed out because she will not have enough time to recuperate back to the team.

Christine Sinclair is suffering from mono. She has had three weeks off. I snuck her back and she has been looking great in this residential camp in Vancouver. She had worked very hard the 14 days before to get her fitness back and we will see how that works. We are very excited to have her back and she looks good. She looks sharp and that is important.

Kelowna Camp

We are now inviting a total of 23 players to join the Kelowna camp and that means that three players have to be cut by September 5th and that is going to be interesting.

First Kelowna Practice
August 18th, 2003

A couple of scary moments in practice.

In a scrimmage 6v6 Kara Lang had the ball and was going to pass it to a teammate and ended up blindly tackled by a defender. She got kicked and went down crying and screaming. We thought it might be a fracture. She never goes down. When she is down it's very serious. I think we all held our breath for a couple of minutes when the official assessed her injury and issued a water break in the middle of practice. I was waiting for Paolo's (Bordignon-the trainer) assessment. It turned out to be just a kick and soft tissue injury in the lower part of the leg and, of course, a lot of swelling and pain. So far, everything looks positive and she can start playing again. Ice and treatment.

Just before we started the practice Christine Sinclair went down in a 1v1 warm-up with Randee Hermus. She was hit in the face. We were kind of scared about a broken nose, chin, or jaw, but she came back in and everything was fine.

So our first practice in Kelowna was very scary and, as a coach of a World Cup Team, you are always nervous and concerned with balancing your practices, trying to build intensity and competitiveness to have the right level and, at the same time, always aware of an injury just days before the kick off to a big event. (It's a fine line creating a competitive team and avoiding injuring each other.)

Tuesday, August 19th, 2003
Day 2 of Camp in Kelowna

Practice was good today. There was more speed in the girls. More intensity, more passion. We were still working on team shape in the back four, mid-three or mid-four. Making the players ready for different formations and different approaches from game to game and in games.

No injuries today. We are still missing Sharolta Nonen and Charmaine Hooper who are playing in the Final Four for Atlanta (WUSA) on Sunday and coming sometime next week.

Brianna Boyd is still out with her concussion and, of course Breanna and Sharolta out affects the team shape because they are starters. But, it is a great opportunity to practice and play the back-up players in the same spots.

We used Candace Chapman, Clare Rustad, Sasha Andrews and Randee Hermus at the back today. Randee looks really sharp. I think the four of them are close to peeking, playing very close to their best level. The question will be, "will it be good enough at the highest level we are about to encounter".

Andrea Neil struggles with infected bruises on her foot so we are a little short in the midfield but Kristina Kiss came back in yesterday from the Pan-Am Games. She is of course a bit tired, but okay to go.

Linda Consolante (d) and Rhian Wilkinson (f) arrived this morning from the Pan-Am Games, also, and they will be good for us and provide more players in practices and it will be easier for me to work on team shape.

Wednesday, August 20th, 2003
Day 3 of Camp in Kelowna

Golf in the morning and practice in the afternoon.

The coaches had a discussion last evening about our first formal review of the roster. This discussion has been ongoing for a year, at least, since we qualified for the World Cup.

One of the conclusions was there is one player who needs to be released. We will let her go prior to our upcoming Sunday. She just isn't up to the standards, can't compete, is intimidated and will not be playing in the World Cup. We are also seriously considering writing a new addition to the roster, Katie Thorlakson (mf/f). She played well on the U19 team last year and has showed good progress in the Pan-Am Games. It is a tough decision to take for the player that has to be released and will be sent home, but those are the decisions you need to take if you are going to create the best chance to win.

Later...What a day!

Not a good day...well, it started well. Golf in the morning and players happy, staff happy. Three hours on the golf course, 9 holes, pretty course. Good performances, bad performances. Great fun.

We had lunch and a rest in our rooms before our practice at 4. Tanya Dennis (d/f) came in from Nebraska. Kara Lang went down again. Everything pointed to a broken leg. Same leg as before, same spot. Concerned staff, concerned players, concerned physiotherapist. She went to the hospital and came back 3 hours later with no fracture. Happy faces. The physiotherapist was very concerned but all the tests were negative.

Linda Consolante (d) went down in the middle of practice after a bad hit from another player. She went to the hospital and came back to the hotel with three stitches, a black eye, blue face, didn't look great at all. But, it ended up well.

Not one of those days you enjoy or appreciate as a coach.

Thursday, August 21st, 2003
Day 4

Nothing dramatic in practice today thank goodness. Warm-up, then work on defensive shape: 50 minutes, then finishing 20 minutes.

Andrea Neil and Kara Lang remained on the sideline. Other than that it was a live, fun practice. Good shooting. Good mood, good spirits.

At 4 we are scheduled to play a guy's team and we will see how we can play against them. We played 4-4-2 first half; 4-3-3 second half. We are looking at shape and formation in practice. I have one concern. I am a little bit concerned that Candace Chapman is my best stopper. I would ideally like to use her on the flank or as a fullback. Great talent. One of our best players-fast, good vision.

I hope that Sharolta Nonen, who comes in next Wednesday, and Brianna Boyd, who is back in after her concussion, can sort that out. I still have the suspicion today that Candace will be a stopper in the World Cup because Candace and Sharolta would be a great combination.

Brianna Boyd can play fullback. She has played there for Carolina all season so she can play there. So maybe it will sort itself out.

Randee Hermus is a good candidate for the left fullback position, also. In competition, we'll have all the players, of course, but at the moment it feels more to me that Candace ends up as a stopper in the upcoming World Cup.

Friday, August 22nd, 2003
Day 5

Quite an eventful camp, today. 300 forest fires around us and threatening residential houses a few kilometres away from the hotel. We had a boat cruise yesterday evening with the team but you didn't see much because of the smoke. It was all back around us and it was quite scary. Barbeque on the boat. A nice experience but, of course, we missed the site from the boat.

Today, we are again seriously discussing leaving Kelowna to go to Edmonton a couple days earlier than planned to avoid nervousness and fear in players here and in those trying to get in. The fires are a daily topic of discussion and parents of players are concerned.

It is described as a messy situation and we need to concentrate on our preparations.

We have made the decision to leave Kelowna tomorrow morning, Saturday, to go to Edmonton two days earlier because of the fire which is more and more going out of control and coming closer and closer to downtown Kelowna where we are. We are now heading into our last session.

The game against the boy's team. Great game yesterday. We had 500 spectators. We are expecting the same today.

We have more and more players getting back but we are still missing a few. Sinclair came in and I need to get more out of her and she is an accepted young leader in our team and she should know that is the case and this can be a symbol for her to get the captain band and see if that can lift her and lift her teammates another step.

We need more intensity, more speed, more enthusiasm in the team than we have had so far. It was great in the summer, we need it back and that starts today.

Friday Evening after the game against the guys

We won. I think we played an excellent game. I am very happy with the progress of the team but some sad news. We lost a player. We lost probably our best player right now, Candace Chapman with an ACL injury, and I just feel terrible for her. This talented, gifted defender/midfielder that has progressed so much and is now out of the camp and it is a bad feeling.

This was supposed to be a nice team building week, but today we feel we are recreating the town problems (fires) with all of our own small disasters. We all go up to the seventh floor looking up at the hills around Kelowna we see the fires streaking down the hills. I don't know what to say. It's coming in our direction pretty fast. It is pretty scary and we are now leaving the hotel in a few hours and going to the airport.

There are rumors that the airport is closed. What would happen then, we don't know, but we would probably find our way to another city and rent another bus. At the moment we have the team bus outside. Our driver is a volunteer from Kelowna. He is a soccer guy on vacation but concerned about the safety of his home himself so we don't know if he is able to drive with us this night.

Just to be prepared we have another set of keys for the bus and we have a licensed bus driver, Ian Bridge our assistant coach. That should be interesting.

Preliminary testing of Candace Chapman's knee: so far no certain signs of ACL but that doesn't mean it isn't ACL. She is up trying to walk on it. Our physio is doing an amazing job with her helping her come back. We will see tomorrow. Tomorrow she will go for tests. I think meniscus or something serious is damaged in that knee for sure. The question is how much and how long will the recovery time be.

The players have been great. They appreciated our plans and team building events. We now have a team project to evacuate from the hotels and fires. Everything is packed. Everything is on the bus. We will get another couple of hours of sleep, hopefully, before we head for Edmonton tomorrow morning or early tonight- we are ready to escape the forest fires in BC, the summer of 2003.

Sunday, August 24th, 2003
Day 7 -- Edmonton

We came here, yesterday, after fleeing the fires in Kelowna the day before. It turned out to be excellent timing getting away at the Kelowna airport. Just after we departed, Saturday morning, the airport was closed down because of threatening fires. And, we are happy to be in Edmonton.
We are working with further tests on Candace Chapman.

Rudy Gittens (CSA medical director and orthopaedic surgeon) was in Finland for a FIFA committee meeting and we are sending Candace back to Toronto for surgery as fast as possible.

There will be meniscus surgery for sure and the chances for her playing in the World Cup are slimmer than slim. But, we are keeping it quiet. We are not expecting anything positive but we are hoping and we will do our best to get her back as soon as possible, World Cup or not.

Monday, August 25th, 2003

The situation with all the events around the team concerns me. It is not good right now. We have been through a lot in a year. We have had good results, good performances, good health situation, no medical problems. And now, we are having all sorts of problems. It's coming all at once and we have a job preparing for the tournament in front of us.

Candace Chapman is back in Toronto to see a surgeon. We have a lot of other problems, as well.

Silvana Burtini (veteran forward and all-position player) may have release problems with the police force in Vancouver, where she works. Sharolta Nonen has hamstring problems coming into camp after the WUSA final and can't practice. Goalkeepers are okay.

Kara Lang has not trained yet. Andrea Neil has not trained yet. Both have short-term problems, but still annoying-hard to predict.

Many of the players have minor problems. They are still training and training hard but they are tired all the time.

Brianna Boyd came up to camp today from Calgary, but cannot train until she has seen her doctor for her concussion assessment. That takes place on Thursday.

My main concern is the situation in the back. It worries me a little bit that a brand new player, Tanya Dennis, is, at the moment, considered to be a starter. She has never been in before. She is a newly selected 18-year-old and the fact that she is considered to be a starter reflects the injury situation. Normally a forward we've turned her into a defender and she has to face all of these expectations and the pressure of being a starter.

Just now Christine Sinclair came into my room to have a meeting. Her coach in Portland, Clive Charles, is reportedly very, very ill with cancer and they are expecting him to pass away in a day or two and Christine will go back for his funeral on Sunday.

With Brianna Boyd's concussion problems and Sharolta Nonen's hamstring problems we have a lack of pace in the back four. The most experienced player by far at the moment is Randee Hermus. Isabelle Morneau is also there competing for a spot and recovering from her surgery so she still has a long way to go before she is a starter on this team.

We need to take a little break here, from a practice standpoint, and go fewer practices. Let the players recover. Hopefully that will help the health situation.

I just hope that will change in time before the real work-up to the World Cup begins.

Tuesday, August 26, 2003
Day 9

In the season so far, the smoothest season of my life, the changes, the fires, the travel, the injuries, they take the form off our very good results this season.

Sharolta Nonen is asking to come later to camp on Friday, instead of Wednesday, because of several reasons, from being sick to being mentally drained to her hamstring. Christine Sinclair just came to see me. Her coach from Portland, Clive Charles, passed away and she wants to go back immediately to see her friends in Portland, which I think is a bad idea, but she is emotional about this and we will see what happens. This is definitely a very bad idea from a team perspective. It's difficult because this seems personally important for her. I have to discuss with the staff. Not an easy decision in the middle of so many challenges.

Wednesday, August 27th, 2003
Day 10

Another eventful day from a bad start to a good finish.

The bad start came with Sharolta Nonen and Charmaine Hooper expected to land and attend camp. The team manager went out to the airport and nobody showed up. After a long time Charmaine came without luggage and she still has no luggage. She came to practice and did a great job. A great inspiration to have her back. Sharolta Nonen never showed up. She was still sick back in Atlanta and we are still waiting for her to attend, hopefully tomorrow.

A great practice this afternoon. Very inspired, very concentrated, very interesting for me as a coach. A lot of skills demonstrated, a lot of speed. Very fun to watch, very inspirational. Practice from all girls great. It made all the staff very happy and we are back in business from that standpoint. Still no word on Silvana Burtini on her job commitment.

Brianna Boyd is back in Calgary for a doctor's appointment about her concussion. She will be reporting back to camp tomorrow and we will know tomorrow (Thursday).

Candace Chapman had her MRI in Toronto, today. We are expecting the results tomorrow-expecting bad news, but let's wait and see.

We went to a fundraiser supper at the West Edmonton Mall today. Two hundred and fifty kids showed up. Very good event. Happy, excited young girls coming to see our players. We stayed there from 6:30-9:30 and it was a great event for everyone. Happy players back on the bus, they sense the build up and things seem to change in a positive way despite the problems we have gone through.

Thursday morning, August 28th, 2003
Day 11

It is now early. I've had a short workout on my bike, and am sitting in my room with my note pad and jotting about possible line-ups for our game on Sunday against Mexico here in Edmonton. I'm looking forward to the work up and seeing the difference in areas we've worked on coming for the upcoming game on Sunday.

The back four: Tanya Dennis, Randee Hermus, Charmaine Hooper and Brittany Timko is a newly composed back four. Brianna Boyd is out, Candace Chapman is out, and probably Sharolta Nonen out. So I need to be creative on this one.

We are now approaching the tactical/technical preparation. This fall camp for two to three weeks before the world's biggest women's soccer event is where it all has to come together. The problems have to be worked out now and the team fully prepared. We are recovering and tweaking once the tournament starts so now is the time to get things right.

First we look at where we are physically. One level is general fitness. The second level is soccer fitness. And the third ultimate goal is game fitness. All three things have been on the agenda for the last six weeks working up to the World Cup and it's our job as a staff to build them and peak them for the WWC. Our general fitness at the moment is right where we want it. Most of the players have been working hard for years. With the addition of younger players they have not been through the same machine, but they are at least playing in pretty high-level environments. The general fitness is good. All test results are strong. Soccer fitness is also, if not peaking, getting there. We have a good summer behind us with good results, strong performances, consistent play, and the soccer fitness is good. Game fitness is taken care of during the spring and summer games and they have proved to be great. Now it is more about getting players recovered from injuries, building them up again in a balanced way so they can peak in a few weeks.

Friday, August 29th, 2003
Day 12 -- Edmonton
Technical/tactical practice

Our warm-up was a combination of runs, stretching, sprints, and long ball passing.

The next half-hour was played on a field 90m x 55m (shorter than normal field size). The coaching session was with 9 players plus a goalkeeper. Back four, three midfielders, plus two strikers with focus on defending shape in midfield and in the back. Main priority is how to shape up when the fullbacks are challenged to play on the ball wide. Cover from inside from stopper. Cover the other side from the midfielder, create a "sandwich" to make the fullback constantly going in hard to win the ball on the sides.

The last 30 minutes a shorter field but same width. 4-3-1 formation and coached with the same priorities, but in a match speed situation-competitive or game situation, competitive with shorter field, so situations are coming faster and quicker and the players need to react in kind to manage the situation. Special priority, again, on the back four shape.

Also in the 30 minutes before that, I implemented different situations with balls coming in from different locations. We are slowly but surely working through a game, game shape and line-up and I use different players in different position to see who is best fit on Sunday's game.

A very typical tactical practice and a set up I use a lot.

Evening

Quite a day. I has been a great day with the team. Everything felt good. A good practice. Great spirit. Team meeting at 5. We went through the style. We went through scripts from games against Mexico and also from our recent games against Brazil. Our playing style and guidelines. Great response. Happy players.

I was called into a meeting with executive committee, vice-president, president, and chief operating officer (of the CSA) telling me that the men's coach and technical director, Holger Osieck, was going to be resigning. They are all here in Edmonton. Apparently they will be selecting a new men's coach coming in soon with new plans for the future so we can't ever escape the politics.

Our old team manager Kathy came back to the team after having time off to marry and the staff was very glad for her and celebrated that event for her by inviting her for dinner. We came back to the hotel and I met the president, Andy Sharpe, in the lobby. We had a couple of beers together and talked, again, about the recent events and the support for the women's team and the banquet last night.

Tomorrow (Saturday) we have a practice at 2. Before that, at 10 o'clock I will meet the Alberta Soccer Associations' coaches with my coaches and spend an hour talking soccer with them. This is something I feel is important and we should do more of.

Saturday, August 30th, 2003
Day 13 -- Edmonton
Day before game

I am pumped up now. The real goal is two weeks away. Healthy players. Many players. All 19 players in camp are available. 15 plus the goalkeepers. The only player on the sideline is Brianna Boyd with her concussion. Everything looks good with her. She will soon be able to play I hope.

Practice:

Warm-up -- a combination of runs, extensions, stretches and normal passing, 20 minutes.

20 minutes, Individual technique. I set up posts by myself. Corner kicks. Set up in the box for corner kicks. First post headers - Sinclair. Second post headers - Lang. Services from left - Kristina Kiss inswingers from right. Charmaine Hooper and Brittany Timko from left.

Long-ball passing - Matheson, Tanya Dennis, Lynda Consolante, and Sasha Andrews. Finishing - the rest of the group against the goalies, 20 minutes of individual skills based on position on the field and the confidence they need in the game.

Scrimmage - 11 vs 11 including deadball situations and tactical information 30-40 minutes.

We finished off with a shooting competition. 20 minutes "Bending far corner shots". We introduced some technical and tactical pointers on how to shoot. It is my experience in the women's game over the years that the female goalkeepers are not as tall as male goalkeepers, making them more vulnerable to shots in the far corner. The goals are as big, but the players are smaller, so we are working again on forcing the plays and encouraging them to use bending shots in the far corner. They're hard for the female goalkeepers to reach.

Sunday, August 31st, 2003
Game Day against Mexico Game Number 1

Some exciting news from yesterday. I had a managing problem with the day staff and we finally have a solution. I received the board's approval yesterday to do something with our situation. That is really good news and the whole team is looking forward to that. I am hoping the change can allow us to give the players a full work-up as well.

The line up for the game today will be minus 3 starting defenders (Nonen, Boyd, and Chapman). We had to compose a new back four. This will be Tanya Dennis, Randee Hermus, Charmaine Hooper (first game as a defender), and Brittany Timko (second game as a defender). I hope that will go well. It's exciting and you need some guts to do that type of position change but I think the players are up for it.

Karina (LeBlanc) will be in goal. The midfield three - Kiss, Matheson, Neil. Up front - Lang, Latham, Sinclair.

Evening

Canada 8 Mexico 0

Of course a disappointing Mexican team performance (what coach is ever entirely happy with any result) but, at the same time, of course, an excellent performance from Canada. Very dynamic. Very lively. Strong performance from the strikers. Charmaine Hooper was a defender for the first half, striker second half. Good team performance. Very consistent.

We think that this will force Mexico to bring in some new players for the Mexico/Canada game in Vancouver on Thursday, so we look forward to that.

All the players got in to play today. Only Sharolta Nonen (injured) and goalkeeper Taryn Swiatek didn't see the field. All the others got in and that's important.

Our starting line-up today was: Dennis, Hooper, Hermus, Timko in defense, Kiss, Matheson, Neil at midfield, and Lang, Latham, Sinclair up front.

Second half, Consolante came in as stopper. Charmaine Hooper up front for Kara Lang.

Five more subs. Sasha Andrews for Randee Hermus. Rhian Wilkinson for Latham. Clare Rustad for Timko. Isabelle Morneau for Neil.

Same formation for the whole game - 4:3:3

For most games, players who are not playing at all or are playing less than one half are working out with our assistant coaches on the side of the field or after the game so they always go home with a little bit of feeling that they have been active and they have been doing exercises so they can always be focused and feel fit. Everyone has to be fully prepared now.

Monday, September 1st (Labor Day)
Day 15

Today we flew from Edmonton to Vancouver to prepare for the second Mexico game on the 4th. We arrived in our new hotel in Vancouver. The players are happy, relaxed, focused and having a quiet afternoon session-recovery, restitution from last game.

Tuesday, September 2nd
Day 16

Mexico is bringing in a couple new players. They were not happy with the performance in Edmonton and my colleague in Mexico is upset with their performance and effort last night.

It is good for us though because I think we will have quite another opposition on Thursday and we should be good for all preparations for World Cup.

I have a difficult leadership situation to deal with. I will have to let my manager go and that decision and talk has to come up by Thursday. We have changed the manager now and that decision is taken. I'm not looking forward to it. To release a player is always tough. To release a staff member is harder. This person has done a good job for us but there have been too many smaller than bigger problems over the years that have been incriminating and I have to deal with all the staff members to keep them focused. I will do what I have to do in order to have a focused staff and players entering the World Cup.

Wednesday, September 3rd
Day 17

The day before the game. Again, players relaxed and focused. Practicing at the main stadium in Swangard. Always a challenge to come in and deal with cities. But, we're feeling good and we had a good practice. More work on shape and dead ball situations.

Thursday, September 4th
Day 18

I am not as focused as I should be or normally am due to the change in managers. I have to deal with this situation when we are playing an important preparation game. The players are heading home almost immediately following the game and at the same time I will have a meeting with my new manager. Our exiting manager has worked hard for four years to qualify for the World Cup staff, as have all the staff members, but changes are a part of this game, as emotionally tough as they can be.

From the 5th - 11th of September the players went home to recover and carry on their workouts with direction from me. Not too much hard training. More focus on recovery/mental training and being ready. Sprints, touch the ball, and come back happy and recharged.

The staff and myself have to deal with the selection problem and one of them is Carmelina Moscato. Whether she is ready or not to come in with her bone fracture.

Monday September 8th
WWC Team Roster Announced

Morgan Quarry and Richard Ivan, CSA media, prepared the following press release for the 4th Women's World Cup. Canada's third qualification.

Canadian Women's World Cup Team

Canadian Women's World Cup Team Head Coach Even Pellerud announced his 20-player roster for the upcoming FIFA Women's World Cup in the United States on September 8th, 2003.

Silvana Burtini, Isabelle Morneau, Andrea Neil and Charmaine Hooper have been selected to their third consecutive World Cup while Sharolta Nonen and Karina LeBlanc are the only other players who have World Cup experience, having played in 1999 in the United States. Morneau was named to the 1995 squad in Sweden but did not play in any games while LeBlanc backed up Nicci Wright in goal in1999 in the United States.

There are six players from the Under-19 team which won a silver medal at the FIFA Women's World Championship in 2002: Christine Sinclair, Erin McLeod, Sasha Andrews, Carmelina Moscato, Kara Lang and Brittany Timko.

Others include 18-year-old defender Tanya Dennis who impressed in earning her first two caps against Mexico recently; WUSA defender Sharolta Nonen (who was named to the All WUSA First Team), Randee

Hermus and Kristina Kiss who play for Floya in Norway, 19-year-old Diana Matheson who earned her first cap earlier this year, goalkeeper Taryn Swiatek who played for Canada at the PanAm Games and striker Rhian Wilkinson who made her debut against the US in April. Christine Latham, the WUSA Rookie of the Year, rounds out the squad.

Goalkeepers: Karina LeBlanc is coming off a fine WUSA season where she was named a finalist for Goalkeeper of the Year and led the league in saves. She was also twice named the WUSA Player of the Week. She had a stellar career at the University of Nebraska and has played two seasons with the Boston Breakers.

Erin McLeod shot to prominence with a strong showing at the FIFA Under-19 Women's World Championships in Edmonton in 2002 where she helped Canada win a silver medal. McLeod was named to the tournament all-star team and became a fan favourite in Edmonton with her hairdos.

Taryn Swiatek attended the University of Calgary and has played two seasons with the Ottawa Fury of the W-League. She was Canada's No. 1 goalkeeper at the 2003 PanAm Games and led Canada to a silver medal.

Defenders: Sharolta Nonen is the experienced defender, having played at the 1999 World Cup. She is also coming off her finest WUSA season, being named to the All WUSA First Team in her third season with the Atlanta Beat. She has been capped 45 times for Canada and has scored one goal.

Tanya Dennis is the newcomer to this group. Only capped three times, Dennis impressed head coach Even Pellerud in the few games she has played to earn a berth on the World Cup squad. She is extremely fast and is a regular on the Canadian under-19 team. She has played at right back and in the middle of the back four for Pellerud.

Silvana Burtini has been converted from her normal position at striker and has played at left back and on the left side of midfield for Pellerud in recent games. Burtini has had an exemplary international career, scoring 38 goals in 74 games, third all-time in goals and caps. She once scored eight goals against Puerto Rico in 1998. She played one season in WUSA with Carolina and is now a police officer in British Columbia.

Sasha Andrews played a prominent role with the Under-19 team in 2002 and scored the winning penalty against Brazil in the FIFA Under-19 Women's World Championship semi-final last year. A native of Edmonton, Andrews is one of Canada's more dominant players in the air and has recently shown an eye for goal, scoring a goal in each of the lopsided wins over Mexico.

The wild card in the defense is captain Charmaine Hooper, only because she has started the last three games in this position and the Canadian team is loaded up front. Hooper had never played defense in her first 98 appearances for Canada, but that all changed in Edmonton on August 31st, 2003, when Pellerud started her in the middle of the back four. She then moved back up to striker. It remains to be seen where she will play in the World Cup.

Brittany Timko could see some playing time at fullback or in the middle of the pack. Timko became a regular member of Pellerud's squad following the FIFA Under-19 tournament where her fierce tackling and solid play earned her many admirers. She had a very strong Gold Cup in 2002 and Pellerud will no doubt rely on her versatility.

Randee Hermus made her debut with the World Cup team at the same time as Pellerud, making her first appearance at the 2000 Algarve Cup. She has played in the majority of Pellerud's games as head coach of the Canadian team, earning 44 caps in less than four years. She scored game-winning goals in both victories over Brazil in July. She usually plays at left back but can also play in central defense. She is still recovering from a stress fracture in her leg but will stay with the team throughout the tournament in the hopes of taking part at some point in the competition.

The veteran of the back four is Isabelle Morneau, who is appearing in her third straight World Cup. She was named to the 1995 squad and did not play but was a regular of the 1999 team. Morneau has recovered from a bad shoulder which caused her to miss the 2002 Gold Cup and part of the 2003 Algarve Cup. She had surgery in the spring and is now fit to bring her steadying influence to the left side of the defense.

Linda Consolante is a relative newcomer to the team, having earned only three caps since making her debut against Brazil on July 20. She is predominantly a centre back and plays with the Ottawa Fury of the W-League.

Midfielders: Pellerud has been playing a 4-3-3 in recent games with Andrea Neil and Kristina Kiss and Biana Matheson likely to figure in the middle of the pack with Timko, Carmelina Moscato and Burtini all able to play there as well.

Andrea Neil is one of the team's leaders and she will rely on the experience of two previous World Cups as she drives the team to success in the 2003 tournament. Neil is a player who commands respect and her 18 goals in 87 appearances is a testament to her abilities. She is a 13-year veteran and is second only to Hooper in appearances for Canada. She is a ball winner in the midfield and her determination can be inspiring.

Diana Matheson burst on to the national team scene in 2003 and hasn't stopped. She has earned a remarkable 13 caps in less than seven months as a member of the national team after impressing Pellerud at a National Training Centre. Matheson may stand only 5'2 but she has the heart of a lion and is extremely tenacious. She has been a revelation in recent months and her vision for one with so few caps is striking.

Kristina Kiss has become a player to be reckoned with and has built up a solid reputation as a free kick specialist. Hampered by injuries in the past year, Kiss has emerged as one of Pellerud's regular starters in the buildup to the World Cup. She is a threat from anywhere around the 18-yard box and is one of the team's better players at splitting defenses with her passing and vision.

Carmelina Moscato is recovering from stress fractures in both feet, which caused her to miss several preparation games this summer. Moscato played a starring role during the FIFA Under-19 Championship last summer and followed that success by getting a lot of playing time in the 2002 Gold Cup.
Forwards: It's probably safe to say that Pellerud has an abundance of riches up front. His strikers are probably the envy of every coach at the World Cup. Even if Hooper (who has scored more goals for Canada than any other player-58) plays defense, Pellerud can throw Christine Sinclair, Christine Latham, Kara Lang and impressive rookie Rhian Wilkinson at the world's best defenses.

Sinclair had an almost impossible to believe year in 2002. She was the MVP at the FIFA Under-19 Women's World Championship after scoring a tournament-leading 10 goals in six games and then went on to score the golden goal in the NCAA championship game, winning the University of Portland its first national title. She was named the Globe and Mail's Top 25 influential sports figures in December of that year. She reached 40 goals in an astonishing 49 games earlier this year and has fully recovered from a bout of mono which sidelined her for two months.

Christine Latham returned to the National Team in 2003 after not playing in 2002 to focus on her scholastic studies. She ended an impressive career at the University of Nebraska by being signed as a discovery player by the San Diego Spirit and went on to be named the league's Rookie of the Year in 2003. Her aggressive style combined with her touch around goal makes her a player to be feared.

Kara Lang burst onto the National Team in 2002 at the Algarve Cup as a 15-year-old and scored goals in bundles. She hasn't stopped scoring and has a tendency for the spectacular. Despite her youth, Lang possesses one of the strongest legs in the game and remarkably can hit with power from distance with either foot. She has played wide and up front for both Under-19 team head coach Ian Bridge and Pellerud, and has remarkable confidence considering her age. She can be a menace to defenders when she runs at them.

Rhian Wilkinson earned her first start for Canada in their last friendly prior to the World Cup on September 14th against Australia and caused a stir. Her strong runs off the ball and her deceiving pace have given Pellerud yet another option up front. Wilkinson has already managed three goals in her first six appearances and seems destined for a bright future.

"We have a strong roster with a good balance of youth and experience," said Pellerud. "We have also a good mixture of speed, skill and leadership. It's a very flexible and versatile roster which can be changed to play certain formations. We are ready to play the way that is needed depending on the opponent. It's a team with an excellent fitness level and a healthy level of confidence."

The Canadians are coming off a 2-0 win over Australia on September 14 and consecutive victories over Mexico (by a combined 14-0). Canada has registered three consecutive shutouts and have not lost in 10 games, dating back to a last-minute friendly against the United States on April 26th. Since then they have won nine games (win over Australia, two-game series sweeps over Mexico-twice, England and Brazil) and drawn once (1-1 against Ghana on August 16).

Canada has played six World Cup games, in 1995 and 1999, losing four and drawing twice.

Canadian Women's World Cup Team Roster

Name	Pos	Hometown	D.O.B.	Caps	G/S	Club
Sasha Andrews	D	Edmonton, AB	14/2/83	18	2	Vancouver Whitecaps/U. of Nebraska
Silvana Burtini	D/F	Williamson Lake, BC	10/5/69	73	38	Unattached
Linda Consolante	D	Montreal, QC	23/5/82	3	0	Ottawa Fury
Tanya Dennis	D	Brampton, ON	26/8/85	2	0	U. of Nebraska
Randee Hermus	D	Langley, BC	14/11/79	44	4	Floya (Norwegian Premier)
Charmaine Hooper	D/F	Ottawa, ON	15/1/68	100	57	Atlanta Beat
Kristina Kiss	M	Ottawa, ON	24/3/81	43	5	Floya (Norwegian Premier)
Kara Lang	F	Oakville, ON	22/10/86	29	19	Vancouver Whitecaps
Christine Latham	F	Calgary, AB	15/9/81	28	9	San Diego Spirit
Karina LeBlanc	GK	Maple Ridge, BC	30/3/80	33	12	Boston Breakers
Diana Matheson	M	Oakville, ON	6/4/84	12	1	Toronto Inferno
Erin McLeod	GK	Calgary, AB	26/2/83	12	3	Vancouver Whitecaps/SMU
Isabelle Morneau	D	Greenfield Park, QC	28/4/76	57	6	Ottawa Fury
Carmelina Moscato	M	Mississauga, ON	2/5/84	14	1	Vancouver Whitecaps
Andrea Neil	M	Vancouver, BC	26/10/71	86	18	Vancouver Whitecaps
Sharolta Nonen	D	Vancouver, BC	30/12/77	44	1	Atlanta Beat
Christine Sinclair	F	Burnaby, BC	12/6/83	50	39	Vancouver Whitecaps/U. of Portland
Taryn Swiatek	GK	Calgary, AB	4/2/81	5	2	Ottawa Fury
Brittany Timko	M	Coquitlam, BC	5/9/85	21	0	Vancouver Whitecaps/U. of Nebraska
Rhian Wilkinson	M/F	Baie D'Urfe, QC	12/5/82	5	2	Ottawa Fury/ U. of Tennessee

Staff

Les Wilkinson	Head of Delegation
Even Pellerud	Head Coach
Ian Bridge	Assistant Coach
Shel Brodsgaard	Goalkeeper Coach
Paolo Bordignon	Athletic Therapist
Cathy Campbell	Team Doctor
Jamie Fales	Equipment Manager
Kim Sebrango	Manager
Bob Birarda	Scout
Holly Mair	Massage Therapist
Morgan Quarry	Media Officer

* Addendum

Injured starters out of tournament:	Candace Chapman	D
	Brianna Boyd	D
Other injured outs/doubtfuls:	Amber Allen	F
	Carmelina Moscato	M
	Randee Hermus	D

Veteran Isabelle Morneau meeting the press

The team in its last home warm up before WWC2003

Pellerud

The press conference - WWC 2003

Even Pellerud making a coaching point

Future Canadian Nationals watching Canada prepare

September 11th
Kingston

Carmelina Moscato is coming back from a bone fracture. Is there time enough to count on her as a healthy player? Brianna Boyd with concussion, still a question mark. She is still recovering and being monitored by a doctor in Calgary on a day-by-day basis. If no considerable improvement she will be replaced by Linda Consolante, who reported to camp yesterday and is ready to go. Now Randee Hermus with a pain in her legs with a possible fracture. Not training yet.

The practice yesterday, the first practice of four before heading to Kingston for the Australian game we are not training Randee; partly training Carmelina, half an hour only, on a positive note Sharolta Nonen looked stronger and better than last time, in Vancouver. She was in the entire practice.

The numbers mean I still have to look into Charmaine Hooper as a defender for this camp. There is much to do but she knows the game.

Practice

One and a half hours, starting late from 7:30-9:00. The first half hour was a warm-up of skills, passing. Then we split into two groups for free kicks from the side pylons. Charmaine Hooper will be very dangerous. She is accurate and strong. In the south end, connecting passes, flicked to the sides, flick behind, running to the ball or crossing for a finish.

The third part, 8v8, short wide field. Good sharp 50 minutes.

September 12th, 2003
Practice at Kingston

Two hours practice on a bad, dry field. Long grass. Disappointing preparations for the last camp. The match facility is nice enough, but playing surface is decent, at best.

First, a warm-up 10v5 passing, regaining the ball. Sprints.

Second, we split into two groups. I worked on the defenders' ability to read, when to drop down, when to stand high. Key triggers for dropping down. Right to midfielder challenging defense combined with diagonal runs, drop down, tuck in, force the ball to go wide.

Third, for 20-25 minutes we worked on crosses and finishing.

Fourth, we worked on team shape the back four plus goalkeeper and three midfielders. We combined attacking patterns with counter attacks with wide left and right. 45 minutes.

We finished off with a shooting practice, 15 minutes, Old versus Young. A surprisingly easy win for the young team-the "old" team wins 9 out of 10 competitions.

September 13th, 2003

Practice at the Stadium -- Kingston

Plans are changing because the back four is not great and still needs big improvement. So the practice that was supposed to be 20-25 minutes on shape, turned out to be an hour on defensive shape. This was very much needed as it was a big concern the day before. We solved some problems in this practice, and I was pleased with the improvement from Sharolta and Charmaine in the middle (center back).

I had a problem with getting information through to Taryn (Swiatek), which confused her, and frustrated her and made her confidence go down, but she will gain from this. She will grow after this exercise. And, we can't leave this alone. The goalkeeper has to know what we want.

We finished off the practice with some shooting. The players were smiling and cheering and laughing and having fun. It lasted about two hours. We also included some dead ball situations after the team shape.

Saturday Evening
Team Meeting at 6PM -- Kingston

In my motivational speech to the group before heading into our last preparation game and World Cup.

I highlighted:

a) The preparations we have gone through - what we have done, lifestyle, priorities, soccer lifestyle. Injuries, sickness, out of shape, out of form, good performances and bad performances. Fitness, team building. Friendship, travel. Challenges on and off the field. Playing style. I highlighted the sacrifices of the players. Why they are here. Why they have been selected to go to a big event like the World Cup.

b) How great soccer as a sport is. How great top performance lifestyle is for these players. The opportunity to get recognized and to realize their dreams as people and players. The friendship, the team spirit. The challenges. The opportunity to take the best of themselves as individuals. The ability to achieve something for Canada.

c) I also highlighted that going into the World Cup, you never know if you will achieve your dreams or not. And what would happen with the media and pressure we are facing now after our summer successes. How we have to handle it as a team if we play well and if we do not play well.

It was more or less to let them feel good about themselves by the preparations we have been through, the camps we have finished, and let them feel good about being selected to play for one of the best teams in the world, we believe, and let them feel mentally relaxed going into the World Cup. We have prepared and stayed focused for one thing and that is the first game against Germany.

It turned out to be a success. I finished off with a movie about the team. 10 minutes.

We decided to play the game against Australia with some starting players not in our planned starting line-up to hide from potential German spies. We started the game without Diana Matheson in midfield. Christine Latham played the first half and Christine Sinclair played the second half. Now the game is on and every edge is important for the upcoming WC tournament.

Sunday, September 14th, 2003
Game Day-Kingston

The crowd is great-sold out. Our last warm-up game. Beautiful day, but steady wind near the lake.

Starting line-up: Goalkeeper: Karina LeBlanc; Defenders: Tanya Dennis, Sharolta Nonen, Charmaine Hooper, Silvana Burtini; Midfielders: Kiss, Timko, Neil; up front: Wilkinson, Lang, Latham.

Substitutes decided before kick-off: Sinclair second half for Latham.

A good, very intensive first half. We created a lot of good chances, but no scoring. Australia also had a couple, but we totally dominated the game. There was high pressure, high intensity, good focus, good concentration level. Very good performance from Neil, Wilkinson and the whole gang really.

Strong wind for us in the first half. Strong wind against us in the second half. The first half ended 0-0. We were a little concerned with the wind against us in the second half, but we dominated even more than in the first half and scored two good goals--one off a corner kick by Charmaine Hooper with a great header on the far post; the second goal when Rhian Wilkinson won the ball from a defender and scored herself. After that we started to sub a lot of players in. Timko was moved to left full back for Burtini, Matheson put in for Timko. Charmaine Hooper went up front for Lang. Sasha Andrews in as a stopper. Kristina Kiss then had an injury and I moved Timko into her spot again in midfield and Isabelle Morneau at the back.

In the finishing minutes Taryn Swiatek in for Karina LeBlanc.

Good game. Good performance. Great, solid shape performance. I saw a lot of what I wanted to see-what we were working on.

Monday, September 15th, 2003
Day off - Players shopping, resting.

The World Cup Tournament

Tuesday, September 16th, 2003 - Leave for Columbus.

I have decided to call Clare Rustad to Columbus just in case we don't have Brianna Boyd and Randee Hermus (everything points in that direction). Rustad has come into Columbus, today.

Later, Brianna Boyd had a doctor's appointment and had a very negative result. She will not play in the World Cup and has now officially been replaced by Linda Consolante.

We came into Columbus at 6:00 with a practice at 7:15 to 9:00. Great facility.

Warm-up - Technical: skills, sprints. Players looked very sharp.

Team Shape and Defense 4 + 2 midfielders, same thing as in Kingston on Saturday. Very sharp defensive shape with LeBlanc, Tanya Dennis, Sharolta Nonen, Charmaine Hooper and, this time, Brittany Timko as left fullback, she did very well.

We had some finishing and then some sprints and the mood is good. Spirits are high, and things look good. We feel more set.

As coaches we are concerned about players not starting due to injuries; is our defense strong enough with so many defenders out with injuries (Boyd/Chapman/Hermus); possible reduced performance due to short recovery or work commitments (Morneau/Nonen/Burtini)

Wednesday, September 17th, 2003
Practice-Columbus, OH, U.S.A.

After a sharp, intense practice yesterday, today's practice was very disappointing. Slow players. They looked tired, indifferent, and I was quite upset by the practice. We had a meeting tonight and I addressed the issue and demanded another approach tomorrow and on Friday to be prepared for this big game on Saturday.

Morgan Quarry, media coordinator in the CSA, spoke to the players about dealing with the media and possible media angles for this World Cup. One concern was the talk of expectations and just being prepared for those types of questions. We agreed that as our "general approach in the group games there is an ambition to go through to the quarterfinals. That is realistic, challenging, and reasonable for a team that hasn't won a game in any World Cup before. With the good run we have had this spring and summer, and recent results, with the increased media attention, Canadian soccer fans' raised expectations of the team we need to have the guts to say to the media, "We are ready to go on, we are good enough to go to the quarterfinals and then we live with that pressure." At the same time there is no reason to go to the media and say, "We are going for gold." That could come back to haunt us later. We may believe and should believe that (and I am thinking this way more). We know that internally the players are hungry, ambitious. We know anything can happen. But, to the media we should have an approach that is a little more humble in expectations for the World Cup.

Now our main focus is game-by-game and the next game is against Germany on Saturday.

Thursday, September 18th, 2003
Columbus, OH

A quiet morning. We (the coaches) have done some work analyzing the German team's playing style, taping and extracting some clips from the Germany/Czech Republic game a couple of weeks ago. We will show it to the players at 3:30 before our own practice.

We are still waiting for a tape of the last game against England where they had a full team. It is supposed to come in Friday morning and this will end our preparations.

After practice - Good, sharp practice; one hour, forty-five minutes. A lot of skills, long ball passing and then an exercise in passing, cross balls into the box around some strikers and finishing. We work on first balls, second balls, third balls. Good for goalkeepers, as well.

We finished with 11v11 on a short 80m long field and full width (65mm). We did as we often did-filled positions with staff members and based on our team shape and Germany's shape and possible starting line-up for Saturday's game.

The staff is taking Mr. Bridge out for dinner. He is 44 years old today.

Friday, September 19th, 2003
Evening before kick-off against Germany
World Cup 2003

A quiet day for the team. Bowling in the morning, after breakfast. The coaches mostly spending the time in the morning and noontime waiting for Germany/England tape to arrive from Germany. It will be converted to the American system this morning, then sent to the hotel where Ian, Shel and myself will watch it.

The tape is armed and ready, we made a scripted edition for the players and we showed it between 1 and 4pm.
Practice at the stadium - 50 minutes. A lot of media present. German, Canadian, American media. Coming to a beautiful soccer-based stadium at Columbus. We have heard there may be 22,000 seats sold for tomorrow. The practice itself is on a beautiful pitch.

Warm-up was just moving the ball around, stretching, passing, juggling the ball, fun in the mid circle.

Then we moved to long ball passing across some bodies. Bridge and myself in between passing the ball and then the players crossing the ball over the top of our heads.

From there we went to three groups. One group working on finishing with the strikers. Another group working on set plays Sharolta Nonen, Andrea Neil, Kristina Kiss, and Silvana Burtini - corner kicks. The third group was based on defensive plays and covering in the back four. Balls into the box, fight in the air and cover for each other for penetrating runs.

That was 20 minutes in three groups based on the specific skills and qualities. Game-related.

We finished the practice with a dead ball situation, the defensive zone, defensive corner kicks, defensive walls, defensive free kick set-ups. The offensive part was taken care of yesterday. Today was the defensive approach.

We went back to the hotel for a team dinner and meeting at 8 o'clock where we went through the Germany game against England. The scripts were presented for the girls. Here are the German strengths and weaknesses. On game day, tomorrow, we will sit down in groups (defenders and goalkeepers in one group, midfielders in one group, and strikers in one group) to make it a little bit more informal. And I will sit down and discuss the game plan with them.

Before lunch and after, another team meeting and team preparation meeting at 2:00.

Saturday, September 20th, 2003
Game Day--8:10

Early wake-up from Sam (author reminding coach to keep tape running). Thank you, Sam. We are looking forward to the game. The weather is nice. I think we are ready. I am preparing the group meetings. I think this is probably the mentally toughest team I have ever coached. A lot of winning mentality. We have prepared for three and a half, soon four, years for this. The best caliber preparations are possible. We are ready to perform. We are ready to beat Germany, I think.

Breakfast at 9:00 and a team walk after that and then meetings in groups:

10:15 Goalkeepers/Defenders
10:45 Midfielders
11:15 Strikers

Then the coaches will head off to a sports bar to see Norway and France at noon from Philadelphia. The opening games are on and we have already seen Norway beat France 2-0 in an even game. It could have gone both ways. And now the first half of North Korea against Nigeria. 1-0 for North Korea. Not surprising to us because we know how good they are.

2:00 Short team meeting. The last reminders. Game plan

2:15 Match meal

4:00 Head off to stadium

We had a very short team meeting at 2:00 before the pre-game meal. Everyone was calm. But, of course everyone was internally nervous. I think we all sounded confident and my last word to the players was "Do not commit fouls close to the box, because they are good shooters on free kicks."

We have stressed our playing style, our commitment to fast, aggressive attacks, and high intensity defensive soccer. We have also stressed "Defending the Box".

Nonen vs Prinz

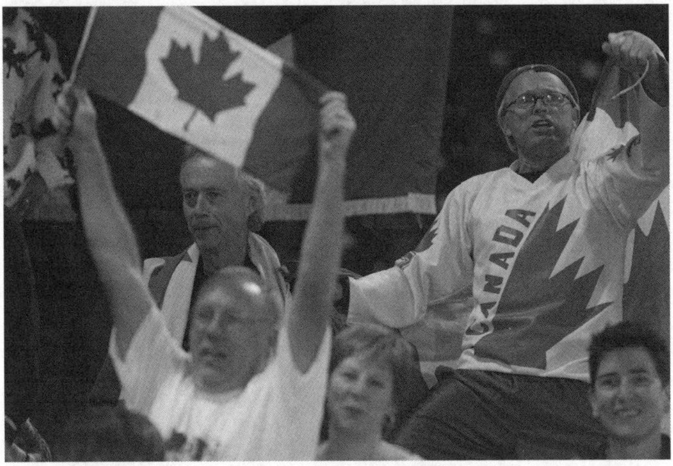

The 12th player - Canadian fans traveled to support the team

Ian Bridge with the Boss

Sunday, September 21st, 2003
After Game Against Germany

What a wonderful start and what a disastrous game after that.

Good start. Scored early in the first three or four minutes by Christine Sinclair. Everyone was happy. But, the game never went our way after that.

The shape was not good and it never looked really great even with the great start. The German defense was vulnerable and didn't play well at all, but we were not able to penetrate often enough. Defensive-wise we lost our shape pretty early.

The three strikers were to pressure hard and high, but couldn't do it effectively, then weren't able to help out in midfield at all. Our midfield three had too much space to cover and too much running and got tired. Unlucky timing on the goals against. They scored the tying goal late in the first half and we had enough to just keep the score even until the interval.

Then unlucky timing again. I decided to go to a deeper 4-5-1 formation in order to help the defensive shape in midfield and the unlucky thing was that they scored directly from the kick off and from there on we lost a lot of confidence. We lost our composure. The players were tired and looked frustrated and, despite the fact that the shape was better, we weren't able to play at our normal performance level at all.

Then we elevated our play again and we almost scored a couple of times. In the 72nd minute I decided to go for the tie and put Charmaine Hooper up front with Rhian Wilkinson right and Christine Latham and Christine Sinclair above the two midfielders with Andrea Neil back in the center stopper position. (We had big problems there.) Almost immediately they scored a third goal and we were out of the match. Final score 4-1.

The worst way of starting a World Cup is what just happened. Now there is the challenge of finding a way to get the players up to standards again. It is going to be tough. We are disappointed.

They are disappointed and maybe confused. I have chosen to be direct. We have assessed this team to be mentally strong and will try to fire them up by being direct and challenge them with direct feedback on the game from good to bad and we will be pretty honest.

After meeting

We have given the players feedback. We have seen the game again. We have seen the goals against and there are a lot of bad feelings among the players. Maybe I have been too hard. Maybe I was too direct. Some players came to me and asked for individual feedback and I was direct again. Maybe too much. There are some sad faces and some sore feelings out there and I am not, at the moment, convinced that I chose the right way to go with it. Maybe I should have gone with a softer way. We will see how they respond.

Monday, September 22nd, 2003

We feel better, but we are under pressure in our group. Japan won 6-0 versus Argentina. We, of course, have to beat Argentina on Thursday and I am pretty sure we will do that. Argentina seems so far to be the weakest team in this tournament.

In the other groups we are surprised by the even games between China and Ghana, for example, only 1-0 for China in a very even game. Ghana was expected to be one of the weaker teams in this tournament and they look strong.

Brazil and South Korea 3-0. Expected.

So we are going into a very exciting week with a lot of pressure on our shoulders. We know that we have to win the next two games and the game against Japan on Saturday is going to be a big game with a lot of pressure.

We will also see on Wednesday what kind of influence the goal difference will have from the last game.

We had a morning practice after breakfast that was on a very wet and heavy field and it was both a combination of sore bodies and sore feelings and wet field. So we shortened our practice tremendously and made it easier for them and we went home pretty early.

Out in fresh air, the discussion of the staff has been partly about some concerns that players are going up and down in moods, from being very happy and relaxed to not looking comfortable and confident, and we need to change that before the game against Japan at least. I assume we will beat Argentina and another discussion these days is will the goal difference be important. Should Japan beat Germany, for example 1-0, we will have to score a lot of goals on Argentina.

It could happen because Germany is in the driver's seat in this group. They can now sit back and rest players. Maybe, they will be too comfortable going into the Japan game and, who knows, maybe they will lose that game. It is not a thing you would like to think about, but we need to be aware and we are playing after them. So we will know what we have to do.

At kick-off time on Wednesday we will have to address that thought based on the result of the game before us between Japan and Germany. Our hope is to be in a position where all we have to do is beat Japan on Saturday in Boston.

Tuesday, September 23rd, 2003

A quiet day. The team walked after breakfast and then, after lunch, optional time-off at a shopping mall. About half the players followed on that shopping trip and most of the staff. We were back for dinner and then a late practice at the stadium at 8:15.

It is now 7:30 and we are preparing the last practice before the game tomorrow against Argentina. I am planning an offensive/attacking style. Hoping to score an early goal and still focus on winning the game if we are lucky enough to ensure that. We may have to start thinking about scoring as many goals as possible, and that will be mostly dependant on the outcome of the Japan/Germany game before us.

I can feel players are mentally not fully recovered from the poor performance last game. We will see how we react tomorrow.

Wednesday, September 24th, 2003
Game Day against Argentina

9:00AM
At 8:30 pm we play Argentina. We have a long day preparing for that game. Maybe too long. We are all expecting, I think, to play a team that is less athletic, less powerful, and less experienced than our team. We have the mental challenge of finding a way to win, finding a way to score goals, building up our confidence again, which is still hurting from the first game.

We will see Japan and Germany first and the result of that game will determine, to some extent, our immediate plans for this game. Should Japan beat Germany there are going to be big problems because it will come down to goal difference and we will then go into the Argentina game tonight with a whole lot more pressure on the shoulders of the players knowing that Japan has a very strong goal difference and Germany has Argentina in the last game. That could happen. Germany is a much stronger team than Japan, but we know in soccer anything can happen in one specific game.

Should Germany win or at least tie the game then it will be Canada and Japan on Saturday where we would have to win and I think is an okay approach for our team to have that pressure. I think it will come down to where FIFA ranking and early game results don't mean a thing. It will come down to guts-which team has the greatest will to win.

3:00
It is three hours before kick-off. I decided to go with a very offensive formation. Almost old fashioned 4-2-4 in hopes of running over them and running through them with our flanks with Rhian Wilkinson right and Kara Lang left. Up front Christine Sinclair and Christine Latham. In the middle, Kiss and Matheson. In the back, Dennis, Nonen, Hooper, and Timko. Swiatek will start in goal. She is the better keeper off the line in counterattacks and I am expecting a counterattack game from Argentina.

For the game preparation meeting Shel had produced a very good tape for us. He is a high-tech goalkeeping coach now with advanced tools and also a very nice motivational tape from our recent games and nice goals and celebrations combined with music. It worked very well. I think it was appreciated by the players and the staff.

After the Argentina Game

It was quite a game against Argentina. We did not succeed with the tactics and the game plan as we had hoped. We needed good services from our defenders to succeed with the 4-2-4 formation and that didn't happen. The players were totally influenced by the first game. Heavy legs, slow brains and a lot of uncertainty and I have seen that more in the women's game than in the men's game after a bad game. The mood, mentality, goes down. The self-confidence was affected and this was far, far away from the normal Canadian team. We struggled with almost everything from team shape to concentration, pressure on the ball, and easy passes. And, Argentina kept the ball much more in possession than we hoped to see.

It was easy to see how completely unfocused the team was and this was one of the toughest games I have ever coached. Against a team that we easily should have been outplaying we lost 1v1 fights all over the field. We didn't create goal-scoring opportunities in the numbers I had hoped to see. We didn't see the penetration on the sides where we could run over them with our fast aggressive players on the flanks and mainly because the service was not in place. This turned out to be a game where

Christine Latham was important for us. She never gave up a ball and was fighting up front in order to create chances for us and happily she got one of those chances where she was able to turn and take on a defender and approach the sweeper, passed by her with a nice touch and was taken down inside the box. A penalty kick for us. A penalty kick in a situation where a goal was desperately needed. Charmaine Hooper stepped up and scored. A nervous bench and nervous players on the field. One up at half-time.

Second half, somewhat better, but not our best yet. We had more domination though and we were more in the box. We created more free kicks and dead ball situations and looked more dangerous without ever playing well. We were better controlled in the back and more aggressive, tighter on the Argentinian strikers. We felt better. It was hard to imagine that we could lose the game, but in the situation we were in with injuries we were all very nervous that something bad could happen in the back.

It was one of those games where you, as a coach, feel 10 years older after two 45-minute halves.

Going home from the game was very hard for us, because there are so many mixed feelings. Of course the win was extremely important. The way we won it was less than pleasant. We had really hoped to hold play against Argentina, win easy and get the confidence back before the last game against Japan. We didn't. You can see in the bus. A quiet team with very mixed feelings and I'm afraid that the confidence level is not better, but may be worse than it was after the Germany game.

Tough start in the big event. The question is, can they recover. I tried to cheer up the players by complimenting them on the game and the result and, of course, mentioning the first ever World Cup win for a Canadian Senior team. They responded very quietly to that. No cheering. No clapping. The reaction proved that the team is not in great balance right now. It is going to be a challenge for the coaching staff to get them up to par before the crucially important Japan game. But, that's our job.

Thursday, September 25th, 2003
Boston

Practice in the afternoon. The speed of the team is still not as it should be and I am concerned. The players organized a team meeting, players only, to discuss some internal issues within the team before we went to practice. We went to Wellesley College for practice. A great field, good technical practice, good quality and some scrimmage with good intensity.

Some minor bruises and injuries. Kara, Kiss, Sinclair. Hermus tried yesterday to do some harder work outs-running on the field and she looked good.

Friday, September 26th, 2003

Today, practice at the stadium at 3:30. Randee Hermus will have a full practice. If that goes well she will be available for the game tomorrow. She might start at left full back. We might move Timko to midfield and keep Charmaine in the back from the beginning of the game and move her up if we need a goal. Charmaine has been playing well this World Cup and I am very impressed with her.

She scores goals in every practice so we desperately need her up front, as well, but we need her even more in the back.

Japan plays 5-3-2 or 5-2-3. They have two good front players with skills and pace. A striker up front and Sawa, the star, behind her. Skillful midfielders but typically possession style and we should be able to cope with them if, and that is a big IF, we are ready to play. It is a psychological thing now.

After practice

Today, we practiced at Gillette Stadium, which, by the way, is a beautiful stadium with the potential for 60,000 spectators. Twenty players for the first time. Randee Hermus with the cooperation of the medical staff took a calculated risk for a full practice and that lasted for 8 minutes before she had to go out. She re-stressed her stress fracture and she is out for the rest of the tournament, that's for sure.

Tanya Dennis, who was moved to right full back was nauseated and was throwing up after something happened with her food at lunch time, I guess. So she was in and out.

Isabelle Morneau was placed in the left full back and she looked very sharp and we put Timko in midfield for Kristina Kiss who has not performed so well so far. Strikers up front: Lang, Latham and Sinclair.

For 40 minutes team shape, different situations in the stadium and we will see tomorrow if this is good enough.

Saturday, September 27th, 2003
Game Day Against Japan

A very challenging day. You go through all these emotions as a coach. Are you optimistic or pessimistic? Are you nervous? Are you relaxed? This turned out to be one of those days where you had to take a position and I took the position to just let it go in the way of deciding to relax. We had done the work, the players had been out for a team walk and I thought they were pretty relaxed, the focus seems to be back. The coaching staff looks okay. I had my wife and my two twin girls visiting the hotel. They just passed by. I don't want my family around when I work. My wife wanted to know my feelings and my thoughts and I said I have reached a level where I am very focused and very balanced and I had a feeling that the players are as well.

September 28th, 2003
Morning after the game against Japan

What a wonderful day for soccer in Canada. As I said in my last report before kick-off, my optimism was growing and it was justified. Immediately after kick-off we had good shape. We looked eager. We looked aggressive and we started the game with three or four solid scoring chances without scoring a goal.

We weren't fantastic but much, much better than before in this World Cup. Then all of a sudden Japan went on the counterattack and scored 1-0. It was devastating for us, but we didn't panic. The players were down for two or three minutes, but they came back fast and we scored a wonderful tying goal, Christine Sinclair to Latham. And we were tied until half-time.

In the half-time talk I outlined the plans for the second half based on the result after the next 15 minutes. I will put Charmaine up front and play 3-4-3. After 60 minutes, if we had the lead we would go 5-3-2 to keep the lead and that is exactly what happened. After 50 minutes we scored a second goal and we changed quickly to 5-3-2 and it worked very well.

All the strikers scored and Isabelle Morneau as a starter was a big hit. She was a great player as a left back in the first half and then she played center defender with Charmaine in the middle and Sharolta right. Tanya Dennis was wide right and Silvana Burtini wide left. That was a very good combination, optimizing our qualities with five backs.

We had good control of the game. We had one goal denied early on with Latham, according to the ref, pushing the goalkeeper on the goal line-a wrong decision, I believe, but this particular referee allowed no contact of any sort.

Then our midfield had problems, Andrea Neil with her hamstring injury started to limp more and more and had to be substituted. Diana Matheson didn't win enough balls. With Timko in midfield this time she was a big hit and one of our best players in the game, together with Charmaine Hooper who was fantastic as a defender and Taryn Swiatek who was very impressive in goal-a real solid keeper.

Timko produced pace and tempo in our midfield and we really needed that yesterday because Japan has tons of impressive passing and possession game and we had to chase a lot and most of our midfielders were not quick enough to cover the field, but Timko was great.

We had a great night. A lot of fans from Canada were at the game and may come to the hotel. I was happy to see my family in the stands. They came down to see me and they are going back to Toronto in the morning.

We made a decision to scout the China game so the coaches were at the airport at 5:00 this morning to go to Portland to see the last group game in Group D, which is our quarterfinal opponent. It will be either Russia or China (and I think China). It will be a very difficult possession, quick, skillful team to play against but, on the bonus side, our goal for the tournament to get to the quarterfinal has been achieved and we are now just looking forward to the next game.

It is always a good feeling to see the coming opposition live. A game tape can give you a lot. For example, their approach to deadballs. Live is very different. It gives you a lot more. It was a good feeling to go and see them. We of course have a lot of information on China. Line-ups, good player profiles. We have confirmed that the real threat is up front with Sun Wen, behind striker Bai Li who is very fast, very quick, explosive, brave. Sun Wen is a smart tricky player that can decide every game with her smarts and skills. Other than that, the typical Chinese team-possession, a lot of possession. A lot of passes. Good balance in the back four. Playing very high with fullbacks. Very high with the flanks. So, when the left fullback has the ball, the left flank goes up almost to a high striker on the left hand side. Tricky to play against because their formation is good in stretching our team over the length of the field. It is important to get shape that can compete with that kind of structure.

Monday, September 29th, 2003
Practice, Portland, Oregon

The optimism and energy, the performances are back. The passion is back. There are a couple of minor injuries. Andrea Neil had to heal her hamstring. Tanya Dennis is still out, we are seeing symptoms of possible concussion, but we don't really know where that concussion came from. Hopefully, tomorrow she will practice.

Tuesday, September 30th, 2003
Practice

At 10:00 we showed the players a scripted edition at 10:00 from the China/Russia game, based on China's offensive shape, defensive shape, double situations and special players Sun Wen and Bai Li, the two strikers. We started practice at 11:00. We spent one hour and 50 minutes on team shape and probable line-ups and formations for the China game. Back to the hotel for lunch and the team had the rest of the day off.

I am still looking at the final decision about team shape. I think the selection of 11 players is pretty easy with the same starting 11 players as last time, but with different formation and tactical approach. Either two wide strikers taking care of the high full backs, with Latham and Sinclair in a 4-4-2, or an uneven 4-3-3 with Christine Sinclair moving up higher in her right flank position than the two other strikers. That will take care of the left side of their defense. That means we have a higher right side and a lower left side and that's a good fit for the Chinese formation and we can also use Christine Sinclair as offensively as possible. So, we will look at that team shape tomorrow at practice and we will confirm that tomorrow afternoon in the team meeting.

Wednesday, October 1st, 2003
Press Conference - As usual in the lobby - a lot of interest from Canadian press.

Thursday, October 2nd, 2003
Game Day Quarterfinal against China

The quarterfinal is ahead of us. It is 10:00am, I went into breakfast and then a chat with Gerry Dobson of Sportnet preparing for the game. I gave him information on how we are planning to play and the line-ups and all that. We are now shortly heading to the movie theater to spend a couple of hours before going back to prepare for the game at 7:30pm.

I am feeling confident. Things look great. The players look relaxed but pumped up at the same time. That good feeling is back. We will play the same line-up as in the game against Japan. We will play an unbalanced 4-4-2 with Sinclair high and we are, at the moment, pretty confident.

1 Hour 50 minutes to departure for stadium...right now is the kick off for Russia and Germany in the other Quarterfinal here in Portland. Again, Germany should win comfortably, but having in mind that there are a few players with injuries. Steffi Jones the midfielder, and Briesonik the left full back.

We have just finished off a game meeting with the game plan, line-up formation and following the plan I mentioned yesterday with Kara in the high out midfield position, Sinclair out front. Same line up. Ian followed me up with a motivational short speech. Great input. The team that has the strongest desire to stay in the tournament will win. We watched a short film. It was motivational, emotional, goal scoring films based on our goals this season.

We are relaxed, balanced, focused. We have reason to be optimistic.

Midnight, October 2nd

We have beaten China in the quarterfinal! We won 1-0, after an amazing team effort. The goal was fantastic. A header on a free kick from Hooper, who else? Taryn Swiatek was fantastic in goal. The defensive effort, shape, organization saved us for the last 85 minutes after scoring the goal early. The players are back near where they were in the late preparation. They played as a team and executed our game plan. More injuries (Morneau) and still they came back together. A tremendous team effort. A good day for Canadian soccer. A great day for Canadian women's soccer.

A nervous coaching crew before the China game

Sharolta Nonen thwarting the Chinese in the Quarterfinal

The winning goal - Charmaine Hooper heads home the set play in Canada's 1-0 win over China

Celebrating Canada's biggest win - Quarterfinals WWC 2003 vs China

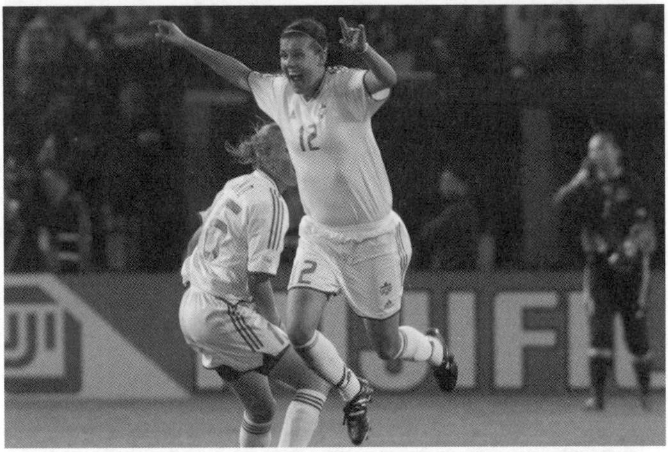

An ecstatic Sinclair as Canada gains it's biggest win ever

A happy Pellerud after Swiatek "lifted" the team to victory over China

Friday, October 3rd, 2003
Day after big win against China

Press conference 9:30. Big media attention from the Canadian media and from Swedish media, we are staying in the same hotel and people from newspapers know me from Norway and there were lots of questions about the Canadian and Norwegian teams.

It was in another way a bad night for most of the players and staff. Not much sleep. Too much thinking about the game. Excited, happy, but tired today. Practice at 1:30. I am sending Ian in to be in charge of that practice with Bob Birarda, as the assistant coach. Shel and myself will stay in the hotel making a tape of Sweden and thus preparing the team for playing Sweden in the semi-final.

I am fairly sure that Isabelle Morneau will not be able to play on Sunday. We are looking into a substitute for her and deciding whether to go with five or four in the back. We don't know, yet, but we will think and discuss and come to a conclusion Saturday evening, based on a combination of gut feeling and the Swedish team's strengths.

Saturday, October 4th, 2003
Press Conference & Team Meeting

Team meeting will focus on clips of the Swedish games. After that stadium practice and outdoor activity later this afternoon after lunch. A marketplace or something like that downtown.

Afternoon

Just finished a team dinner outside the hotel with Andy Sharpe, CSA president, and everybody was present and sharp and I think it was a good idea to take the team out to dinner. An important thing for the presidency (CSA) to take that initiative and, after some pressure from the management of the team, they realized that it was a good thing to do and we went out. It was a very successful, relaxed, focused, fun dinner. I think it was good for the president, as well, to feel that he was involved with the team and good variation in the life of the team. A lot of laughs and relaxation.

Sunday, October 5th, 2003
Game Day - Semi-Final against Sweden

Kara Lang was back at the hotel vomiting last night. We will find out how big that problem is this morning.

2:00pm
We will play 4-3-1-2 formation. Swiatek, of course in the goal, maybe the best goalkeeper in the tournament. Tanya Dennis, Sharolta Nonen, Charmaine Hooper, Silvana Burtini at that back, Timko, Neil, Matheson, and Christine Sinclair as the withdrawn striker, Lang and Latham up top.

We are the underdogs. Sweden is highly favored to win the game. I think most people here on a neutral basis are considering U.S.A., Germany, and Sweden as far better teams than Canada and that is a good thing for us. We can use that as an up side and we are going to do that.

After Game

We lost to Sweden 2-1 and it was a tough loss. We were leading the game until the 75th minute. That said, Sweden was sharp and slightly the better team. The disappointing thing is, of course, that we gave away two goals late in the game. But, the goals came because we weren't alert enough in defense. We were sleeping on the free kick and also, part of this was because Canada lost another defender, Silvana Burtini, and had to put Britanny Timko as the full back. In some quick situations a midfielder does not have the same defensive genes as a defender and that hurt us in some situations yesterday. This has nothing to do with Brittany, she is a great soccer player and very talented, but overall too many new players in new positions.

We were very close to making the World Cup Final 2003 and it is, of course, sad to have missed that golden opportunity. That said, did Canada become a Top Two Team in this World Cup? I don't think so. Top four, top five, yes. I think we achieved all that we could possibly achieve. I think we should be looking back and be pretty happy being in that semi-final and we should be excited about the future.

This team is still too young to perform at the highest level. It is extremely promising as the players are all gaining world experience. It has been a big take off for the team. We are not running up in the air, yet, but we will get there.

Monday, October 6th, 2003
Practice

Practice and workout was more fun. It was a very good mood. I think the players have shifted to being pretty happy about their achievements, but, at the same time, a little bit sad because they know that that lack of focus for that few minutes was enough to lose the game. There is still a lot of media attention. We just heard that there is a lot of attention in Europe for this World Cup, which is a big turning point in Europe, and perhaps for Canadian soccer, at least for the women's program. We hope that the men's program comes around, as well, because it should be about the game of soccer not just a certain program. I know that will take more time, though.

It is hard to achieve the same in the men's game as with the women. The history and the competition and the programs are just so much more developed. It is a lot of hard work and, of course, the right coaching.

At this FIFA World Cup we have put the team stamp on the world of soccer though. I think that is what we can express, today. We are heading into the Bronze final on Saturday against powerhouse U.S.A. (We are officially out of defenders, but I will discuss that later.)

The program has taken off. It is not up in the air at high altitude, yet, but we are narrowing the gap. We are creating confidence in the team. We have created self-esteem in Canadian soccer again. We have created confidence in the player group that we will take advantage of in the future. Nobody can take that away from the players. For our upcoming big games and Olympic qualification in Costa Rica in late February/early March, we hope to have some of the injured players back again and we will then have a strong team. We will probably miss Candace Chapman after her ACL surgery, on October 17th. I still think that she would have made a big difference for us. Especially considering the fact that Brianna Boyd and Randee Hermus were out. We then lost Isabelle Morneau and Silvana Burtini. Charmaine Hooper became a defender and a great one, but that took something away up front.

We found a new goalkeeper in Swiatek. Tanya Dennis struggled the whole tournament with head pain and possible concussion. She played in most games but only few practices. Amazing and astounding achievement for a young 18-year-old player not being involved at all before. So the future certainly looks more than promising.

I read in the newspaper today that the U.S.A.'s youngest player, Cat Reddick, is 21. That is the age of my oldest player other than Charmaine.

Tuesday, October 7th, 2003
Los Angeles

Flew in yesterday evening and this morning we had a sharp workout in the park house by the hotel conducted by our physiotherapist Paolo Bordignon. We gave them the rest of the day off and also tomorrow. I think the team will go to Disneyland tomorrow, but we will be off from any kind of soccer thinking and come together again on Thursday morning for preparing for the last game on Saturday.

Teamwork - German defender and goalkeeper combine to deny Mia Hamm an opportunity

Canadian fans trekked south in droves to support the Canadian Women

German defender Steggeman fights off Abby Wambach

An airborne Latham teaming with Andrea Neil to demonstrate some Canadian physical dominance

Swiatek rising above once again

Kristine Kiss' last game with Canada. The talented midfielder resigned with injuries a few months after the tournament.

Wednesday, October 8th, 2003
Day Off - Disneyland

Some of the staff went, as well. It was a good day off. I went to get gifts for my family and find cards for colleagues. Kevan Pipe, Chief Operating Officer for the CSA, came in yesterday. I had a chat with him this morning. I also have meetings with the vice-president to discuss next year and to talk about staff and staff improvements. Les Wilkinson (CSA VP) has been around my team and other teams here at the WWC and he has seen with his own eyes how important it is to update the staff. We have seen Germany and Norway and all the teams have large groups of specialized members supporting the team, including three or four therapists and managers and scouts. It would be good for the future for us to have our politicians around so we will have more understanding that life in top performance sport has changed.

The fact is the past is not good enough for today and certainly not for the future. We have to review some of the things we have done and do things better next time, even if things have worked very well for us. We can do better with the right mixture of people in the right jobs. Our staff has been determined with a huge workload and they are all fantastic workers. A very good group. We have done the most with what we have, but we can do more.

Thursday, October 9th, 2003
Evening

Back to work after two days off (Tuesday and Wednesday). We are starting to prepare for Saturday's game.

This morning the media came back to the hotel and we had a press conference at 9:30 and there is still good attendance from the Canadian media. The Swedish and German teams are staying in the same hotel as us and the international media interest from especially the Swedes and Germans is great.

We conducted individual meetings with the players and then practice at 1:00 at one of five or six fabulous training facilities outside. They were all like carpets, fantastic practice. 1 hour 45 minutes, sharp. Practice was based on intensity and coming into shape again after two day's break, focus on the game. The players did well. Injury problems: Tanya Dennis has a concussion for sure, Silvana Burtini will not play with her meniscus. Isabelle Morneau did practice and did surprisingly well, but is still a long shot for Saturday's game, which means that we are out six defenders for that game.

We based practice on the back five with Sharolta Nonen, Sasha Andrews and Charmaine Hooper and Kara Lang and Timko on the flanks and I think that will be the approach for the game on Saturday.

We met with FIFA, the players and the staff, in preparation for Saturday's game. We are guaranteed the Bronze medal trophy winning or losing the game. Both the third and fourth placed teams get that.

We went out for dinner with the CSA people. The staff went downtown for seafood dinner. It was very nice and we are now heading into Friday's preparation practice at 1:45 at the stadium. Before that we will have a press conference, again, as usual and I will talk to Sportsnet at 10:30.

Friday, October 10th, 2003
Day Before Bronze Medal Game

Last practice before game. I think things are pretty calm and relaxed. It is a big game, but there are no major consequences involved in it any more than status, prestige and the big rivalry between Canada and the U.S.A. I have already discussed the different line-ups from 5-3-2 to leaning more into a more offensive shape 4-3-3 and use the "three monsters" up top...Lang, Sinclair, Latham. And then, if that happens, because of injuries I will use Sasha Andrews who is strong in the air, but not strong on the ground, and may be put her in the middle of our back four with

Charmaine, Sharolta Nonen out and more speed on the flank together with Timko as midfielder in the fullback position. Midfield will be Kristina Kiss who is coming back very sharply in practices now and she could be an important player tomorrow with her sharp services on free kicks and corner kicks, with Diana Matheson covering the whole midfield in the middle and Andrea Neil at left center-mid.

There is of course a lot more pressure on the American team after losing in the semi-final to Germany. There is criticism about their team in the media, especially the fact that they are playing with an older team and may have made changes too late. I am not sure that is correct, but there is pressure on the coach to make the changes and we are now speculating whether they are coming with 4-3-3 or going back to 4-4-2 formation with Wagner behind the strikers. She looked very sharp in the game against Germany and it wouldn't surprise me if they came out with 4-4-2 with the diamond again. That is their preferred formation and then they can use Wagner in that spot behind the two strikers, either Parlow/Wambach or Wambach/Hamm. Maybe Parlow in midfield, maybe Hamm in midfield on the right side.

Afternoon

We are back in the hotel after practice. We are preparing a team meeting after dinner and then the game tomorrow and things are pretty good. Short practice at the stadium today at the Home Depot Center, a beautiful soccer stadium, wide and short.

We tried 4-3-3 with Taryn Swiatek. Sharolta Nonen and Britanny Timko left and right fullback, Sasha Andrews and Charmaine in the middle. My philosophy behind that is to stop Parlow and Wambach and hopefully Timko and Nonen are quick enough to take care of the rebounds and reduce balls to Mia Hamm. Three in the middle-Kiss looked sharp, Diana Matheson, always sharp, and Andrea Neil, an important leader for us. Up front, the three monsters, Lang, Sinclair, and Latham.

Saturday, October 11th, 2003
Bronze Final Game

Before departure for the stadium - our last team meeting. The team looked very relaxed. The coaching staff is as well. This is a bonus game. The pressure is on them, not on us. And we decided to go out with a pretty offensive minded team 4-3-3, attack them and see how that works.

After the game we will go home to the hotel to have lunch and then have a team meeting looking ahead to next year, the training programs, and start looking forward to the next challenge, which is the Olympic qualifications in February and March in Costa Rica.

After Game

We lost 3-1. A very respectable performance. We should and could have scored early. Good goal scoring opportunities for us in the first half. I think even more important for our team in that situation with all the injured players and substitutes, it had been very important for us to score early to get the advantage on the U.S. team, but we didn't score on many chances and when you don't do that you know, as a coach, that the U.S. team will soon come in for the game and they did, scoring their first goal. It was a fantastic long shot from their veteran Kristine Lilly. Impressively for us we came back and scored the tying goal by Sinclair, late in the first half. At that time it was a pretty even game. And, most importantly, we were able to perform all day long. I had some questions before if we would be able to do that, but we were and I think that is one of the greatest efforts from this young team.

Back at the hotel - There was a lot of praise for the team from our fans, media, and also from CSA bosses. Very nice. Appreciated by the staff and players. We will focus on next year and the development the team needs to go through to take another step.

Sunday, October 12th, 2003

We watched the final game. It was exciting, very end-to-end. Germany was a little bit less energetic than before. Both teams could have won. It was even-back and forth. Sweden had big chances in the end of the second half. It went into overtime. Germany won on the set plays. In total assessment of the tournament, I think the best team won. Germany was the better team overall in this tournament and Sweden was a very worthy second place team.

Both teams were very professional with good staff, very skillful, quick teams. They play with a lot of intensity. I think this is the last time we will hear about the weakness of goalkeeping in women's games. We have seen fantastic goalkeeping here. The Swedish, German, Canadian, American, Norwegian, Chinese goalkeepers almost without mistakes, very strong goalkeeping and it is a very nice step forward for female soccer.

There is one trend that concerns me. The women's game has been a very honest game and this time we saw more tricks, more play acting. In the Bronze medal game, Abby Wambach was play-acting the whole game and fell down as if she were dead. That was disappointing and hopefully not a trend, but I am afraid we will see more of that because you see more and more that the women's game tends to be like the men's game, physical battles, air fights, and more tactical (which is good), but I would like to see less of the acting we have seen creeping in.

Players and coaches involved in the women's game should and must copy the good things from the men's game, but ignore the downfalls. Play acting is definitely one of the things that should not be integrated into the women's game.

Chapter XIV

The International Game

When Even Pellerud first came to the women's game, he was in a unique position. He had not seen a women's game, nationally or internationally, in his 30-odd years of playing the game. He was totally immersed in the men's side of the game. It was his open-mindedness that served the women's game well because in developing the programming through the Norges Fotball Forbund (NFF) he was insistent that there be no discrimination between the men's and women's programs.

He was in a unique situation to watch the game evolve on the international stage, participating in the first FIFA Women's World Cup in 1991 and 1995 and again in 2003. A great believer in the community of practice, Pellerud has been involved in Olympic Committee work in Norway and coaching organizations throughout the world.

Interested in the international development of the game he has been involved in FIFA Technical Committee work, as well as UEFA. He has made a great number of friends in the international coaching ranks on both the women's and men's side and maintains his vested interest in where the game is going internationally. He has a genuine interest in seeing it promoted.

FIFA, the Federation of International Football Association, is football international. It was Helen Wille and the Norwegian delegation who made their voices heard with Joao Havelange in the '80's that finally brought about recognition of women's football. In agreeing to a world championship leading to a World Cup, the Norwegian delegation got the ball rolling for the way the international women's game is played today. The European Women's Championships had existed for over 20 years representing the strongest international showcase for the women's game to that point in the late 80's.

The next strongest group is CONCACAF with the U.S. and Canada enjoying the most consistent success and a surging Mexico (2004 Olympic qualifier) closing the gap. Brazil remains the lone South American powerhouse and in the Asian Conference China is now being more closely followed by Japan and North Korea.

FIFA has continued developing the women's game with structures similar to the men's side. The second official FIFA World Championship added was the U-19s, which was inaugurated in Canada in 2002. Soon to be converted to a U-20, the women's game continues to blossom under the auspices of FIFA. The struggle to gain a place for women in the international game of soccer over the past 100 years has to be acknowledged. Programs throughout the world have had to fight through the male-dominated bureaucracy. In developing football countries it remains a problem for the women's game. While national cultures for the game have to be developed those cultures have been predominantly male and the change has come slowly.

Some of the first serious inroads made by the women's game in soccer began in England during the First World War. Although the first recorded soccer game was in March 1895 in Crouch End, England, it wasn't until 1916 that the game really emerged. With the industrial war machine "manned" by women primarily, teams were formed at munitions and manufacturing plants. They started in the north of England as early as 1916/17 at the Vicker's plant. Organized by women, but primarily coached and managed by men, the game became popular and grew throughout England. Although initially conceived as a morale booster for the factory workers, the game caught on with the fans as they appreciated the athleticism and technical and tactical understanding of the game demonstrated by the players. Admittedly filling a void left by the cancellation of the professional men's game during WWI, the women's game continued to flourish after the war. International matches (with France) became a yearly event. Lily Parr, a beautiful actress, also became a great player-the Mia Hamm of the time. In 1920 the Dick Kerr Company ladies team (trained at historical Preston North End) played a match at Goodison Park, Everton's home field, in front of no fewer than 53,000 fans. It was to be the last significant women's game played on an FA club's field. Worried as to how the parallel league would affect the men's game, women were banned from playing on these professional pitches and the promising development withered. It wasn't until over 50 years later that any significant organization began in women's international football. Indeed, the ban was officially lifted in 1971 and the first official women's international game was played in 1972. (For a history of the early women's game, see The Dick Kerr's Ladies, Barbara Jacobs, Constable and Robinson, July 2004)

A parallel situation occurred in North America in the early 90's when the principals of a strong U.S. women's program, led by Michelle Akers, were able to secure sponsoring of a professional women's league in North America. The USSF did not support the early implementation of the women's league fearful of the erosion of the fan base building for the fledgling Major League Soccer.

One of the dozens of professional men's league efforts over the past 50 years the success of the MLS was considered critical to moving the game forward in North America - particularly leading up to the World Cup in 1994. The women's attempt to start a league was clearly a distraction to the USSF. After an acrimonious few months an understanding was reached with the women's game primarily represented by the U.S. Women's National Team players.

With a promise to delay recruiting until after the 1999 Women's World Cup, the non-believers in the USSF acquiesced and the league was sanctioned after the world tournament. The Women's United Soccer Association (WUSA) was born offering a platform for development female footballers. Credibility was secured with Tony DiCicco named as commissioner and Lauren Gregg in charge of player personnel. Primarily designed to promote the American Women's game, limited internationals were placed on each team.

Dozens of the world's best, first seen in North America at the '96 Olympics then the 1999 World Cup, became household names to soccer families around the country. Meinert, Riise, Store, Aarones, Prinz, Sawa, Sun Wen, all previously unknown in North America gained a supportive following in their adopted cities.

Canadians Sharolta Nonen, Charmaine Hooper (Atlanta Beat), and Brianna Boyd (Carolina Courage), Christine Latham (San Diego) and Karina LeBlanc (Boston) were stand out players in the new league. Now, playing beside the Mia Hamms, Kristine Lillys and Tiffy Millbretts of the USA - these fellow internationals brought the game forward. The USA had been the crucible for developing talent with impetus from Title IX and the burgeoning college programs and now WUSA complemented player development. Other countries also recognized the need for these pyramids of play to develop the game. Well-run senior professional leagues in Norway, Japan, and Italy had begun to emerge in the 70's and 80's. These players, seeking to continue to hone their games after college or university, frequently rearranged their lives to pursue their dreams.

Lauren Gregg

One of Even Pellerud's friends and international coaching colleagues is Lauren Gregg. Gregg, presently involved as a consultant with the Women's United Soccer Association as it attempts to restructure itself, was a player on the U.S. National Team from 1986 to 1989 and served on the National Team coaching staff from 1989-2000 when she took over the position of Vice-President of Player Development with the new WUSA. Author of The Champion Within as well as an upcoming book on developing youth players, Lauren Gregg was a U.S. coach during the first three World Cups. She went on to be chiefly responsible for international recruiting and player personnel as V.P. of WUSA.

She has an excellent insight into the international game, having traveled extensively among the developing soccer countries. A member of FIFA's Technical Committee and very active in the international sporting world, Lauren shares with us her unique insight on how the game has developed.

In reflecting on how the game has developed in the various countries in an international sense, she recently gave the following summary: *"In 1991, the dominant teams were Norway and the United States. You have to look at what qualities the various teams had. China was the most technical team in the world at that point, whereas the U.S. and Norway were the most physically and psychologically strong, and maybe a little edge to the U.S. in individual athleticism. Tactically, I would say that Germany was the most impressive team. Those were the top four countries in 1991. Each of those national teams brought something to the competition that made them exceptional. I know we in the U.S. modeled our combination play after Germany's influence on us in 1991. They were just brilliant at it. Norway was dominant in the air and their service ability was unusual in the women's game. China's technical ability got squandered to some extent because of the lack of psychological and physical dimension of the game.*

"With Norway and the U.S. in the final, I think you saw the two psychologically- healthy teams. Both had winning attacking mentalities and this physical, tough psychological play was enough to override the other dimensions that other teams in the competition may have held an edge in.

"As far as that game goes, I think it was a coin toss who won. I don't think we were necessarily that much tougher psychologically. There were some incredible battles in that game and I think we were probably more athletic. Norway was a bit more organized so I would say our edge to win that game was probably on athleticism, fitness, and psychological hardness. We were certainly the fittest team, then, and I think that was something the other teams learned from as well.

"After that we began to see an evolution and I think every country responded very differently-it was an interesting phenomenon. I parallel that in my mind-that is the evolution of the game-as being relevant to where women sit in status in their own home countries. Sweden with such gender openness was certainly up there competitively. I think China may have gone backwards after 1991. Instead of investing more in them the country ignored

them to some extent and they went a little in retreat. Other countries such as Germany felt that the U.S. shouldn't win. Being soccer countries, they were insulted when what they perceived as non-soccer cultures came to win. It's a world game now and although they recognize we are a women's soccer culture now, they still use that to elevate their play. I think Norway felt the same way.

"In that period of time as a National Team, I think we may have stood still in terms of our evolution. We stayed man-to-man. We stayed competitive because of our work rate and fitness and we relied on that a lot going into the '95 World Cup. We pushed the transition game, the quick counterattack. We stuck with that. Norway evolved more than any of us, I think, and get credit for leading international women's soccer into the next phase. The U.S. may have set that standard that women could be athletic and fit and that psychological hardness dimension, and the hardness of the game is every bit a part of the women's game as it is the men's game, but Norway took the biggest leap I believe. In the '95 World Cup, in terms of organization, they introduced a very solid, strict zonal defensive back four. In 1991, we saw a lot of sweeper systems either in front of the zones, like Sweden did, as well as Norway, and then our team with the man-to-man sweeper. That was eliminated after '95, for the most part, by reading from Norway's success and performance.

"The other advantage that the U.S. and Norway had over a lot of the other countries, was an attacking mentality and that's what made women's soccer appealing to the fans. It wasn't just sit back, it was very offensive and Norway was the most direct team in the world and it always was under Pellerud. And now, Canada is gaining a reputation for the same game.

"So, when we look at China, Norway, the U.S., Germany, and Sweden, they were also good at what they did. They knew what they wanted to accomplish. That's the argument-Do you pick the system for the players or the players for the system. And Even was very adamant for picking the players for the system he believed in. He believed in aggressive direct play, as well as a strict zonal defense. They were very well trained, almost

machine-like, and they executed incredibly efficiently. Where it broke down for our team was, we didn't have a lot of options being in the man-to-man system against their incredible mobility, we could try any system and think this shows that the style is more important than the system. You could play 4-5-1 as a defensive system or you could play as an attacking system. The Norwegian midfield, much like the Chinese, was just mobile. Players were shooting forward right and left and if you are playing a marking system out of the back, they spread your shape and players are coming through the midfield and then the midfield's retracting. It really threw us out of our rhythm. It was that constant coming at you, direct style of play that teams have difficulty coping with.

"Another second part of the evolution was where defenders had to do more than just defend. They had to build a set play and I think the U.S. were deficient in that regard in that we couldn't hold the ball, so teams would drop their restraining lines. This was a new piece of the puzzle that was coming into the women's game. We see a variation where teams initiated their pressure forcing the defenders to set play, which made it much more difficult for us to attack.

"Another consistency with Norway was their effectiveness on restarts or deadball plays. We lost on a corner kick and that became part of our focus after '95. Even in practice if we gave up a corner kick we would award possession to the other team as a constant reminder that we can't give up so easily.

"China and Germany continued to evolve their technical efficiency and, I think, are still technically superior even though neither team had won a World Cup to that point (1995).

"I would say that we used China as a model for our organization in the box and for playing service. I think what we, as a coaching staff in the U.S., and myself personally have tried to do is to garner something from each country and I think China would be our model for attacking in the final third. They were just deadly in their point play, box organization, and their numbers forward on a pass. The Germans were machine-like.

Backtracking to '91 they had, like our team, in a little different way, no flexibility in how they wanted to play the game. They wanted to build it out of the back every time and they became predictable. We organized our system to a high pressure one and we forced turnover after turnover. They didn't want us to play direct or play long so we saw an evolution over a decade in their program. They had found a balance between what they were exceptional at (possession and combination play) and more direct play (changing the field and playing forward). They learned where and when to play each style and that's what makes them exceptional (Germany were the 2003 Women's World Cup winners).

"From the psychological side, I would still say that Norway and the United States remained strong until '99 and then we saw that Germany had it all. They had the psychological dimension really for the first time in every player on the field. Their technical prowess, the combination play-everything was running on all cylinders.

"I think other teams did what we did, kind of borrowed and picked different components from everyone. You knew where your weaknesses were, where their strengths were and you tried to match up. After '95, going into the '96 Olympics, we made changes. We went into the zonal defending system. Our whole attitude at least in our time as a dominant team, was premised to some extent that we were the only team in the world at that time that really played with a true front three. We wanted to keep that, but what we needed was a more secure defense. So we shed the man-to-man system and went to three backs. That allowed us to play zonal in the back and maintain the pressurized attack up front that we wanted, but we became more versatile as well. We had other systems that we could go in and out of. For instance, we chose to mark Hege Riise in the game in the'96, which was an unusual decision in the system. You essentially go to 10v10 and decide whether or not you can win the game that way.

"I think a big part of this is the players becoming more tactically mature. I think the fact that we were better soccer play-

ers and, again, the system is less important than the style. In particular, if you have players who understand the game, you can be a man-marking team or zonal team, as long as you have the ability to be both, the ability to understand the game.

"In 1996, we were more prepared and we had defenders that could attack as well as defend and we had multiple systems to use.

"Another element of evolution in the game that Norway brought was the goalkeeping. We really followed their lead on that. Our goalkeeper, until we saw Norway play, would sort of lag behind and I think, even around the world, Norway really set the standard for goalkeeping in terms of foot skills in the box. When Even Pellerud brought that approach to his game and his goalkeepers played that way, it made a difference.

"We were fortunate in that we traditionally had great goalkeepers. Great athleticism. So we then began to develop them on another level. By '99 (World Cup in the U.S.) China had put it all together as well. They, once again, had drawn on the strengths of some of their opponents and they came in as psychologically hard as any country. That was the best Chinese team ever and it made for a terrific World Cup and this helped bring the game forward tremendously.

"It was at that tournament that we also saw the German team that had that toughness, that desire to win. They had players in place and you knew they were going to be a force in 2003.

"Goalkeeping was getting stronger and stronger. I think by 2003 we saw that as an overall improvement and again directly contributed to the soccer culture. They are immersed in performances in the World Cup and the Olympics bring another dimension to the game in the individual creativity.

"I think Canada is a good example of how important it is to have support in programming. In the early days Canada was very competitive with the U.S., but they stood still while other teams evolved. It takes a financial investment and time and

effort from the national organizations to bring the programs forward. We see that, in countries who have put the effort and investment in, that those teams continue to evolve. When China fell off it was because there was some withdrawal of investment. Again, the reinvestment coming to the U.S. to beat the States on their soil was probably a big incentive for all teams.

"Bringing Even Pellerud to Canada showed the rest of the soccer world, and certainly it hopefully showed Canada, that there was a serious approach to the women's game in Canada. I would imagine that he knew the programs he wanted to put in place and demanded that was part of his contract and I think we are already seeing some big changes with the success of the U19 team and I would imagine the programs are going to support the game in the years to come. Even's a coach who will fight for his team, fight for what he believes in in the way of programs and I think we have seen the result of that. Without a doubt, Canada in the last five years is a much more organized team. They're a fitter team. They are more combative. They have a purpose and a confidence and that comes from being together, a supportive coach and the people behind him. It is interesting that for much of the development that has taken place, you have to give credit to the individual players themselves, because most countries didn't have a lot of support while this female game was evolving and it was those players who put us on the map in the first decade. Because really, up until 1995, we didn't have much of an organized entity in the world of women's football and the players themselves had to take the responsibility of the development. I know, having been involved in international recruiting for the professional leagues, many of those players were the ones who were running from work to training and doing whatever it took to be successful. I know that coach Tina Thuene-Meyer has done an incredible job recognizing what their players are going to be best at, how much time she has to be with them, and what it takes for these players to be successful individually, and as a team. I know she fought for more programming and it was reflected in the program and I think she is a very good coach. I have a lot of respect for her.

"As far as the future goes with the teams, I think Brazil is finally putting it all together. People think they have come out of nowhere, but if you look back, they have been in all of the events. But there are more countries developing and becoming more competitive. Look at Sweden now, Norway, Germany, Denmark, U.S., China…they are all committed to their programs and now we see Canada, Brazil and Mexico with a new commitment. What we're seeing, and what we're going to see more of is a high level of technical play and I think greater sophistication on the ball. Just watch Brazil and you know the game can be more technical and they have set the standard. We might have to look at our coaching, even here in North America. Are we too robotic? Why can't we produce some of these magicians, these creative 15, 16, 17-year-olds? Then, when you've got more technical players you can have a more tactically sophisticated game. That's an area we really have to improve in. You look at the Brazilian men's game and some of the sophisticated play, the ability to deliver under pressure and in the penalty area. In the women's game, we still have to get to that point of dropping a ball between defenders. It would just open the game up. That's what I would like see…more deliveries in and around the penalty area in the women's game.

"As for goalkeeping, we're getting there, but that can still grow.

"I think one of the real factors that is going to make things that much better is the greater number of competitive teams. It was great to see Spain beat the German U19 team in the European Championships. The women's soccer culture is growing. The parity's not there worldwide yet, but it's getting there. The Federations really need to support their programs on a level necessary to compete.

"The necessity for competition to keep the level of play developing higher is where WUSA was very helpful. As I said, previously players took responsibility themselves. They went to the Japanese league (which doesn't exist anymore), they went to Sweden, Norway, where the semi-professional leagues allowed them to play with elite national and international players.

Sweden still has an excellent semi-professional league. Norway has an excellent semi-professional league. Germany has an outstanding semi-professional league and China has a good league system. In many ways that's what helped them out. In North America, our model doesn't help us in that we keep our 13-year-olds together, our 14-year-olds and so on where other countries have more of a men's model where the top young players get into the semi-professional environments as early as they can. This teaches them very quickly. We need to strike a balance where we have a foundation below it (a youth program) but we should also try to get our players into more competitive environments earlier or we're going to lose something in their development.

"I believe you also use the marker of yourself, an internal competition versus external. It doesn't matter whether you lose against the team. It's whether your performance reflects what you know you're capable of. I like what Canada is developing in young players like Christine Sinclair. She is truly an outstanding young lady and an exceptional talent. It is important. Teams like Norway had their personality players. Under Even they had Hege Riise, Heidi Støre, Bente Nordby. Canada has had Charmaine Hooper who is truly an icon of the '90's. If you look back at our team and how it has developed around Karen Jennings and Michelle Akers and now the overlap of Mia Hamm and Kristine Lilly. All the great teams have players that can carry them. I think you have to be careful about being a little generic. That was Germany's problem for a long time. When Maren Meinert and Birgit Prinz came out of the mix in the last few years that seemed to carry them over the top. That's why it is exciting for a country like Canada to have young players like Sinclair coming along who you could build programs around. You have to have someone day-in and day-out like Hooper who sets the standard. It's good for Canada that she is not alone any more. There are other players who are starting to set standards with her and that can become contagious. You need those players. You need players who can break open a game. They can carry a game."

Prinz wreaks havoc

Steggeman closing quickly

Canadian FIFA Referee Sonia Denoncourt explaining a baffling call to US Internationals Wambach and Millbrett

Workhorses Meinert and Prinz - "connected" forwards

Prinz drawing a crowd as she finishes against the US

Abby Wambach - a huge physical presence -
USA vs Germany WWC2003

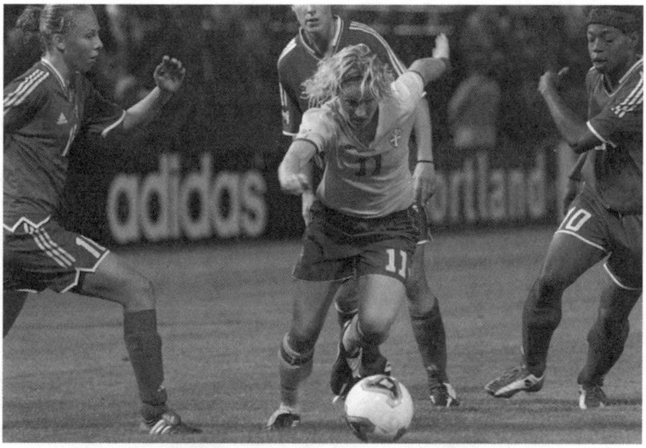

The ever dangerous Svensson gaining a step
on the Canadian Defenders

Meinert - the brilliant German midfielder preparing to cause
problems for US goalkeeper Brianna Scurry

Prinz's percentage of play involvement won her the
MVP at WWC2003

Kara Lang's strength and speed gave her success vs Japan

Norwegian striker Mariann Pettersen extending herself

Sinclair scored the opening goal for Canada in WWC2003

One of the players who rearranged her life to pursue her dream was Charmaine Hooper. Acknowledged to be one of the finest women players in the world, Hooper, to this day, claims she was born too early, as women's soccer has grown during her career. She was in a unique position to witness the development of the women's game when you had to scratch and claw your way to respectability and keep working to the point where programs were supported by their countries and a reasonable living could be made in the game.

Charmaine Hooper: A True International

Charmaine Hooper represents the consummate international. Born in Georgetown, Guyana in 1968 and playing her first soccer game in Zambia, she came to Ottawa in 1978 and developed as a youth in Canada. As a young girl devoted to the game, she rode her bicycle everywhere in Nepean, a suburb of Ottawa, Ontario, Canada. Her parents were also significantly involved in transportation to practices and games. Her very talented older brother played in the National Team program (Linden Hooper) and also in college and was capped over 66 times on the Canadian National Men's Team, including in 1986 for Canada during the Men's World Cup.

The story is told that her dad, exasperated at being pulled away once again from a household task to deal with Charmaine's soccer obsession, pointedly let her know that he thought this effort was fruitless. He could see where, in a men's game, a player was gearing towards making a living or profession out of the game, but he didn't see the women's game going anywhere. At that time (1980) Canada's National Team was newly formed, there were no professional, even semi-professional, leagues in North America and Charmaine's father, arguably in a chauvinistic way, indicated that these incredible efforts she was putting into the game could be better spent on another career direction.

In a moment of insight into Hooper's character, she clearly recalls that exchange with her father and how it strengthened her resolve to make soccer her life. A few years later, she presented her father a set of keys to a new car, purchased with the proceeds from her ongoing successful career as a professional in Japan. "I guess there is something in the women's game, Dad, and now we're both benefiting from it."--Charmaine had never forgotten that earlier moment with her dad in the driveway.

Pioneers in life are those who forge their own way, making it easier for others to come after. Hooper's spectacular success as an international was capped in February 1999 when she was named MVP in the U.S.A. vs. the World match in California. Scoring both goals in a 2-1 victory over the U.S., coming back from a 1-0 deficit, scoring on a free kick and a pure striker's goal, that moment validated the long journey Hooper had taken. After excelling in Canada at the club and Provincial level, Hooper went on to the United States, to play on a scholarship for North Carolina State. She was also an All-American at North Carolina State twice.

A critical factor in the development of any country's program and, indeed, any player's individual development, is playing at the highest level possible. The World Cup presented that opportunity for female players but, unlike their male counterparts, they did not continue to hone their skills at similar levels in professional leagues in between yearly camps or events. This has produced a significant problem in the women's game internationally and players had to have an extremely high level of commitment to train and develop successfully outside of the National Team programs. An outspoken critic of Canada's lack of preparation in the early '90's (there was a five-month gap between winning CONCACAF and qualifications and the next Team Canada event in Australia) and a continual proponent for a more stable, predictable schedule for Canadian internationals, Hooper went abroad where opportunities existed for women players. Her career saw her seek out professional and semi-professional positions in Norway, Italy, Japan, and, finally, in W-league in WUSA. Hooper recalls: *"Playing in Norway, Italy, Japan, Canada, the U.S., the level of skill and competition has been very high, but each place was different in some way or another. Norway produced different athletes. The girls were bigger, taller, and there was a lot of time spent practicing. They were definitely committed physically and mentally to the game. In Italy, the mentality was different. The players on my team in the league were good, but the players would always complain when it came to working hard or having to do fitness. Also with the Italian and Mediterranean machismo attitude, women's soccer took a backseat to men's soccer in the media and in the public. So things didn't get done too quickly when it came to developing the game or bringing the game forward for women's soccer in Italy.*

"In Japan (L-league 1994-1998; W-league in the off-season: Rockford Dactyls and Chicago Cobras), the level of play was very high, but the players themselves were not very big, strong or fast. That's changed rapidly in the last few years, especially after the success of the Men's World Cup in 2002. In the U.S., the level of play has definitely been their highest, and I think that's simply because most of the world's best players were playing in WUSA. We could also see where the strengths of other nations were and I had to say I think the Japanese players were the most technically sound (it is noted that Charmaine Hooper played with the great Japanese International, Sawa, on the Atlanta Beat WUSA team)."

Hooper has some serious concerns about the state of the women's professional league. *"WUSA shutting down has been a disappointment for many. The league gave young girls everywhere the hope to some day be a professional soccer player. Just as young boys dream to one day be like their idols in the MLS or the Premier league, the WUSA league has been great for our National Team players to hone their skills and to keep fit during the year and, as a result, I know the National Team is better. It would be nice to see this type of league in Canada or at least a Canadian team in WUSA, if the league resurfaces. It is important for this league to come back in some form, as this is the best way for the National Team both in Canada and the U.S. to continue to improve because without the league it will be very difficult for teams to maintain their high level of play for the future."* (Hooper was the leading goal scorer for the very strong Atlanta Beat in all three WUSA seasons 2001-2003.)

Charmaine Hooper, the most capped and prolific goal scorer in the history of the Canadian game, continued to add international recognitions to her resume when she was selected for the first all-star team for the 2003 Women's World Cup, playing at a position she had never played before--center-back. This outstanding player has remained committed to the international game throughout the years and is presently a female representative to the FIFA Player Development Committee, sitting around the table with icons the likes of Franz Beckenbauer and Michel Platini. With FIFA's public commitment to further invest in the women's game with solid experience from internationals such as Charmaine Hooper, Canada can look forward to a bright future. There will be another soccer-rich Hooper on the horizon in the future, as Charmaine and her husband, Chuck Codd are expecting their first child in early 2005.

Even Pellerud embraced the International Women's game early in his career. The success of Norwegian football's development model attracted international attention and Pellerud paid close attention to what was going on in other countries as well. In 1990 when he joined the NFF, Norway, Sweden, China, and the U.S.A. were the "big four" in the international game. Germany, Italy, Russia, as well as Canada were also competitive sides. A close eye was being kept on the young Brazil program as well.

With the advent of a FIFA sponsored championship, close scrutiny was given to the game. Technical analysis, reports, and committees were formed as FIFA prepared to give equal attention to the women's game. In a frank discussion about the state of the women's game, former U.S. National Team coach (1989-2000) and WUSA Commissioner Tony DiCicco agreed that there was an early naiveté in the game at the '91 World Cup. The evolution of playing styles, zone defense and an attacking mentality led to the emergence of Norway as the pre-eminent team at the '95 World Cup and a very dominant team in the '90's.

The U.S. Team's response to tactical play in '95, their introduction of zonal defense, their six-month training camp and long-term rededication led to one of the strongest U.S. teams ever fielded ('96 Olympic Team). The Chinese regrouped in 1999 at the World Cup in the U.S. and, although they lost in overtime, were arguably the best all-round team with the host U.S. a close second.

DiCicco in Success in Soccer and the FA's Insight magazine, reported on the technical state of the women's game. Even Pellerud and he agreed that an accurate and effective flank service was one of the deficiencies in the women's game. Finishing out of the air was an area that the women's game needed to become more technically proficient in. Both coaches agree that though parity was improving with the addition of Brazil, Sweden and Canada to the mix of the big four (U.S., Norway, China, Germany), there are still large gaps that need to be filled. The U-19 World Championships are serving to both introduce the higher level game on a larger scale to the world and develop the players who are the future National Teams.

With programs once again strengthening in England, France, Italy, Russia, and more recently the U-19 Spanish squad, the Europeans will be a strong component in the future of the women's game. In Asia, both coaches were impressed with what was happening in the Koreas as well as Japan. The Men's World Cup in 2002, with the addition of facilities and the raising of the consciousness of the game in that part of the world, has also been extremely helpful to the development of the game.

While the U.S. college programs remain a strong area of player development, Pellerud is selective when advising his young talent on programs. A strong believer in the importance of consistent challenge and competition, he pays attention to the schedules and coaching standards. Excited about the potential of Kristina Kiss a talented Canadian midfielder from Ottawa, Pellerud advised her against a U.S. college career to optimize her development as a player. Preferring a strong Canadian training schedule, Pellerud advised Kiss and defender Randee Hermus to look to Floya in Norway to improve their games.

Both Hermus and Kiss had positive experiences and Kiss improved to the position of starting midfielder in the 2003 World Cup. Hermus, a potential starting back, was sidelined with a stress fracture in her foot. Both of these players came out of the Canadian development system unlike the vast majority of National Team players who attended U.S. College programs. Playing in a small town in the semi-professional Norwegian league, Kiss and Hermus played for the Floya team. Now in her second year, Kiss (who has since left the Canadian National Team following the World Cup) found the joy in the game-the culture of soccer-very positive. Well north of Oslo, Kiss described Floya as a *"community that is involved completely in soccer, and the press as well. It's such a different environment. Soccer is in the people's hearts there. It isn't that way in Canada and you know that just spending some time over there. It's difficult to describe, but when you win people truly celebrate from the heart and you do a dance after you win and they dance to a song. Here it's more like, 'Oh, just another goal.' It's a much better soccer environment there. I would encourage any soccer player to go there just to experience that.*

"From a soccer standpoint, technically this play is much better across the board-the players, individually, are more equal technically. In Canada, we might have some individuals who are technically superior, but then the difference is larger between the next player. What I really notice is they all know how to play the game well. They understand the game. They think about when to make a pass and where to make a pass more than we do over here and, although I played on the W-League Fury (Ottawa), and

we were a good team, I think everyone understands how the game is supposed to be played a little better over there. It certainly helps us when we come back and play on the World Cup team because that's the way the international teams play."

While the apparent demise of WUSA (Lauren Gregg and Tony DiCicco are still working to bring it back in some form in 2006) has limited the options for strong individual players, Pellerud has championed the development of the W-league. He recognizes the need for the highest levels of competition to be maintained. While there is still a way to go to improve parity and get more consistent quality in opposition in the W-league, he feels that if allowed to grow it will offer those development levels required for players who are aspiring to be on national teams.

While Even Pellerud has proven to be adept at knowing his way around a boardroom, there is no place he would rather be than in a group of coaches discussing relative merits of playing philosophies. While he leaves the politics to the football bureaucrats he is astute and experienced enough to insist on input. His recent five-year reappointment with the CSA included autonomy over all aspects of the women's game including development from U-15 and up.

While he has coached on the men's and women's side, he has left his legacy on the women's side of the game. A true international, Even has a great love for the development of the women's game throughout the world. He is very active for FIFA in coaching and committee work whenever asked and maintains very close links to his international coaching confreres.

There is one place-and one place only, however-that Pellerud prefers to be and that is on the field with the players. His love of the game and the attention he pays to the players individually within the team stem from a personal passion for the game, but the understanding and love of the women's game has grown over the past 15 years.

Interview: Anson Dorrance
Head Coach, University of North Carolina

Even Pellerud has coached in the women's game during the formative years Internationally. He has had the good fortune of being one of the true pioneers in the women's game. One of the coaching friends he has made over the years is Anson Dorrance. Dorrance was the architect of the original US Women's 1991 World Champions and is widely acknowledged as the most successful women's coach in the history of NCAA Soccer. At the helm of the University of North Carolina Tar Heels for over 20 years, he has been in a unique position to observe the women's game both in the US and Internationally. He recently shared his observations on Even Pellerud's contributions and the state of the International Game.

Dorrance was in trust from his first contact with Pellerud - both from a coaching and a human perspective. *"I first met Even in Canada in 1990 when he brought the Norwegian National Team over for a 3 Nations Tournament. I had the sense that he had brought a lot of young players over for a look, leaving some veterans at home, but I was very impressed with the organization and the intensity of play from his team. We won the tournament but what I will never forget are Even's comments after their defeat - to me personally and to the press. He congratulated us and listed the things we had done well individually and as a team - he offered no excuses for his own team. I have found that extremely rare in the game - to have that grace and analysis - his perception was bang on and I knew he would make adjustments in the future."*

In the International Game as US National Team Coach for over 10 years, Dorrance left the team and Tony Di Cicco took over in 1994. Dorrance was on the technical committee for FIFA in Sweden at the 1995 Second Women's World Cup. He provided an insightful analysis on the strength and weaknesses of the women's game in the final report, which was published by FIFA in 1995. Coach Dorrance recalled the 1991's WWC.

"Meeting Norway in the final certainly proved that they were an elite team but all of us had the feeling that China was extraordinary and they lost versus Sweden against the run of play. I believe they had an exceptional game against Norway - what I credit Pellerud for is the Norway got better at every game - to be perfectly honest our peak game was the semi-final against Germany. Pellerud had his team peaking for the final. After our win Even again impressed me with his grace. Remember the world really didn't want to and wasn't expecting to see the US win a world cup of any sort. Even said something that was wonderfully noble and I believe also accurate - he thought we had had the best world cup. Until that game we had played some spectacular soccer.

"I think the US winning in 1991 was a shock and helped in many ways for countries to pay more attention to the women's program. I think FIFA was excited by the way we played. We attack almost at all cost. In 1995 when Even's team won it was a testament to his incredible well-organized back four, the simplicity of their game plan, and the individual combativeness of the Norwegian players. The thing that impressed all of us over here was how extraordinarily organized the Norwegians were in defending and how incredibly simple and focused they were in their attack Even's approach left a real mark on the American game because over the years our difficulty in breaking down the Norwegian defense led us to think a lot more about our attack. Tony DiCicco and the US National Team were certainly influenced by the Norwegian success. He moved the team toward the zonal flat four which we did not play in 1991. We played two markers and a sweeper and Even's first real contribution to the American game was to get all of us to play zonal defending."

"Internationally we could see Germany was getting better and better and most importantly were gaining greater confidence. China was always impressive but a bit inconsistent. They would seem unbeatable in one event and then plunge a bit and then scream again to a high level as they did in the 1999 WWC and then drop off again. This progression was different from Germany who improved steadily since 1991 to their dominant win in the 2003 WWC. One of the greatest improvements I have ever seen in a team was Norway under Pellerud from 1991 to 1995. They were an incredible machine in 1995."

In discussing the importance of developing young talent for International matches, Dorrance indicated he has been impressed with Pellerud's approach to the quality youth players. It's something that coach Dorrance did in the late 80's and 91's. Even Pellerud will bring a quality player up immediately to the full team if he likes what he sees. This philosophy of accelerating deserving young players on the National's Youth Team and even on the full team is something Dorrance believes creates success.

"Even if it's just watching those kids develop he seems to bring them up regularly and if they play they stay. As a mark of their success I was recently interviewed with Gerry Smith from Santa Clara and Jill Ellis from UCLA at the NCAA Championships - I made the comment that the most impressive thing for me at that College Cup was the play of the Canadians. I coached Angela Kelly and Carrie Serwetnyk and there has been the odd Canadian over the years but since Even's been here there are terrific character players with immense skills. These are experienced players at the age of 19 and 20 that Even has brought in to the National team. Sinclair in Portland, those great players at Notre-Dame (Thorlakson, Tancredi, Chapman) and that wonderful midfielder in Princeton (Matheson). These great Canadian players are now scattered all over the place and it seems if an American College doesn't actively recruit in Canada, they are making a huge mistake. A lot of that has happened since Even came on board."

Coach Dorrance also offered these comments on the women's game and the development he has observed over the years.

"In areas where we've got to do a better job with the women there is a long list that most of us agree on. Obviously, in the women's game, we don't head balls as well as the men. There's a huge difference there. I think the ability to serve balls over distance is also an issue. Those are a few weak areas. We're very poor at picking balls out of the air and getting them out of the box. Even when I was doing commentary for the WUSA for those years I was stunned at how many goals at that level were given up because of a poor clearance out of the back. Heading, serving over distance, clearing balls out of the penalty box, and also things like volleying, picking balls out of the air, playing them on the frame. With the exception of Marinette Pichon, it seems like it is something in the women's game we just don't spend enough time on. Those areas in particular are a bit of a concern.

"On a very positive note, the youth coaching since I began coaching women in the '70s has improved dramatically. The caliber of the average player that comes out of the youth ranks now in this country and in Canada has changed dramatically. The excellent coaching they're getting through their clubs and sometimes their high schools is changing the game. I think there has been a huge positive jump because now there are so many quality players in the American collegiate ranks and I certainly credit the development of these excellent youth players with the fine coaching they're getting."

In commenting on the importance of maintaining the highest competitive environment for National team player development, coach Dorrance provided the following interesting observation on the influence of WUSA on the International Game.

"We generally feel that one of the reasons Germany emerged was with their players in our league, the American players lost their aura. Part of the qualities we had when we set foot on the field was we had an invincibility because of our athleticism, our combativeness, and our intensity, and then all of a sudden the Germans came into our league and they came to the correct conclusion that not only were they playing with us, but in a lot of respects they were so much better in different areas. Certainly technically and tactically they were there. The legacy of the WUSA was actually constructing some of the foreign players that played in our league because they could certainly compete with the American National Team players. The bizarre irony of the American women's professional league is I think we served the World better than I think we served ourselves."

On the strength of the German Team (WWC 2003 - U19 FIFA 2004) and the contribution of the professional club system, Dorrance had these comments:

"We (UNC) went over the summer before last and played some games in England and Germany and I had a pretty good collegiate team that year and we went over to Germany after playing a couple of games in England. I was very impressed with their standards and their game and so I think the German National Team program, if the clubs are competing at a level about, say, Frankfurt, are certainly contributing to the growth of the German club, because the club we played beat us 3-1 in the match, not that they didn't have to concentrate to beat us, but I was certainly impressed with the standard of their average player and their style with club teams of that level the whole program improves.. If the clubs are anywhere near that standard, then they're being served even beyond what the German federation has invested in their National player development."

On looking forward to the 2007 WWC, Dorrance had the following observation on the International Game and coaching:

"A huge curiosity for me and I think for everyone is the emergence of Brazil. Their performance at the Olympics was outstanding. All the Americans have an understanding of the game and obviously the ones who played in it feel like the US in the final won against the run of play. The Brazilians were a bit unlucky, some of their shots were striking the post and they missed some sitters so we feel like the Brazilians created more opportunities and, obviously looking at Marta and other young Brazilians play there is now a bit of a technical separation between the elite Brazilian players, sort of like what has happened on the men's side between the elite Brazilian men and the rest of the world. So we're curious that if they maintain this coach, Rene Simoes who I think has done a brilliant job for Brazil and continue to spread the women's program maybe...the view we have here in the US is there is going to be a changing of the guard. So, obviously some of my motivation in coaching my college kids, many of whom have played for the Olympic or national teams or have aspirations to, is to see if we can make ground with these Brazilians technically.

Rene Simoes did a wonderful job. I mean I'm looking at his Brazilian team and not only were they unbelievably confident, but they were very secure with none of the issues of Brazil in the past.

My feeling is if they can retain a coach of his standard or find one of a comparable standard-because obviously a coach like him is probably dying to get back into the men's game-I think Brazil will be formidable."

When asked, Sylvie Beliveau has made the comment and Lauren Gregg as well; in the women's game coaching still makes a bigger difference than it does in the men's game. Would you agree with that?

"Probably for the reason that women are more coachable. In the men's game it is basically a fight. One of the reasons I bailed out of the men's game is I got sick of getting up

in the morning and putting my armour on to do battle with 18-22-year-old male egos. The thing about the women's game and women in general is they're much more coachable. When you make a coaching suggestion to a women's team or a young woman you're developing, she's going to take your recommendation at face value and try to do it well. In the men's game it is still a fight. From that perspective, they are a lot more cooperative and their coachability is still a lot greater.

"I have to say, of all the coaches I have had the privilege to compete against, Even Pellerud has been superb. The best I have met. His results also speak to that."

What's to Come

Even Pellerud as technical adviser and architect of the U-19 team, recently attended the U-19 FIFA World Championships in Thailand with Ian Bridge and Shel Brødsgaard. Despite Canada's misfortunes in their 10-man quarterfinal loss to China, the tournament was a success for FIFA. Twelve teams participated and Germany's exceptional play continued as they took the gold medal, defeating China in the final. With former players and National Team coaches such as Sylvie Beliveau (Canada), Lauren Gregg (U.S.), and Vera Pau (Holland/Scotland) on the international FIFA committees, the international women's game is in experienced hands. Presently working on the technical development communities and with Futureo, these coaches are guiding issues such as the necessary changes in the international calendar, the FIFA U-19 soon to be U-20 World Championships, rearrangement of the Women's World Cup schedule, and international qualifying tournaments. These changes are being implemented to optimize the strength in women's games. The resurgence of the Scandinavian sides in Sweden and Denmark, the remaining strength in Norway, and now Finland has also recently qualified for the 2005 European Championships. A full Scandinavian contingent will participate in England against the home side, England, as well as France. The final eight for the 2005 World Championship will also include Italy, whose women's program is developing strength once again-in all, Sweden, Denmark, Norway, Finland, France, Germany, England and Italy are in.

The Danish World Cup team gained international reputation when they recently brought the Americans' 20-game winning streak to an end by tying 1-1 and defeating them 3-1 on American soil (November 2004).

On the CONCACAF side, Mexico's surprising advancement to the Olympics and Costa Rica's stronger showings are good signs for the game.

In the international women's game, the personalities and methods of coaching are seen to be a more significant factor for team success than in the men's game. The women's game itself is emerging as the federations and individual countries invest in their female programs. The future is certainly bright internationally and Even Pellerud fully intends to remain a part of it.

Thailand -
The 2004 U19 FIFA World Championships

Even Pellerud recently (November 2004) traveled to Thailand in his position as Director of the Women's Program for Canada. He also had an extended role of coaching along with the U19 National Team Head Coach, Ian Bridge.

Pellerud was with the team around the clock and was able to watch all the Canadian games as well as a number of other games. This allowed him to develop a good overall impression of the tournament.

Pellerud points out that FIFA's decision to initiate a U19 Women's World Championship in 2002 (the inaugural event being held in Canada at the Edmonton, Victoria, and Vancouver venues) had a large impact on the international development of the women's game. The FIFA World Championship brings an instant recognition and a level of prestige throughout the world with the intention of both the highly developed countries, as well as the developing countries in the Women's game to begin to seriously pay attention to their programs and to even launch initial programs in many smaller soccer countries.

Pellerud feels that there has definitely been a palpable change in the recognition for women's soccer throughout the world and, more importantly, significant development of the quality of the game by introducing this high level of competition. As Pellerud has stated previously, the inaugural tournament in Canada was a great start, although from a coaching perspective there was not a consistent or impressive display of quality football.

He notes that there were two teams that were much better prepared than the others, those being the two North American teams-Canada and U.S.. The results bore that observation out in that these two teams went to the final in an evenly fought match to settle the tournament Canada losing 1-0.

In the 2004 world tournament, Pellerud has noted that the team preparation was much more obvious from more nations. Germany (the ultimate winner), as well as China, Thailand, and Brazil were all obviously better prepared. Canada and the U.S. remained at an excellent level, but the other countries were coming from behind.

The coach also indicated that one of the more pleasing observations was the lack of huge "lopsidedness". The results show a developing parity in the 12-team tournament. Very few teams, if any, were not competitive. The play of the host country, Thailand, was exceptional in such a short period of preparation time.

He feels it is good for the game to not only have an outstanding team or two, but rather solid teams with good shape, good team performances, hard-fought games, and a higher level of tactical soccer.

Comparing the U19 tournament with the men's side, there was a much greater number of youth players that played for both the full side (senior WC) teams and the U19 WC teams. The result was a collection of high-profile athletes participating in the tournament. This was good from a media standpoint and in many ways for the future of the various national sides.

The U.S. team is one exception. They fielded a team that had very few senior side caps. Canada, however, in basing its future on the younger players had multiple capped players including Kara Lang, Brittany Timko, Tanya Dennis, Ayesha Jamani, and Amanda Ciccini. These were not only developing players but impact players. Pellerud feels it is hard to overestimate the importance of these players gaining international experience at the tournament level. He feels this will improve their impact on the full squad in the future.

The Brazilian team had a similar large number of experienced National Team players. Their stand-out and rising team star is Marta. Pellerud comments that Marta can turn any game into an advantage for Brazil. Despite the fact that the team wasn't particularly well organized or consistently sharp, Marta seemed to be able to turn up the heat at will. He felt that she deserved to win the Most Valuable Player award (which she did) for the tournament, even though her team failed to advance to the final. Marta is the type of player on whom the future of the game will ride.

On the German team the coaches pointed out that, as is consistent with their playing philosophy and development model, it was a very strong team performance with what would appear to be mature, well-educated soccer players at the U19 level.

Brittany Timko was winner of the "Golden Boot"-the tournament's leading goal scorer (despite going out two games early). The runner up to Timko's Golden Boot, was the Silver Boot winner Anne Meitach. Pellerud also felt Meitach would have a strong influence on the senior team soon and thought Germany's midfield play was very strong.

Pellerud also pointed out that FIFA is under discussion to extend the age to U20 and there is some push from the European side to increase that as high as the U21 level.

He finds the junior team critical to the development model in Canada. He is excited about the impact the tournament has had, how it serves as a goal for the young players with a commitment to trying to win a position on these National youth squads. "We are beginning to see young athletes that are focused on soccer and creating a soccer lifestyle and a large part of that is due to players such as, Lang, Jamani and Timko."

Pellerud's Picks

A great handicapper of talent, Pellerud picked Germany as the favorite for the 2003 Women's World Cup with Sweden a strong contender. That they finished 1-2 was no surprise. Even's greatest moments as a coach in Norway were obviously the World Cup in 1995 and the multiple European Championships. Being on the bench for Canada's first ever win was also a huge moment for Pellerud in WWC 2003 and in many ways this break-through against Argentina fueled the coach and team for their ultimate run to the bronze medal game.

"Historically it is a difficult task to pick a team of all-time greats but I must admit that it is easier on the women's side than the men's because the sport is younger with serious international competition started just 15 years ago. It is natural that, while following the better players, even as coaches, the high profiles are usually the offensive players, the workhorses-the midfielders and, in particular, strikers. I've enjoyed watching these players both for and against my teams over the years and they have brought a lot to the women's game. Here then are my proposals for two teams of the world's best."

As a coach and pivotal builder of the women's game, Even Pellerud was asked to come up with two all-star teams from his years in the game. Given this daunting and highly personal task, Pellerud was excited to think about the players and the games over the years. He points out that these were subjective decisions based on his time in the game and noted that he was back in the men's game for the most part from 1996-2000.

His philosophy leans towards supporting players who had outstanding individual skills or qualities...something special that they brought to the game. By definition, this type of player dominates team selection. He used Mia Hamm as an example. The fact that Pellerud picked her for his second team in no way underrates her massive talent in all aspects of the game. What more reflects his observation is that the other selections may have had one extreme or stand-out quality.

Team A: 3-4-3

Goalkeeper:
Elizabeth Leidinge (Sweden) - tall, athletic, determined, and very important stellar goalkeeper for Sweden in the 80's and early 90's.

Back Three:
Doris Fitchen (Germany) - tall, athletic defender. Strong in the air. Strong on the ground. Skillful. Confident. Always a consistent, world-class defender for Germany through the 90's.

Joe Fawcett (U.S.A) - has always been an impressive, consistent, quiet leader for the U.S.A. defense; fantastic at reading the game; no mistakes; plays all her strengths and hides her one weakness, which is pace.

Gro Espeseth (Norway) - remember her from the rivalry with Michele Akers through the 90's in the series between the U.S.A. and Norway…fearless fighter, leader, and fantastic defender.

Mid-Four:
Maren Meinert (Germany) - great creative force from any position in the midfield; extremely creative; extremely good passer; can kill a team with her vision and passing

Hege Riise (Norway) - (in a deep diamond position) good vision, passion, few touches, poisonous penetrating passes

Kristine Lilly (U.S.A.) - up and down the left flank for decades from the late 80's to the early millennium; fantastic, consistent, running, skillful and lots of passion and determination; an underrated player

Sun Wen (China) - skillful playmaker for 15 years; very intelligent; little touches, one-two passes, deadly finishing; fantastic player

Top Three:
Charmaine Hooper (on the right) - Can play all positions up front; fearless, physical, determined, good finisher, fast when she needs to be, strong when she needs to be...she has the whole package.

Michelle Akers (middle) - perhaps the most impressive female soccer player I have met and seen and played/coached against; Tall, extremely athletic, she can shoot in a net from 30m with left and right foot and also head the ball from almost the same distance; extremely good player in the 90's, too bad she had to stop early. I am a big fan.

Birgit Prinz (Germany) - came up at 16 years old as a strong, fast striker on the left hand side; has continued to be in the middle and on the left, she has always preferred to go to the left; she is a well-rounded, very dangerous striker and goal-scorer. MVP at WWC 2003.

Team B: 3-4-3

Goalkeeper:
Bente Nordby (Norway) - Arguably the best goalkeeper in the World. She had increased competition in the late 90's to the present, and remains active as a senior keeper for Norway. She is still a strong keeper, but her peak is behind her. Her athleticism and experience keeps her as a #1 Norway player. A very skillful player with excellent hands and good feet, and really has developed strong leadership over the years.

Back Three:
Kersti Stegeman (Germany) (right) - a hard defender to beat, almost impossible; solid as a rock; not the most elegant player to watch, but very effective and efficient in her way of winning the ball and passing the ball, makes things look easy.

Pia Sundhage (Sweden) - Swedish captain through the 80's and 90's was a symbol for the Swedish team; consistent, good leadership, played in the middle early on and later on became a defender, always a good player, a pleasure to watch; good captain, good leadership; always a good pass.

Brandi Chastain (USA) - Needed on this team because of her good defensive qualities, but maybe most of all for her offensive qualities; she handles the ball with ease, she can pass with both feet, her left foot is fantastic; sometimes makes too many risky decisions, but we need her skills and qualities

Mid-Four:
Bettina Wiegman (Germany) - Came early to the German team in the 90's and was a striker as a young player, matured in her role as a team leader and has impressed more and more through the years with her skills, her passing qualities and also her penetrating runs after the ball into the box and, of course, for her penalty kicks.

Heidi Store (Norway) - Norwegian captain through the 80's and 90's, same role as Pia Sundhage for Sweden. Centre midfield, used to be dominant in the early 80's because she was more talented than the others. When the other players caught up she changed the game to compensate for her lack of pace and became more of a controlling, holding midfielder with smartness and passes; also very strong in the air

Karoline Morace (Italy) (left) - Dominant player through the 80's and 90's, but it was too much to ask to make the Italian team a top team all alone. But she was always outstanding with her character, her brilliance, her ball skills, her body language, and her poisonous attacks.

Mia Hamm (USA) - I admire her first and foremost for her overall general skills; she is also very well-educated, but it is her passion, her competitiveness, and her consistency which has been an outstanding example for the women's game around the world and nobody can take that away from her. She has had a fantastic positive impact on the women's game.

Top Three:
Dagny Melgren (Norway) - she can score goals in the most spectacular ways, makes spectacular goals look easy, has become more and more of a crucial match winner for Norway; I spoke to her when she was 15 years old and she was a little player that actually the coach didn't believe in at that time, but I was happy enough to invite her to my last camp when I coached Norway in the 90's and I could see her future was great.

Abby Wambach (USA) - Another player I am a big fan of, I wondered why the USA invited her so late into their team; typical target striker, but with a lot of other skills, as well; she sees everything, she flicks the ball through to other strikers, very unselfish, very determined, very tricky, very strong in the air, maybe the best header in the world, right now and has a great future.

Linda Medalen (Norway) - A Norwegian striker through the 80's and 90's, competitiveness, physical, aggressive, running the field from side to side, up and down, fearless, nothing can stop her when she is determined, was crucial for the Norwegian success in the 90's.

Conclusion

A true coach is one who is dedicated to education, not only as an educator of his players, but concerned about his own accumulation and development of knowledge. Even Pellerud has learned a lot from the game and the great people in it. The influence Even Pellerud has had on his players as a coach both in Norway and in Canada has raised the levels of the game played both on the field (as results) and in players (as individuals). When Coach Pellerud agreed to put pen to paper about his approach/philosophy and how he developed it over the years it was an opportunity for players and coaches alike to learn how a successful coach at the highest level of the sport approaches the game. It is hoped that coaches and players will benefit in some small way from this endeavor.

While Even Pellerud is dedicated to winning, he has first been dedicated to his players as well as the game itself. His World Cup Team in 2003 was named Team of the Year in Canada and that has been Pellerud's proudest moment to-date. As is so often the case in the international game, Even Pellerud had to make a big decision in January 2005. Lobbied by the NFF to return to Norway, the Canadian National Coach turned down a long-term (8-year) contract to coach the Norwegian National Team and will remain in Canada to continue his work with the young Canadian program.

His next objective is to win the 2007 World Cup in China and the nation will be watching closely!

Sam Kucey's Acknowledgements

The author would like to acknowledge and thank so many people who were eager to contribute to the success of this book. It was an easy task to secure interviews and comments from soccer players and coaches because of the positive influence Even Pellerud has had on the game.

Special thanks go out to: Tony DiCicco, a true champion of the women's game; Anson Dorrance, who has become synonymous with championships in the U.S. College ranks; Lauren Gregg, whose knowledge and insight on the development of the female player is second to none. In Canada we have so many great contributors to the sport: Ian Bridge, Shel Brødsgaard, who have been through so much with the team at both the National and U-19 levels. Dr. Cathy Campbell who has penned a beautiful chapter in the book, Dr. Rudi Gittens a tireless and always cheerful soccer fanatic and FIFA sports doc, as well as Don Johnson, Ottawa's renowned sports medicine orthopaedic surgeon, as well as my friend Don Kirkendall, a tireless researcher at the University of North Carolina. Special thanks to Colleen Hacker and Anne Marte Pensgaard who are fine pioneers in the field of sports psychology. John Walker, whose Nebraska program has been superlative.

I would like to thank the CSA executives for being so open with their interviews. Karen Espelund, Sylvie Beliveau, and Jeremy Boone from North Carolina who has contributed so much in the way of exercise science for soccer, and PEAK Centre for Human Performance here in Canada for their interesting contribution in training footballers.

Special thanks to the Norges Fotball Forbund and former president Per Omdal, as well as former National Coach Egil Olsen and National statistician Øyvind Larsen, who gave such great insight into the Norwegian game.

Most important, I would like to thank all the players past and present who were so great in contributing to this effort.

I would also make special thanks to Darlene Munroe who has spent countless hours typing and retyping the manuscript. I would also like to thank my secretary of so many years, Nicole Valiquette, for her contributions and organizational skills.

Richard Kentwell and Bryan Beaver at Reedswain have been terrific. Special thanks for most of our pictures to Marion Domonokos, that talented photographer who is also nuts about soccer (good luck at the Masters!) and Mike Stalschmidt, international photographer of Sideline Sports Photography, LLC, who seems to be on the sidelines of just about every big game in the world.

Finally, of course, I would like to thank Even Pellerud. We wrote this book together and Even brings a unique perspective to the game and, most importantly, a well-rounded approach to life. I have enjoyed becoming his friend in this project.

I would like to reserve my greatest thanks to my family, particularly my wife Caroline who gave up even more time than usual, as this two-year project took on a life of its own. Her support and that of our four lovely daughters, Andrea, Amantha, Meredith and Whitney, all fantastic sportswomen and great human beings (who have taught their parents more than they will ever know)-their support is what makes all of this worthwhile.

There were so many other people along the way who helped and I want to thank them all for their contributions and hopefully, in some small way, this book will help the game move forward.

Even Pellerud's Acknowledgements

First of all, my sincere thank you to the people and old friends in the village of Roverud. The Roverud village and its friendly, quiet environment was the best environment to grow up in for active kids like myself. In the local soccer club, Brane, we were all responsible for creating a good learning environment - from pushing the lawn mower every Saturday to arranging our own travel to away games. My soccer heroes are still the Brane senior players from the 1960's.

I owe Kongsvinger Football club and, in particular, the club chair, Erling Engebraaten, a lot for having faith in me as a rookie coach, hiring me as the premier league's head coach following my active playing time. That established a lot of confidence in myself and kicked off a good life in soccer.

Thanks to my wife, Anne, for her support and creative technical input and feedback through many years, and following me from club to club and from country to country.

My apologies to my four kids - Marius and Marte in Oslo, and Hedvig and Tora in Vancouver - for having to accept a dad that was always traveling too much and quite often had soccer tactics in focus even when being at home.

A big part of my development as a coach took place through my eight years in the Norwegian FA. A lot of inspiration and fun was provided by my good friends and colleagues, in particular Nils Semb and Egil (Drillo) Olsen, the Men's national coaches in this period of my life.

Lastly, I would extend a thank you to all coaches that taught me about the game. I was lucky and had some of the best coaches out there, and many times I have used their practices and their programs.

In order to make this book happen, Sam Kucey has invested so much time and effort. My thanks to Sam and his team, including his wife Caroline.

Also, I am happy to have good friends and colleagues in this program and also colleagues that I have played hard games against. Thanks to you all for great contributions. Without you guys, this book would not be what it became. Just reading the articles from these contributors is well-spent time.

So thank you, Ian Bridge, Shel Brodsgaard, Cathy Campbell, Anson Dorrance, Tony DiCicco, Lauren Gregg, Oyvind Larsen, Egil Olsen, Anne-Marte Pensgaard, Colleen Hacker, John Walker, Sylvie Beliveau, Jeremy Boone, Mike Stalschmidt for his great photos and all those who work so hard for the game.

Even Pellerud
Canadian National Women's Team Coach

References

Fitness Training in Soccer: A Scientific Approach. Jens Bangsbo. *Reedswain Publishing. (2003)*

The Girls of Summer: The U.S. Women's Soccer Team and How it Changed the World. Jere Longman. *HarperCollins (2000)*

The Vision of a Champion. Anson Dorrance and Gloria Averbabuch. Reedswain. (2002)

Catch Them Being Good. Tony DiCicco and Colleen Hacker with Charles Salzburg. *Penguin Books (2002)*

Embracing Your Potential. Terry Olick. *Human Kinetics Publishing. (1998)*

In Pursuit of Excellence. Terry Orlick. *Human Kinetics Publishing. (1990)*

National Soccer Coaches Association of America Soccer Coaching Bible. *Human Kinetics (2004).*

Positional Play Series on Strikers, Defenders, Midfielders. Alan Wade. *Reedswain (1998)*

Performance Conditioning Soccer: A Guide to Soccer Field Testing.

An FA Guide for Coaches. Wade

The Champion Within: Training for Excellence. Lauren Gregg. *JTC Sports Soccer Publishers and Reedswain. (1999)*

"Four Phases of Player Development, The curriculum for development of player skills must be appropriate for each age level". Soccer Journal. *July/Aug 2003*

Endurance and Strength Training for Soccer Players, Physiologic Consideration. Jian Hoff and Jan Helgerud. *Faculty of Medicine, Norwegian University of Science and Technology, Trondheim, Norway. 34: (3) Page 165-180*

Frank Cass Journal Soccer In Society. Vol. 2, No. 3, Autumn 2001, *Page 58-78*

Glossary of Acronyms

CONCACAF - The Confederation of North, Central American and Caribbean Association Football

CSA - Canadian Soccer Association

NAIA - National Association of Intercollegiate Athletics

NCAA - National Collegiate Athletic Association

NFF - Norges Fotball Forbund (Norwegian Football Association)

NSCAA - National Soccer Coaches Association of America

NSCAC - National Soccer Coaches Association of Canada

FIFA - Federation Internationale de Football Association

MLS - Major League Soccer

NUSPE - Norwegian University of Sports and Physical Education

USSF - United States Soccer Federation

WC - World Cup

WUSA - Women's United Soccer Association

WWC - Women's World Cup